84278

F
869
S353
A23

Block

The immortal San Franciscans for
whom the streets were named

Date Due

JE 4'73			
OC 12'73			
OC 26'73			
JE 2 '74			
FEB 1 0 '75			
NOV 11'76			
FEB 9 '77			

The Immortal
San Franciscans
for whom the streets
were named

The Immortal
San Franciscans
for whom the streets
were named

by Eugene B. Block

Chronicle Books / San Francisco

To Ruth, with love

Contents

Acknowledgement

THE AUTHOR, WITH deep gratitude, expresses his profound thanks to the many men and women whose help and interest have made this book possible.

Before listing some of them, however, he wishes to make it clear that his selection of individuals for biographical sketches, and the omission of others, in no way implies any judgment on the importance of their contributions to the community. On the contrary, the many whose careers are related here were chosen solely on the basis of unusual, dramatic, and human interest values in their life stories. No doubt scores of others, listed in the appendix, rendered equal services to the city in their time.

In the preparation of these biographies, the author, delving into historical records, often vague, confusing and contradictory, has made every effort to avoid error. Should inaccuracies be detected, he begs the indulgence of his readers.

Of the many to whom thanks are due for assistance in research, the following deserve special mention: Mrs. Gladys Hansen, San Francisco Public Library, Mrs. Irene Simpson Neasham, director, Wells Fargo Library and Museum, Dr. Albert Shumate, San Francisco, Rev. John B. McGloin, S. J. University of San Francisco, Rev. Joseph Brusher, S. J., University of San Francisco, Society of California Pioneers, California Historical Society, Judge Leland J. Lazarus, San Francisco, John Delury, San Francisco, Peter Conmy, Oakland, Rev. Harry B. Scholefield, San Francisco, Pat Frayne, San Carlos, The late John R. Gard, San Francisco, Mrs. Eleanor Rossi Crabtree, San Francisco, Chief Thomas Cahill, San Francisco, George Woo, San Francisco, David T. Loofbourrow, Jr., San Francisco, Edwin J. Block, Kentfield, Hartford Sharon, San Francisco, Robert J. Dolan, San Francisco, Mrs. Arthur Aitken, Redwood City, Marilyn McFarland, Menlo Park, Robert De Velbiss, San Francisco, Harold Gilbert, San Francisco.

Preface

THIS BOOK DEALING with the streets of San Francisco goes far towards filling a real need. Mr. Block's contribution, as indicated, is a solid and worthy one.

For two decades now, the undersigned has enjoyed teaching a course at the University of San Francisco on the history of our city. Among his many perplexities in so doing—and some still remain—is the precise point which involves the naming of the streets, avenues, boulevards, etc. of San Francisco. Eldredge has helped—i.e. *The Beginnings of San Francisco,* Volume II, Appendix where she lists about 130 streets with their historical significance; other pamphlets and occasional brochures have also been of limited use—i.e. *If Streets Could Talk,* prepared by the Crocker-Citizens National Bank; always, though, there has been the need for a more thorough treatment. Mr. Block is in our debt, therefore, for having here given us the most complete guide up to now. It will be used and appreciated by many afficionados of the City. It goes without saying that much research has gone into these pages: the result of such faithful ferretings are evident here.

John Bernard McGloin, S.J.
Professor of San Francisco History,
University of San Francisco

Introduction

THE HISTORY OF San Francisco with all of its rich tradition and legends, is woven into the lettered words on its street signs, beginning with the actual discovery of the Bay.

Some are named for explorers and political leaders in the Spanish and Mexican periods before American occupation; far more honor sturdy pioneers who contributed to the growth and development of the little Yerba Buena settlement even before the gold discovery. Others pay tribute to outstanding citizens of later times — some contemporary figures among them — including notables in politics, science and letters.

Who are the men and women for whom so many San Francisco streets are named? How were they selected? And what did they contribute to the life and progress of the community that has become the great metropolis of the West?

Of the pioneers whose names and colorful careers are perpetuated by streets, some were miners; others were merchants and politicians, living in a flamboyant day when might instead of right often prevailed, when vice of all sorts was rampant, and when great fortunes were quickly made and lost as rapidly.

Through the years the names of many streets have been changed for reasons that are sometimes obscure but today these designations, by and large, have a dignity that was often ignored in pioneer times.

No longer is there a Corned Beef and Cabbage Alley, a Rattlesnake Street, a Cat Alley, a Good Children Street, or a Ghost Alley. Such appellations have been changed, sometimes as many as four times, as the temper of the people turned from the informality and provincialism of early years.

Nor are the first names of women any longer given to newly-made streets, though today close to 100 thoroughfares still retain such original feminine nomenclature.

To trace the origin of most of them is virtually impossible. In some cases, pioneers, far from home and kin, did name streets for wives, sisters and sweethearts. Jessie and Annie Streets, for example, were designated by Charles Christian Russ to honor members of his family. But there are no records to explain why Caroline Street became Harriet Street or why Blaine Street supplanted Eugenia Avenue. Nor do records disclose why Cherubosco Street was renamed for Elsie, whose identity remains a mystery.

Many of the feminine names, undoubtedly, are those of less than virtuous women who in pioneer days won the hearts of early settlers but the secrets behind such honors have gone with them to their graves.

Apparently, those who undertook to name San Francisco streets in days gone by followed no carefully designed criteria. Aside from the designation of streets for pioneers and those who later assumed distinguished roles in community life, some have been given the names of presidents; others are called for trees; patriotism is recorded in such as as Lexington and Liberty Streets, while Blackstone and Gutenberg are not forgotten. But the identity of such individuals as John, Harry and Carl, each with a street in his honor, is not to be found in records.

Strangely, there is no street named for Andrew S. Hallidie, inventor and builder of the city's first cable car. David Belasco and David Warfield, whose great theatrical careers had their debut in the city by the Bay, have also been overlooked.

Maiden Lane, the colorful little thoroughfare running into Kearny street between Geary and Post, deserves special mention.

Before the 1906 fire it had the name of Morton, a disreputable redlight alley lined with brothels whose painted inmates continually called through open windows to passersby.

Today as old-timers walk by the street, observing its attractive shops and eating places, they often look at its present name, laugh and wonder who with a warped sense of humor or ironic taste conceived the idea of calling a by-way with such a past Maiden Lane. But it didn't happen that way.

In 1909 the street was renamed Union Square Avenue because of its proximity to the downtown park. A year later it received a new name—Manila Avenue—which someone thought would better fit the spirit of the Dewey Monument in Union Square.

After a time there came another change, the third, merely because Albert S. Samuels, a jeweler with a store close by, believed it would be appropriate to give the street the name of one in New York that is a center for jewelers and silversmiths — Maiden Lane. No one seemed to disagree.

Favorite streets in the home cities of early settlers received attention, probably for sentimental reasons. Broadway, Lombard and Greenwich were taken from New York; Pine, Filbert and Chestnut from Philadelphia. Market Street, of course, is a common name in many cities.

Humorous incidents played their part in the titling of some streets, McAllister for instance. Hall McAllister, the distinguished lawyer who was so honored, liked to tell how it came about:

"I was walking along this street, then only a few blocks long, when a General I knew approached me. 'Hall,' he said to me, 'for a bottle of champagne I'll give this street your name.' So we walked over to the Golden Horn saloon and I bought the bottle. We baptized what instantly became McAllister Street and drank what remained. If I had ever dreamed there'd be a cable car line on this street, I'd have bought up the sand dunes beyond it; I could have had them for practically nothing."

No less amusing is the story of Golden Gate Avenue, once called Tyler Street for the President of that name. The change was made because Irish conductors on the old Tyler Street car line were in the habit of calling out at the transfer point for Taylor Street, "Change here for Tyler and Tyler Streets." Some passengers laughed; others were badly confused. It was easier to give the street another name than to substitute conductors without a brogue.

Curiously, some streets of San Francisco are still under water. Mostly located on submerged lands off Hunter's Point, the city map shows Alvord, Texas, Pollock, Olney and others — all well-covered by the tides of the Bay.

Despite the casual street-naming procedures of pioneer days, when settlers were free to designate streets as they chose, San Franciscans no longer take the matter so lightly. A developer, opening a new tract of land, first makes his own selection of names for newly-made thoroughfares. Initially, he must check through the long alphabetized lists of names already established.

When this has been done, the suggested names are submitted to the city engineer who designates a member of his staff to pass upon the proposals. Once the recommended name has been approved, the city engineer decides whether it is to be a street, avenue, boulevard or perhaps only a court or alley.

After that official has acted affirmatively, final approval must come from the Board of Supervisors by resolution.

Illustrative of the city's growth which constantly requires new street names and changes of others for diverse reasons, is the fact that in the short interval between the time the Post Office's 1969 Zip Code Directory of Streets went to press and its final publication, new thoroughfares were added and new names given to others.

One new street became Banneker Terrace, honoring Benjamin Banneker, the famed Negro surveyor who played a major role in laying out Washington, D.C. Others included Nautilus Court, Atoll Circle and Albatross Court — all the result of new developments.

In the same period, because of downtown business changes, Savings Union Place became Security Pacific Place and Gaines Street was changed to Ice House Alley, appropriately titled for the two brick buildings so named and now tenanted by leading interior decorators and designers.

In earlier periods, name changes were made mostly to avoid confusion in postal deliveries. Sproul Lane, intercepting the north line of Sacramento Street between Mason and Taylor, is a good example. Half a century ago it was called Yerba Buena Street. The designation doubtlessly would have remained indefinitely had not someone, without knowledge of the name, chosen it for a new street in the Twin Peaks area.

So, for a time, there were two Yerba Buena Streets — until postal authorities discovered the duplication. Serious differences developed as to where the change should be made. The issue was finally settled by changing the name of the Nob Hill thoroughfare to honor the then president of the University of California.

Street names in the Hunter's Point area have undergone changes, often as many as three or four. Time was when such titles as Korea and Formosa were acceptable but toward the end of the nineteenth century residents began to protest, claiming that such appellations were "ugly and unacceptable." Some of these took numerical designations like First and Second Avenue South but in time confusion developed as to whether "South" referred to South San Francisco, a different municipality.

There also were streets titled for letters of the alphabet like A, B and C but again residents demanded change, so that A Street now bears the name of Arthur Avenue for the former president of the United States; B Street has become Burke Avenue for the great English statesman; and C is called Custer for the famous General.

Confusions continued, however, and with them came protests, mostly from the Post Office. The result was the appointment of a Commission in 1909 by Mayor Edward Robeson Taylor to make the exhaustive study of the entire problem and to recommend changes.

Although the Commission labored long and conscientiously, perhaps even taking its assignment a bit too seriously, its recommendations aroused some opposition, largely because of proposals that the names of early Spanish officials, explorers and politicians be substituted for titles that were considered innoccuous, meaningless and lacking in "musical quality."

Among those most vociferous in opposition to such changes was Charles W. Polk, an outstanding citizen of the time, who objected vigorously to naming streets for people he referred to as "Spanish robbers and free-booters."

Such protests resulted in rejection of many of the recommendations of the Commission but a large number of substitutions were made, sufficient to satisfy many of the major needs for change, especially the most serious problems in which the Post Office was concerned.

Today, street names continue to change but at a steadily decreasing rate, perhaps because the growing city, faced with many more serious matters, becomes less concerned with issues such as the names on its street posts.

However, students of San Franciscana — and they number in the hundreds of thousands — continue their deep and serious interest in the whys and wherefores of street names. There may be some, less sentimental, who merely shrug their shoulders with the casual question: "What's in a name?"

But are they REAL San Franciscans?

Ortega
Discoverer of San Francisco Bay

The Yerba Buena Ortega Saw

JOSE FRANCISCO DE ORTEGA, pathfinder for Don Gaspar de Portola's exploring expedition, deserves first place among those in whose honor San Francisco's streets have been named. He is credited with the discovery of San Francisco Bay on November 1, 1769.

Zoeth Skinner Eldredge, recognized as one of the foremost authorities on California history, not only positively names Ortega as the discoverer, but sets the precise time as between two and two-thirty o'clock in the afternoon of that historic day.

From all accounts, Ortega's first sighting of the Bay was accidental. At the time he was leading a small party of scouts under the general command of Portola, who had been sent north to take possession of the ports of San Diego and Monterey and to fortify them. Portola's assignment came from Don Jose de Galvez, visitador general of Spain and a member of the Council of the Indies.

The expedition comprised two divisions; one traveling by sea, the other by land. They converged at San Diego and decided to proceed north to Monterey Bay but for reasons that remain uncertain they failed to find it, probably because of faulty maps.

Ortega and his group were sent northward for further explorations and it was while on this mission that he first sighted the Golden Gate and the waters of the Bay. Not long afterward they discovered Carquinez Straits.

Why the Bay was not discovered at an earlier time by Spanish navigators has long been the subject of conjecture among historians. Some say that it is a question beyond explanation; others theorize that the Yerba Buena harbor was probably obscured by dense fog most of the time. And there are writers who believe that from a far distance Angel Island may have appeared as part of a continuous coast line. Actually Ortega then regarded the Bay as an obstacle to his progress.

His career, as a soldier and an explorer, was colorful and exciting. He was courageous and imaginative.

He was born in the city of Celayo in the State of Guanajuato in Mexico in 1734. Soldiering was in his blood at an early age for he had barely attained his majority when he enlisted in the company of the Royal Presidio of Loreto in Lower California on October 1, 1755.

His aptitude for military service was soon apparent, for less than a year after his enlistment he was made a corporal and advanced to sergeant only months afterward. He still held this rank when he was assigned to the Portola party. Apparently his discovery of San Francisco Bay made little or no impression on the high command for he was not promoted to a lieutenancy until August, 1773 when, over vigorous protests, he was placed in command of San Diego.

His chief supporter for this post was Junipero Serra, who had been at odds with the commandante of California, a Captain Fagas, and recommended that Fagas be replaced by young Ortega.

This brought serious opposition from Viceroy Bucareli who argued that the position should go to one of considerably higher rank. In the end, he compromised by recalling Fagas, appointing Captain Fernando Rivera y Moncadoas as commandante of the Presidio of Loreto, and placing Ortega in charge of San Diego with his new rank.

Ortega's first year there passed peacefully with no thought of impending trouble with Indians for he was confident that he had won their friendship. The unexpected sanguinary attack that occured late in the night of November 4, 1775 came without warning and the mission guard was wholly unprepared.

The raiders may have even known that Ortega was away at the time. He had left a day before to establish the Mission of San Juan Capistrano and had taken half of his little force with him.

Only a few men were guarding the Mission in the dead of night when they suddenly were startled by war whoops and other wild discordant cries from the approaching mob. Minutes later a band estimated as more than 5,000 descended on the helpless Mission.

The church and other buildings in the compound were set afire. Fierce fighting followed and the invaders finally departed after they had finished their ghastly work.

On the ground lay the bodies of a priest, a carpenter and a blacksmith. All of the defending soldiers were wounded, some seriously.

A courier was dispatched to apprise Ortega of the attack. He hurried back and took vigorous measures to avert any further trouble. The invaders did not return and Ortega was not troubled by Indians again.

He continued as head of the San Diego Mission for the next six years after which he was sent to Santa Barbara to establish a Presidio. A year later he founded the Mission at Buenaventura. Other and more exciting work lay ahead, assignments that would better challenge his ability as a pathfinder and his love for adventure.

For three years, from 1784 to 1787, he carried on explorations along the wild and rugged frontier, an assignment that ended when he was put in command at Monterey.

In 1791 he was transferred to Loreto as a successor to Captain Arrillaga, who later became governor of California. This post he held until 1795 when he had reached the age of sixty-one. The Spanish authorities then believed he had done his share of service.

He was retired with the rank of Brevet Captain and sent to the Santa Barbara Presidio. He died February 3, 1798 and was buried there with full military honors. Surviving were his sons who had become the owners of large ranchos. His granddaughters had married governors. His widow, Maria Antonia Victoria, succumbed May 8, 1803.

Ironically, the street honoring Ortega was not named until 1909, more than 111 years after his death. The belated tribute came on recommendation of an official city commission that frowned on the designation of streets by single letters of the alphabet and what had been merely O Street was given the name of the man who discovered San Francisco Bay.

de Anza
The
Conquistador

Captain Juan Bautista de Anza

IN THE YEAR 1776 history was being made on opposite sides of the American continent though events on the Atlantic Coast far overshadowed those in the Far West.

While the spirit of rebellion in the thirteen colonies was leading to the Declaration of Independence, a little band of intrepid travelers, led by Captain Juan Bautista de Anza of Mexico, was pushing its way to the shores of San Francisco Bay to establish the Presidio and to select a site for Mission Dolores.

Accomplishing his purposes, de Anza left behind some 30 members of his party, the first colonizers of little Yerba Buena. Thus began the settlement of what later became San Francisco.

Two years before he had led his first party from Mexico over tortuous trails to Northern California, reaching as far north as Monterey before returning home.

The two Anza expeditions had their origin as far back as 1769 when the King of Spain, Carlos III, ordered the building of a chain of forts from the Gulf of Mexico to the Gulf of California and the fortifying of the Pacific Coast. Establishment of the San Francisco Presidio was one of the objectives.

The plan captivated the imagination of the adventurous Anza who petitioned for the privilege of leading an expedition into Northern California. Though he offered to defray all costs personally, his request was denied.

He later renewed his plea, stating his desire to travel overland from Sonora by way of the Gila and Colorado Rivers despite the risks he knew would be encountered. This time, having won the approval of the King and of Father Junipero Serra, he started out January 8, 1774 with a party of 34, including 20 soldiers and made western history.

The exciting details of his two perilous expeditions are highlighted by the personality of the man himself — a soldier and explorer, eager to face great dangers and to overcome them.

Born in 1733 in the Spanish port of Fronteras in Sonora, Mexico, he donned a military uniform with the rank of lieutenant at an early age. In 1760 he was made a captain and put in charge of the Presidio of Tubac. Evidently, he also had won the respect of superiors for at about this time one of them referred to him in an official report as "an all-round good officer because of activity, valor, zeal, intelligence and unselfishness."

He was also known as a restless man, craving excitement. Therefore no one was surprised in 1769 when he grasped what he saw was an opportunity for adventure, even though it involved grave dangers. Spain then was making plans to occupy the Pacific Coast as far north as Monterey, believing that either the Russians or the English had similar intentions. And the Spanish were anxious to get there first.

Anza, of course, was elated when he received authority to launch the first expedition but even the early days of his journey were beset with more difficulties than he had anticipated. Not only was he forced to travel over many miles of wilderness, but he constantly faced the need for water, and his animals were in poor condition.

Before reaching the Gila range, the party was attacked by savage Indians who killed some of Anza's horses. There were other clashes with Indians as they proceeded and on one occasion Anza narrowly escaped with his life. He and his companions no doubt would have been killed had not Palma, the chief of the Yumas, sent a courier to warn him that a large number of hostile tribesmen, whom he could not control, were prepared to ambush the party.

With amazing courage, Anza continued on his way but was relieved a day later when he was met by five naked Yumas with word from Palma that the trouble-makers had been expelled from the tribe and that all now was safe and peaceful.

Overcoming great difficulties, the party some time later forded the Colorado River and met another gathering of Yumas, all of them entirely nude. Apparently Anza had misgivings as to their friendliness, for Eldredge wrote:

"He (Anza) was much troubled by the multitude of naked Indians in the camp. He presented them with an ox, trinkets and tobacco, hoping to get rid of them, but they remained to sleep with their new friends. Anza describes the Yumas as tall and robust . . . with their faces disfigured with paint. Their ears were bored with from three to five holes in each of which they wore a ring. They also pierced the cartilage of the nose and through it passed a bunch of feathers. They went naked for they considered it womanly to be covered."

So friendly were these Indians that many of them accompanied

Anza as guides for a considerable distance but after they turned back the party again was forced to work its way over desolate land as best it could, constantly facing the need for water.

They finally reached Monterey and, considering their mission accomplished, undertook the long trek to the starting point in Mexico where Anza was hailed as a hero, complimented by the King, and honored with significant military promotion.

Of the importance of this first expedition, Eldredge wrote:

"Anza had conquered the desert and had overcome the natural barriers between a paternal government and its feeble establishment in distant California. He had realized his cherished dream and had opened the King's Highway. He had secured for Spain the friendship of the powerful tribes of the great river. . . . He was now to establish a presidio and mission worthy of the serafic patron and father, Saint Francis, to found a city that, in the fullness of time, was to dominate the great ocean and take its place with the mighty ones on the earth."

Now regarded in Mexico as a famous man, Anza was commissioned some months afterward to form a second expedition and retrace his steps — this time with the definite purpose of establishing both the San Francisco Presidio and the Mission.

To encourage colonization, it was provided that the party should consist only of married men who would be promised large grants of land after serving an enlistment period of ten years.

Anza started out on Monday, October 23, 1775 but it was not until Spring of the following year that he reached his destination. Again he met with many problems. He suffered a serious leg injury on the way and there were more skirmishes with hostile Indians.

Hazards continued even within miles of the party's goal. Nearing the present site of San Mateo, the travelers were attacked by an enormous bear which was killed only moments before several of Anza's men would have lost their lives.

Once encamped on the shores of San Francisco Bay, Anza selected the Presidio site and formally established the military reservation. He then turned his attention to a location for the Mission which he chose to designate as Dolores, because his decision was made on the Friday of Sorrow — Viernes de Dolores. The site he first selected, however, was later changed.

Before departing, the intrepid leader decided that he would plant a cross to mark the most suitable spot for the erection of a fort. After carefully surveying the area, he chose a place where the entrance to the Bay was narrowest. He named this the Point of the Steep White Rock, later to become known by its present name Fort Point.

With the cross in place, he turned his attention to finding suitable locations for those of his party who would remain as first settlers and who were not to be joined by others until a lapse of fully 60 years.

Then, with his mission fully accomplished, Anza started back to Mexico in June of 1776.

On his return he again was welcomed as a hero and appointed Governor of the New Mexico territory, but his popularity was destined to end.

Four years later colonies that had been established by Spain along the Colorado River were savagely attacked by Yuma Indians and almost completely annihilated. At once Anza was bitterly criticized for having wrongly assured the authorities of the friendliness of the tribe. He was summarily relieved of the governorship and soon afterward disappeared. However, San Franciscans, many years later, gave his name to a street that had been known only as A.

Richardson

Founder of Yerba Buena

Yerba Buena, from the Bay

ON THE MORNING of August 20, 1822, the sparkling black eyes of an unusually attractive Spanish señorita changed life's course for William Anthony Richardson. The result was his place in history as the founder of Yerba Buena.

Richardson was also the first to develop commerce on the Bay and for fully twenty years his vessels carried merchandise and produce from one rancho to another.

An Englishman born in Kent in 1795, he put into the little Yerba Buena cove as the first mate aboard the British whaler *Orion,* whose master had no intention of remaining there. An acute food shortage had developed and Richardson, the only member of the crew speaking even a smattering of Spanish, was sent ashore in a dory to purchase supplies.

A tall, imposing figure with deep blue eyes, he was warmly welcomed by the few people standing about the Presidio. Sight of the strange whaler anchored offshore had created much excitement.

The dark-eyed girl was the first to greet him and it did not take him long to decide that he had reached the end of his voyage. He was offered refreshments and even horses but when he explained that he wanted only ship supplies, the Spaniards shook their heads and beckoned him to follow them.

"Supplies you can get mañana," they told him in their native tongue. "We're going to have a fiesta in honor of your ship — and we don't do business on fiestas." He was urged to visit the Commandante at his adobe home for a gay night of dancing but the newcomer said that he must return to his ship; he would be back early the next day.

Richardson, who already was determined to remain permanently in a settlement housing so beautiful a girl, rowed back to the *Orion* in darkness to report that he would not resume the voyage. The captain, angered by his mate's failure to bring supplies, struck him a blow that sent him sprawling to the deck and told him to go back to the shore and stay there. "If I ever see you again I'll kill you," he warned, as Richardson hoisted himself over the rail.

Richardson's sole desire now was to remain near the señorita and to find some kind of work. He soon learned that she was Maria Antonia Martinez, a daughter of Ignacio Martinez, Commandante of the little Presidio and the most influential man in the area. It was quite evident that she returned his affection, though he did not know that she had whispered to a sister, "That handsome man, he'll be my husband some day."

As he looked over his new surroundings, eager for work and money, Richardson learned that the law forbade foreigners from settling or even trading in the area. He applied for permission from Governor Pablo Vicente de Sola, the last Spanish ruler, and was told that he might remain pending formal permission on condition that he teach shipbuilding and carpentry to the native children.

Richardson found his opportunity. Only three small boats were carrying on trading about the Bay. From scant savings he purchased the largest vessel, *El Rey del Mar,* and went into business. Next he bought a dilapidated rowboat and a derelict whaler that were drifting offshore. With these he established a trading business that brought profit as well as friendship with the natives. Indian crews manned the vessels.

Three years later, having been granted citizenship on condition that he be baptized a Catholic, he married Maria Martinez at the Mission of San Francisco deAssisi. It was a colorful ceremony, the bride with a lace mantilla over her dark hair, the groom in the uniform of the British Merchant Marine.

For a time Richardson continued his ship service around the Bay, his bride often at his side. Occasionally they picnicked under the willows of what is now Sausalito or sailed leisurely into the calm waters that took the name of Richardson Bay.

Later, on a ship that he had fashioned from the hulk of the abandoned whaler, he went north to Sitka on a profitable trading expedition. Returning six months later, he was met by Maria who proudly displayed their daughter, Mariana, who had been born in his absence.

Again leaving his wife with her family, he sailed to Los Angeles in 1831 and from there to Peru, on another trading venture that yielded still greater profits.

Richardson, whose early dream of taking Maria to the altar now was realized, began to dream again. He envisioned a new commercial town on Yerba Buena cove, an opportunity that he believed had been overlooked and for which he determined to obtain support. The family, about this time, had been staying in San Gabriel in Southern California and he availed himself of the chance to disclose his plan to Governor

Figueroa. In doing so, he explained that he had made the same proposal to the previous Governor but to no avail. Figueroa, in contrast, was greatly impressed. He told his visitor to return to the north, draw up rough maps for such a town, and submit them as soon as possible.

Traveling with a mule pack, the Richardsons slowly made their way back, encouraged by the assignment. On the day of their arrival, June 25, 1835, he accompanied his family to a sandy spot on what is now Grant Avenue just north of Clay Street, and stretched a sail over four wooden poles. It became the first civilian home on Yerba Buena — a location now designated by an historic tablet.

In this abode, such as it was, Richardson mapped the little town he had foreseen, extending it over sand dunes between ravines. A few streets were sketched with a trail leading to the Presidio. Governor Figueroa was elated. He not only dispatched word of his approval but designated Richardson as master of the harbor. It was a post that would become increasing important as well as profitable, especially after the start of the Gold Rush. As vessels approached the entrance to the Bay, their masters would fire two shots to notify Richardson that he was needed to pilot them into port. His response, three long whistles, was the signal for his crew of eight oarsmen to meet him at the shoreline and row him to the incoming ship.

In spite of these demanding duties, he found time to open a store, dealing in hides and tallow which he gathered from neighboring ranchos.

Earlier he had made valuable contributions to the commerce of the port. During his trading trips around the Bay, he had often dropped his plumblines, enabling him to chart the waters and to mark dangerous rocks and shoals. All of these he turned over to the authorities.

Domestic responsibilities were not neglected. After occupying the sandlot tent for three months, he erected a better home on nearby land that had been granted him.

It was one of his proudest boasts that although born an Englishman, he had co-hosted the town's first Fourth of July celebration in 1846. In this event he shared honors with an American, Jacob Leese, who had arrived from Ohio only days before the holiday and urged Richardson to join him in suitable festivities. The Alcalde having consented to the affair, Leese turned his attention to erecting a home adjoining Richardson's but it quickly became apparent that even a crude house could not be completed by Independence Day.

"Don't worry about that," Richardson told him. "Go ahead and finish your house; I'll go around in my boat and invite all the people around here to the fiesta."

"Fiesta?" Leese questioned. "Isn't that a funny way to describe a Fourth of July celebration?"

Richardson laughed. "Don't forget," he explained. "Practically all of our guests will be Spaniards."

With the help of sailors from the ship that had brought him to Yerba Buena, Leese finished his home in time, driving the last nail early in the morning of the Fourth. The celebration was a rousing success, attended by Richardson's father-in-law, Martinez, Commandante of the Presidio, and more than 60 other guests. Actually the fiesta continued until early in the morning on the sixth.

For the next ten years Richardson devoted himself to his duties as master of the port and to his business responsibilities. He died Sunday, April 20, 1856 in Sausalito where he owned a large rancho. Reporting the funeral, which took place three days later, the then California Chronicle referred to him as one of the community's "most respected men."

Arguello

A Romance of Old California

Mission of San Francisco

ALTHOUGH DON LUIS ANTONIO ARGUELLO relinquished his duties as the second governor of California under Mexican rule in 1825, it was not until 1909—84 years later—that a boulevard was named for him in his native San Francisco.

Even then, he may have remained unhonored in this way had not a city commission been appointed to rename many streets, including some that were numerically designated. Otherwise Arguello Boulevard in this city's Western Addition might still be known as First Avenue.

While Arguello enjoyed a successful two year term in office, he is best remembered today not so much for himself as for the tragic romance of his beautiful daughter, Concepcion, a poignant episode on which Bret Harte based his well-known poem with the girl's name as its title.

In the days when Arguello was commandante of the Presidio at Yerba Buena, before he had assumed the gubernatorial post, Concepcion had many suitors. None were to her liking until the sudden appearance of Nikolai Rezanov, who came into San Francisco Bay from one of the Russian settlements in the far north to purchase supplies.

Trade between the few American settlers at Yerba Buena and the Russians in settlements at Sitka, Alaska and in the Aleutians already had been established, and American ships occasionally voyaged there to hunt sea otter.

It was not surprising, therefore, that Alexander Beranov, the head of the Russian American Fur Company, who was known as the "little czar" of the Russian settlements, should look to Yerba Buena for relief when he found large numbers of Alaskans starving and many of them suffering from scurvy.

He ordered the ship *Juno* to make the voyage. In command was Nikolai Rezanov, tall and handsome, with a brilliant mind and unusually gracious manner.

Arriving in the Bay, he dropped anchor and went ashore. His first call was to the Presidio to present his credentials to Commandante Arguello. It was there, on his first visit, that he met 16-year-old Concepcion, known as the most attractive girl not only in the settlement but in the entire region.

Only days later they were ardently in love, fully convinced that they were intended for each other. Rezanov's proposal of marriage was accepted without hesitation but Concepcion's father was neither pleased nor satisfied. For one thing, his daughter's suitor was 35 years her senior. For another, there were religious differences, Concepcion being a Catholic and Rezanov of the Orthodox Eastern Church.

The girl pleaded with her father, insisting that she could never love another. The padres were consulted and Arguello finally relented, agreeing to the marriage if Rezanov could obtain approval from Rome. Rezanov had explained quite frankly that he would need the consent of religious leaders in St. Petersburg and perhaps even that of the Czar, but he brushed off these difficulties as far from serious.

The lovers made their plans together, apparently oblivious of the time that would be needed to overcome their problems. When Rezanov announced, six weeks after his arrival, that his ship was loaded and that he must depart, the couple was resigned to the situation.

Concepcion was at the water's edge when the *Juno* weighed anchor and moved slowly into the open Bay with the Russian master at the bridge returning the kisses she was blowing from the shore.

Then began the interminable wait — a wait that would end only at the grave. Rezanov had promised to write from every port he touched. No word came.

A month, two months slipped by and then a year. Concepcion was unconsolable. With the arrival of every ship, she was at the shoreline, frantically awaiting the first seaman to come ashore. Eagerly she would ask for the letter that was not there.

Two years passed and more. The girl, her suspense unbearable, feared disaster, yet she was certain that in this event some news of shipwreck would have come. Still she never lost faith in the man she loved.

Her plight was discussed in the settlement for a time, some questioning Rezanov's sincerity; others were certain that his intentions were honest and sincere.

Some years later Concepcion decided to change her life; she would become a nun and devote herself to a secluded religious life. She took the vows but her veils and her duties failed to assuage her sorrow.

Not until nearly half a century later did an answer come — if that it was. Many years had passed since Rezanov's departure when a famous English traveler, Sir George Simpson, chanced to arrive in Yerba Buena. He knew nothing of Concepcion and her grief but in casual conversation he remarked one day that a Russian ship captain named Rezanov, who once had anchored there, had met death in a fall from a horse in Siberia.

The sad news reached Sister Concepcion who said prayers for the man she still loved. But she wondered to the day of her death why he never had written to her.

Concepcion's father, Luis Antonio was born in Yerba Buena in 1784. His father, Jose Daro Arguello, had been commandante of the Presidio by the Bay and in 1815 became governor of Baja California.

The son, Luis Antonio, had won recognition as early as 1821. On an exploration expedition to the Columbia River he discovered Lassen Peak.

After Mexico had achieved independence from Spain, he was chosen governor of Alta California in 1822, being the first native Californian to hold that office.

He died in San Francisco in 1870.

Leese

The Pioneer
Merchant

Jacob Primer Leese

JACOB PRIMER LEESE was a grocer and for some years his store in Yerba Buena was known as the largest and most popular of its kind in California.

Around its hot pot-bellied stove, men of affairs would sit nightly, discussing the business of the town and the politics of the West. Though he never held public office, Leese assumed an important place in the early life of California and his name frequently appears in its history. Without doubt he had gained prestige by his marriage to the attractive dark-eyed sister of General Marciano Vallejo, who was commander of all of the Mexican forces in the north.

Leese, broad-shouldered with thick black hair and sideburns, had come west from Ohio where he had been a trader of some means. Like many others, he soon was attracted by accounts of the western country with its wealth and opportunity.

He left his native state in 1835, landing in what later became Los Angeles. He was short of money and far from pleased with his new surroundings. Looking for a way to better his situation, Leese decided that profits were to be made from transporting mules. This he did for a time, his work taking him into Mexico and as far as South America.

As soon as he had accumulated sufficient funds, he moved north to Monterey, where he once had planned to settle, but hearing of Yerba Buena and the Bay, he began to consider that location as his final destination.

He was preparing for that northward move when by good fortune he met two men of his liking. One of them was William Hinckley, formerly of Massachusetts, who had arrived in California as master of the bark *Volunteer* in 1830. The other was Nathan Spear, like Leese an energetic trader. All three were destined to leave their mark on the young settlement.

Their conversations led to a partnership. Together they decided to establish a grocery business in Yerba Buena and acquire cheap property as fast as profits would permit. The idea was especially pleasing to Hinckley who was disgusted with what he termed "Mexico's absurd customs regulations." He believed that they would be less severe in the northern town. Leese was pleased on another count—he had visions of becoming Captain of the Port.

He arrived in Yerba Buena alone, the partners having decided he should go in advance and find a home. In his initial efforts for a land grant he met with disappointment, although he had brought with him letters of recommendation from Don Mariano Chico, addressed to both the Commandante and the Alcalde.

When they asked where he wished to locate, he promptly pointed out a site on the cove close to the water's edge. To this the officials shook their heads, explaining that the law then in effect forbade any land grant closer than 185 yards from tidewater.

They graciously proposed two alternative locations. Leese stubbornly refused to even consider them, shrewdly realizing that the site he wanted would probably be the first to increase in value.

In spite of the cordial manner of the authorities, he returned to Monterey and complained bitterly to Chico, who apologized and promised to advise the others that Leese's first request should be granted. Meanwhile, he authorized his visitor to select any suitable place for a temporary home.

Returning to Yerba Buena, Leese chose to locate next to the tented home of Captain Richardson, where the two celebrated Independence Day shortly afterward.

Some time later Leese received the land grant he had first requested and built a large and expensive home on the property. The old location was enlarged to become the town's first St. Francis Hotel, which became known as "the fashionable house of the day," probably because it was the first hotel in the town to put sheets on its beds. It was later razed by fire.

For his grocery, Leese found a suitable site on sandy ground not far from his temporary home. He invested $17,000 for the original stock, obtaining foodstuffs from trading vessels that had put into the harbor. His two partners joined him but as soon as the business was well established, it was agreed that they should return to Monterey and operate a store there, leaving Leese to run the grocery by himself.

Apparently he found some time for recreation and at a social he was introduced to General Vallejo's attractive sister. A courtship started and the grocer lost no time in proposing marriage. He often commented that he had chosen April Fool's Day of 1837 to ask the vital question.

They were married a week later and their nuptials was the occasion for a two-day celebration.

A year later their first child, Rosalie Vallejo Leese, was born.

Long afterward a marker was placed where their home had stood, with an inscription stating that the first white child in the town had been born there — a fact disputed by historians who claim that the honor goes to the wife of a soldier who came with the Anza expedition many years before.

The grocery business expanded rapidly. With the profits its owners enlarged their Sonoma store which already was doing a large business with ranchers and with ships masters who came to buy hides and tallow.

Leese invested heavily in land and his properties extended far into what is now Visitacion Valley. The government also granted him a number of other large-sized lots.

As time passed, Leese was approached by agents of the Hudson Bay Company with a fabulous offer for his home. Unable to resist a chance for profit, he sold the property and moved with his family to Vallejo's large rancho at Sonoma. However, he deferred his departure until he had fulfilled a government request to assist Captain Jean Vioget in making the first official survey of the town. This was Leese's one and only public service.

He was living happily in Sonoma when the Bear Flag Revolt occurred. Probably because of his relationship with Vallejo he was taken prisoner along with his brother-in-law and held for a time at Sutter's Fort.

After California became a State, he was obliged to engage in long litigation to uphold his titles to the large land holdings he had acquired under Mexican rule. He was successful and remained, a contented, wealthy man whose name was given later to a street in the Mission District.

Vallejo
The
Californio

Mariano de Guadalupe Vallejo

MARIANO DE GUADALUPE Vallejo, who in 1835 assumed the triple duties of Commandante of the Yerba Buena Presidio, Collector of Port and Alcalde, came into the world as the result of an extraordinary romance, one that seems almost unbelievable, today.

First, let us meet his father, Don Ygnacio Vicente Ferrer Vallejo, scion of a noble Spanish family, whose fascination for a new-born infant was responsible for Mariano's birth.

In early youth, Don Ygnacio had left his ancestral home in Spain and settled in Guadalajara, Mexico, determined to fulfill a promise to his parents that he would study for the priesthood. Many members of their large family, both men and women, had taken holy orders.

Before he could carry out his promise, however, a chance for adventure convinced him that the religious life was not for him. Instead, on the invitation of a Captain Rivera, he joined a military expedition to explore what was then called Alta California.

Secretly he slipped out of Guadalajara and became a soldier, unaware that fighting lay ahead.

The party had made its way to San Diego when word came of an Indian uprising in Monterey. There had been considerable loss of life, including the wanton murder of a priest. Sensing need for reinforcements, Rivera proceeded north and assisted in restoring peace.

It was during this expedition to Monterey that destiny crossed Don Ygnacio Vallejo's path in a most unusual way. The party had stopped at a pueblo for the night and as Vallejo was walking by a small adobe home, a man came running out calling for help. "Please, please," he cried, "Come in and help me. I'm all alone and my wife is having a baby."

The soldier obliged, despite his lack of knowledge of midwifery.

Soon he found himself thoroughly fascinated by a new-born baby girl, the first he had ever seen at such an early age. The little pink-skinned form intrigued him and he felt pleased that he had had a part in her birth. He was still admiring the squalling infant when a call came from his command. "I'll be back here some day," he told the father, perhaps in jest, "and if she's old enough to marry, she will become my wife— that is, if you and she are willing."

The father laughed and nodded. Before long he had forgotten the strange proposal. But Don Ygnacio did not. He traveled far after the hurried march to Monterey, once meeting Father Junipero Serra, founder of the missions, when their paths crossed in the San Joaquin Valley. Yet, through all of his travels and experiences, visions of the infant kept running through his mind.

He met fascinating women of his own age but found them uninteresting. Often he remembered the promise he had made and wondered whether it ever would be fulfilled.

Thirteen years passed, yet the incident in the pueblo was still fresh in his mind; so much so that he decided to return to the place, hoping that he might find the one he had helped to bring into the world.

To his delight the family was still there and the child of whom he thought so often was approaching young womanhood. She was beautiful, dainty, and had charming ways. Vallejo was presented and jokingly recalled the promise that had been made so long before.

He lingered and pressed his courtship, though he was now 40 years of age. Weeks passed before the girl, Señorita Maria Antonia Lugo, accepted him. Their marriage followed.

It was a happy union despite the difference in ages and the couple became the parents of thirteen children. Mariano de Guadalupe, born July 7, 1808, was their eighth.

The family lived in Monterey. Young Mariano studied and worked there, finally moving to Yerba Buena where he became Commandante of the Presidio, Collector of Port and Alcalde. Busy times followed, for the settlement lacked organization and Vallejo began by creating the first ayuntamiento or town council.

Five years later he was ordered to Sonoma where the early settlers were in need of colonization. While carrying out his new duties, a party of more than 400 men and women arrived from Mexico. They had scarcely put down their belongings when Vallejo received orders to send them back. It was a difficult assignment but it was executed with sympathy and understanding, typical of the unusual administrative and military ability Vallejo displayed when problems arose.

He found time for romance, marrying Señorita Benecia Francisca Felipsa Carrillo, the daughter of an old and influential family. She bore him fourteen children.

Reading and study were his principal forms of relaxation. He prided himself on his extensive library and freely loaned books to those about him, eager to advance their learning.

In 1838 he was made commander of all Mexican military forces in California, a position which he held with much distinction. As years passed, however, he realized that U.S. occupation of the territory would be good for the people and he exerted a strong influence to bring it about.

During this time he became a close friend of General Fremont and it was difficult for him to understand why the American took him prisoner during the Bear Flag revolt in June, 1846. Nor could he ever explain why it was Commodore Stockton and not Fremont who finally ordered his release after six days of captivity at Sutter's Fort.

Under American rule Vallejo became active in public affairs and, in 1849, he was elected a member of the convention that drafted the constitution for the new territory. He later was elected to the State Senate.

His last years were spent in retirement in Sonoma where his wants were met by his associates and Indian friends. He died on January 18, 1880, unaware that a city in Northern California and a street in San Francisco would bear his name and perpetuate his memory.

Zoeth Eldredge, the historian, paid him this tribute:

". . . His active life has become quiet — his mature manhood honored and happy. With all, he possesses a fine form and handsome face, a kind heart, courteous manners, and that abundant hospitality for which his countrymen are so justly celebrated."

De Haro
Alcalde
of the
Pueblo

Francisco de Haro

FRANCISCO DE HARO was a shrewd bargainer in real estate. He did exceedingly well on May 12, 1837 when he purchased from Jose Antonio Galindo the Rancho de la Merced — comprising what is now the greater part of San Francisco and San Mateo Counties — for 100 cows and merchandise to the value of $25.

The satisfaction he may have gotten from his purchase was forgotten when the two sons he idolized, Francisco and Ramon, along with their uncle, Jose Reyes Berryessa, were ruthlessly shot to death by Fremont's men in June, 1846. It was a blow from which he suffered until the day of his death, November 28, 1849.

De Haro had come to the little Yerba Buena settlement in 1819 as a sub-lieutenant in a Mexican regiment of infantry. He spent some time at the Presidio and received other assignments that took him to scattered parts of the territory. Later he retired from active military service to make his home by the Bay.

In February, 1834 Mariano Vallejo, the Commandante of the military post, received orders from Governor Figueroa to hold an election for civil officers for Yerba Buena. Delays made it impossible for Vallejo to execute these instructions until December of that year.

The Commandante's home became the polling place. It was quite adequate since the number of votes cast did not exceed 27. De Haro was elected Alcalde. The office of secretary went to Francisco Sanchez. As can be surmised from the size of the community, the Alcalde's duties were not too burdensome. Four years after taking office, De Haro received instructions from Governor Alvarado to have the town surveyed, a task for which he selected Jean Jacques Vioget, a young Swiss engineer. Vioget did not name the streets and their boundaries were designated only by buildings and fences. Zoeth Eldredge writes that Vioget's original drawings first hung in "Bob Ridley's billiard saloon," later to find their way to the walls of the Recorder's office in the City Hall where they remained until destroyed in the fire of 1906.

As Alcalde, De Haro served two terms, the first expiring at the close of 1835; the second running from 1838 to 1840. He had been out of office for six years when the killings of his sons and brother-in-law occurred, a senseless tragedy that remained a subject of dispute for many years with Fremont cast in a villainous role.

The facts no doubt are best told in a statement by an eyewitness, Jasper O'Farrell, the surveyor, as quoted in Eldredge's "Beginnings of San Francisco." In part, it follows:

"I was in San Rafael in June, 1846 when the then Captain Fremont arrived at that Mission with his troops. The second day after his arrival there, a boat landed three men at the mouth of the estero on Point San Pedro. As soon as they were observed by Fremont three men (of whom Kit Carson was one) were detailed to meet them. They mounted their horses and after advancing about 100 yards halted and Carson returned to where Fremont was standing on the corridor of the Mission, with Gillespie, myself and others, and said: 'Captain, shall I take these men prisoners?'

"In response Fremont waved his hand and said 'I have got no room for prisoners.' They then advanced to within fifty yards of the three unfortunate and unarmed Californians, alighted from their horses, and deliberately shot them. One of them was an old and respected Californian, Don Jose R. Berryessa, whose son was the Alcalde of Sonoma. The other two were twin brothers and sons of Don Francisco de Haro, a citizen of the Pueblo of Yerba Buena.

"I saw Carson some two years later and spoke to him of this act and he assured me that then and since he regretted to be compelled to shoot these men but Fremont was blood-thirsty enough to order otherwise, and he further remarked that it was not the only brutal act he was compelled to commit while under his command.

"I should not have taken the trouble of making this public but that the veracity of a pamphlet published by C. E. Pickett, Esq. in which he mentions the circumstance has been questioned — a history which I am compelled to say is, alas, true — and from having seen a circular addressed to the native Californians by Fremont, or some of his friends, calling on them to rally to his support. I therefore give the above act publicly so as to exhibit some of that warrior's tender mercies and chivalrous exploits, and must say that I feel degraded in soiling paper with the name of a man, whom for that act, I must always look upon with contempt and consider as a murderer and a coward."

This statement was published in the Los Angeles *Star* of September 27, 1856 with a letter from Jose de los Santos Berryessa, whose father was shot to death with the De Haro boys.

In his message, Jose Berryessa not only confirmed the O'Farrell version but added still more macabre details at Fremont's expense. He was himself a prisoner, he averred, and his father had come to the Mission on his behalf, accompanied by the boys. Let Berryessa tell the rest in his own words:

"Unfortunately Col. Fremont was walking in the corridor of the Mission with some of his soldiers and they perceived the three Californians (the elder Berryessa and the two De Haros). They took their arms and mounted — approached toward them, and fired. It is perhaps true that they were scarcely dead when they were stripped of the clothing, which was all they had on their persons; others say that Col. Fremont was asked whether they should be taken prisoners or killed and that he replied that he had no room for prisoners and in consequence of this they were slain."

Shortly after the shooting Berryessa observed one of Fremont's soldiers riding by, carrying a serape belonging to the murdered father.

He implored Fremont to retrieve it for him so that it could be taken to his mother but the Colonel refused, explaining that it belonged to the soldier.

Minutes later Berryessa met the trooper and begged for this memento of his father. It was given to him in exchange for $25.

Spear
The Merchant or the Soldier?

A residential street in 1847

IT COULD BE called the battle of Spear Street. For two men named Spear still vie, posthumously, for the honor of having the downtown street named for them. Perhaps the issue has received over much importance for when the street received its name, it was under water and legend has it that its first lot was sold for $25.

Nathan, the merchant, or Willis Bradford, the soldier — who is entitled to the honor? Historians do not agree. Zoeth Eldredge and Henry Carlisle vote for Nathan Spear. J. B. Fitzhamon, the well-known journalist, insists that it was the other Spear, whose descendants in Montana often said that their grandfather boasted of the thoroughfare that bore his name.

Both men played colorful roles in the pioneer days.

Nathan Spear arrived in California from Boston in 1832 by way of the Sandwich Islands. He first opened a store in Monterey with William Hinckley. They moved to Yerba Buena four years later, joined Jacob Leese as partners, and operated a trading post in competition with William Richardson. Nathan built the first flour mill in California on Clay Street near Montgomery. It was operated with mule power. Wheat was collected from ranches around the Bay and transported to the mill on schooners. Customers were charged one half of the flour that their grain produced.

Spear continued in this and other profitable ventures until 1846 when he sold his properties to his nephew, William Heath Davis.

The other Spear, had a venturesome career. He was a native New Yorker, claiming kinship with Governor William Bradley of Massachusetts. After his mother's death when he was sixteen, he wandered over Iowa prairies working at odd jobs, then moved to Arkansas, and finally to New Orleans. There he enlisted as a quartermaster's teamster in the forces of General Winfield Scott. He later became an Army Scout and had many exciting escapades, once being so severely wounded that he was hospitalized for months.

His recuperation in Mexico was cut short by reports of the gold discovery. Starting out at once for California, he rode alone for more than 300 miles before joining a party pushing through the wilderness over the southern route. Indians attacked them on the way and Spear was hit in the head by an arrowhead, receiving a serious wound that left a permanent scar.

San Francisco was facing an epidemic of sickness when he arrived in November, 1849 and for weeks he nursed many of the sufferers. Among them was a baby named Ociana to whom he took such a fancy that years later he gave the name to his first child.

Then, under peculiar circumstances, romance suddenly altered the way of Willis' life. By chance he met his brother John, from whom he had not heard for many years, and the truth about a broken love affair unexpectedly came to light.

Long before in New York, Willis had been infatuated with an attractive girl named Jane Ferguson when his letters to her suddenly brought no answers, Willis decided to go West and try to forget.

Now in Yerba Buena he learned from his brother what actually had occurred. John told him that Jane's aged uncle, a domineering sort with whom she lived, wanted her to marry a tailor named Wood and had deliberately intercepted Willis Spear's love letters — a mean bit of trickery that resulted in his niece's marriage to Thomas Wood.

"Are they still married?" Willis inquired anxiously.

"She's a widow now," John told him. "Wood came to California a few years later and died of cholera."

Willis, his old love rekindled, pressed for more information. "Did Jane ever learn the truth?" he inquired.

John Spear laughed. "Yes, she did," he said. "The old uncle disclosed the whole story on his deathbed. He even told her that if Wood ever died she should hunt you up and marry you."

Willis could scarcely believe what he was told. "Tell me," he demanded, "have you any idea where Jane is now?"

His brother took a worn notebook from his pocket, fingered the soiled leaves, and read an address in Niles, Michigan. "She's living there now with her two children. Going to write?"

Hours later a letter was in the mail. More were exchanged and a short time later Willis Spear was on his way East to marry his childhood sweetheart. They had four children and lived happily until his death at 89.

And that's the story of the two Spears. For whom the street was named does not seem to really matter.

Leidesdorff
The First
Black Citizen

A view of Leidesdorff Street

DESTINY PLAYED CURIOUS, ironical pranks in the life of William Alexander Leidesdorff. One historian, Miriam Allen de Ford, refers to him as one of the most interesting of all San Francisco pioneers.

He was a mulatto. Because of the black strain in his blood, his impending marriage to the beautiful young daughter of an aristocratic New Orleans family was forbidden. So he fled West, a self-proclaimed exile from southern bigotry.

In the young settlement on San Francisco Bay, where everyone was aware of his racial background, he became a wealthy government official and businessman, popular and highly respected. This striking difference in attitudes is relevant during today's time of social revolution and movements for equality.

Leidesdorff was born in St. Thomas in the Dutch East Indies, now the Virgin Islands, the son of a wandering Dane and a dark-skinned West Indian girl. By chance, a wealthy English planter took a fancy to the young child and offered to become his guardian. The offer was readily accepted, young William's parents presumably finding themselves unexpectedly relieved of a troublesome burden.

Under the friendly guidance of his new benefactor, the boy was sent to school and received sound, wholesome paternal counseling. He was in his early teens when a good opportunity came: a gainful job with the planter's wealthy brother, a cotton merchant in New Orleans. Before Leidesdorff left, he was scrupulously admonished never to disclose the fact of his mixed blood — good advice for a boy who was to make his home in Louisiana.

Young William was happy in his new surroundings. He was well paid and he saved his money. When his employer died some years later, his large estate was left to Leidesdorff, now grown to manhood.

With new-found wealth he lived well. He played the guitar, sang and courted pretty girls. Then he met Hortense, the attractive blonde young daughter of a rich and influntial aristocratic family that was proud to trace its lineage to Louis XIV of France. It was the proverbial love at first sight.

Hortense quickly accepted his marriage proposal and proudly wore the diamond ring she received a day later. Her family welcomed him and plans were made for an elaborate wedding.

But beneath the young man's happiness, lurked a heavy, taunting worry. Should he tell his fiancee of his mixed blood? Though swarthy of skin, no one had ever questioned his background. He fully realized the hazard of disclosing his secret, yet his conscience told him that the girl must know the truth before their marriage. For weeks he was tormented by his dilemma. At last he made the fatal decision — Hortense must be told.

The wedding was only a few days off when Leidesdorff revealed the story of his birth to her. The result was even worse than he had expected. In tears, the girl told him that her parents would never consent to the marriage but that she would always love him.

Leidesdorff left reluctantly. The next day a messenger brought him a bulky envelope, containing the engagement ring and a note from the girl's father stating that all relations between them were at an end.

Heart-broken, William Leidesdorff resolved at once to leave for the West and start a new life. He quickly sold all of his possessions. With the proceeds he purchased the 106-ton schooner *Julia Ann* and stocked it with provisions and merchandise for the voyage. The day before his departure, he was on Canal Street when in the distance he caught sight of an approaching funeral cortege.

Out of curiosity, he stepped into a nearby store and inquired who had died. The answered stunned him. "A society girl — poor thing," the clerk told him. "She nearly married a mulatto and she died yesterday of shock."

That night a priest called on Leidesdorff and handed him a crucifix. "I officiated at Hortense's funeral," he explained. "Just before her death she told me to give you this and to tell you that she still loved you."

Hours later Leidesdorff was on his way to California. He landed in the little Yerba Buena cove in 1841 and was warmly greeted in the sparsely settled community. He knew almost at once that this was where he wished to live.

He acquainted himself with his crude surroundings and began to plan his future. There was money to be made. Ambitiously he set to work, determined not only to succeed but to make himself an active part of the settlement as well. Before long he had made a profitable start.

For a short time he engaged in trade along the coast. Then he purchased an old sidewheeler called the *Sitka,* after its place of origin. He brought the *Sitka* from Alaska to Yerba Buena, where it became the first steamboat on San Francisco Bay. Leidesdorff announced the beginning of regular ship service to Sacramento but the maiden voyage brought chagrin and bitter disappointment. For some reason, the trip took six days and seven hours. Soon after he landed, he learned that an ox cart, which had started at about the same time, had already arrived. Leidesdorff abandoned the business and turned to carrying freight about the Bay. But he saw still better opportunities and began to develop them.

He erected a small building at Clay and Kearny Streets, known as the Old Adobe. It became his home and the site of his new general merchandise store and ship chandlery shop. He also built the town's first hotel, a one-story structure on the Plaza. He later sold it to an Englishman. John Brown, who renamed the place the City Hotel. Its spacious billiard room soon became a gambling hall.

Anticipating growth in commerce, Leidesdorff built the first warehouse and wharf at the foot of Pine Street, purchased lumber in large quantities and invested his profits in land. Before long he was accepted as one of the settlement's most respected businessmen. His advice was sought after and his popularity grew fast. It was certain that as the community developed, Leidesdorff would play a major role in government affairs.

He was named Master of the Port and later honored with an appointment as United States vice-consul, a position he held despite the fact that he was not an American citizen.

Later his adobe home was the scene of the first election after the town came under United States rule. A crate once used for shipping lemon syrup was transformed into a ballot box, with a slit cut in the cover for the insertion of ballots. Washington Bartlett, an American, was chosen to be the Alcade, a post combining the duties of mayor and magistrate.

Leidesdorff already had built himself a new, more comfortable home at Clay and Montgomery Streets. It was surrounded by large gardens and the owner, always cordial, delighted in presenting flowers to women as they walked by.

Politics in and out of the town intrigued him and rapidly he assumed more important roles. He participated in Fremont's abortive Bear Flag rebellion and, when Northern California came under American rule, was elected a member of the community's council. Later he became city treasurer. In 1847 he was appointed a member of a committee of three to supervise the building of the first public school.

At the height of his popularity he was stricken with brain fever and died in May, 1848. He was then only 38 years old and had never married.

Despite his successful career, he had incurred debts of fully $50,000 but before his estate was finally settled two years later, the value had mounted to more than $1,000,000 due to Gold Rush inflation. He had left no will.

His death was a shock to the community and all agreed that something must be done to perpetuate his memory. Before long the Gold Rush was under way. Ships were crowding into the little harbor and better facilities were needed. The waterline was pushed back and a street laid out along the beach. It was named for Leidesdorff. Along it rose a two-story building to house the Pacific Mail Steamship Company. The sidewalk was formed by sinking cases, which had come filled with Virginia tobacco, into the mud.

Thirty years later the street had become a crooked alley four blocks long in the heart of the financial district. It was crowded with offices of grain and mining brokers. Gambling in stocks and commodities brought quick profits — and often heavy losses. Because of the latter, the street took the nickname of Pauper Alley and large numbers of women, dabbling in investments, became derisively known as mudhens.

With the passing of time Leidesdorff's spectacular career began to fade from memory until an unexpected sequel suddenly thrust the name of the dark-skinned pioneer into public print. It came in 1854, six years after his death.

It was then that suit was brought in San Francisco by the surviving relatives of a young Hungarian named Wolf Leidesdorfer, who, it was said, had left home in 1817 at the age of 15 never to return. Vague reports had reached his family that he had gone to America and reaped a fortune. Now the claimants insisted that their long-lost kin was in fact William Alexander Leidesdorff and that, since there was no will, they were entitled to his estate.

Captain John L. Folsom was appointed temporary administrator and lost no time in trying to convert at least some of the Leidesdorff fortune to himself. Hurrying to Jamaica, where the claimants lived, he located some of the Hungarian boy's relatives and, after impressing them with the difficulty of proving their case, purchased some of their claims to the estate of William Leidesdorff. Among those who sold their interests was a Negro woman who insisted that she was the mother of the deceased and that his father had been a Dane.

The suit dragged on long after the statute of limitations had expired. To terminate matters, Governor John Bigler ruled that the fortune should become the property of the state. There was a move to recover from Folsom but it was never pressed.

Historians give no credence to the claims of Wolf Leidesdorfer's survivors. They point out that William Leidesdorff, who in California made no secret of his Negro blood, was of dark complexion. Wolf

Leidesdorfer's skin was fair and discrepancies in the ages of the two further support the conclusion that the contentions of Wolf's heirs were groundless.

One hundred and twenty-two years after Leidesdorff's death — on Sunday, July 12, 1970 — members of the San Francisco Negro Historical and Cultural Society honored his memory in a march along the street that bears his name.

Larkin

Searcher Turned Settler

Thomas O. Larkin

UNLIKE MANY YOUNG men of his time who migrated from their eastern homes in quest of fortune and adventure, Thomas O. Larkin was motivated by a far different urge. He might have remained contentedly in his home in Charlestown, Massachusetts but for his desire to locate his half-brother to whom he had been devoted since childhood.

Try as he might, he could get only scant word about the man he sought, John B. R. Cooper. In devious ways he had learned only that Cooper, following the example of their uncle, was a sea captain in the western trade, had commanded a vessel bound for the Pacific Coast and located permanently in a distant land called California. On occasion young Larkin had talked to seamen returning from the West but they knew nothing of the missing Cooper.

As time passed, Larkin became increasingly anxious to find his half-brother or at least learn his fate, for he feared that Cooper had fallen victim to savage Indians. At last, although he was without funds, he decided to go to California and press the search himself.

Fortunately—or perhaps unfortunately—he had no dependents. His father, of British ancestry with kin who had fought at Bunker Hill, had died when the boy was seven; his mother nine years later.

So Larkin's only concern was to earn enough for passage to the far western country. He had just observed his nineteenth birthday when he was told that there were good opportunities in Wilmington, North Carolina. Impulsively, he left his poorly paying job in a book and stationery store and prepared for the southern move. With him went a youth of the same age with whom he had made an unusual pact: they would share a room together and pool their earnings; if one was without work the other would support him.

Both found employment, however, and the relationship continued for more than six years. Larkin then decided they should go their separate ways. He had been earning a modest wage in a sawmill until his health failed and he was obliged to give up his job.

He returned to Charlestown. His savings were meager and he was uncertain of his future, still wondering if he would ever have sufficient funds to journey West.

In desperation he called on the owners of a shipping line for whom his uncle had commanded Pacific-bound vessels. They did not carry passengers but the men who heard his story were touched and agreed to do their best to help him. They finally arranged passage on a ship, the *Newcastle,* in command of a Captain Hersey.

It was a hard voyage, made more difficult by the young man's poor health. But the purpose of the trip buoyed his spirit, despite the fact that he was obliged to sail first to the Sandwich Islands before touching at Yerba Buena Cove.

Finally reaching his destination, Larkin made inquiries and was delighted to learn that his half-brother was well and prospering, living in Monterey. He hastened there and found Cooper comfortably situated and happily married to a sister of General Vallejo.

It was a happy reunion, compensating Larkin for all of his anxiety and difficulties. Day after day, and often far into the night, they talked together, relating their experiences since they had last seen each other.

Cooper was insistent that his half-brother remain in California. He pointed out the opportunities in virgin country and promised to help Larkin find gainful work. A good job was found in a flour mill and the newcomer soon settled down to comfortable living.

A year after his arrival he fell in love. Since he and his fiancee, a British girl, were Protestants, the padres could not marry them. The problem was solved by having the ceremony performed aboard an American ship by the American consul of the Sandwich Islands, John R. Jones, who chanced to be on the mainland.

As Larkin neared the end of two years at the mill, he started looking for a chance to have his own business. He was robust now and somewhat envious of Cooper who was working for himself.

Friends pointed out that there were pressing needs for lumber — not only for home building but for export — and they believed big opportunities lay in that field. He became interested and established a mill to turn out shingles and heavy building timber in large quantites. There were good markets in this region and in Mexico and, before long, he branched out into other merchandise, selling soap and foodstuffs.

His success became known and word of his earnestness reached men high in the American government. To his surprise, he received an appointment in 1884 as United States Consul for all of California. Two years after he also undertook the responsibilities of naval storekeeper.

Somewhat later he assumed the position of confidential representative of the United States, a post given him in the hope of bringing about the occupation of California without bloodshed. At that time foreign countries, especially Russia, were casting covetous eyes on the rich territory and it became Larkin's task to keep the government informed of what he saw and heard.

In his official capacities he exerted a strong influence among all elements of the population. It was to him that Commodore Sloat looked for tactful strategy in anticipation of actual American rule. As Consul, Larkin joined Sloat in signing the official proclamation on July 7, 1846 in Monterey. He felt confident that the change would be accepted by the Californios, but he was unwilling to rely on his judgment without actively working to insure peaceful transition. Moving about and meeting those he knew could be trusted, he succeeded in allaying fears and averting disorders.

At the request of Commodore Stockton, he traveled down the coast on the *U.S. Congress,* stopping at Santa Barbara, San Pedro and Los Angeles to hoist the American flag and confer with Mexican officials. It was delicate business in which Larkin displayed such unusual diplomacy that Stockton named him a member of a small and carefully selected group that met in Yerba Buena to assist in governmental affairs.

Soon after this meeting, Larkin set out for a conference with Colonel Fremont in a remote region in the mountains. As he departed, he was totally unaware of a trap that was being set for him by a band of rebellious Californios. He had been warned by friends to be on his guard but Larkin, always courageous, was confident that no harm would come.

Perhaps he should have sensed trouble when, on starting back to Monterey, a friendly traveler loaned him a fast horse with the understanding that should Larkin be killed, his wife would pay for the animal.

He did reach Monterey in safety, however. On his arrival, he found word awaiting him that one of his children was critically ill in San Francisco and that he was wanted there at once. He was riding northward when darkness fell and he put up for the night, intending to resume his ride at dawn.

Long after midnight he was awakened by a party of Californios, who took him to a camp some distance away and ordered to reveal the whereabouts of an American party. Larkin bluntly refused, even under threats of great bodily harm, but his demands for release were ignored.

The reason for his capture has never been fully understood. It is presumed, however, that those who held him planned an ambush against a large number of Americans and believed that wholesale murder might restore the area to Mexican hands.

He remained a prisoner for several months, well-treated by his captors, until he was finally allowed to go. Seriously worried about his family and government affairs, he hastened to San Francisco where he found his wife distraught and on the verge of collapse. Their child was dead and the mother had feared that she would never see her husband alive again.

Larkin resumed his official duties and received the personal thanks of President Polk for the astute manner in which he had helped to bring about the change in government.

The strain of office under trying circumstances had taken toll of his health and spirit and Larkin longed for an extended rest in Massachusetts. He resigned his posts and left with his family in 1850.

They were gone for three years when love of California induced them to return and establish a permanent home. This they did and settled again in San Francisco.

Hinckley

The Yankee Merchant

William Sturgis Hinckley

WILLIAM STURGIS HINCKLEY, a successful pioneer merchant, who became Yerba Buena's Captain of the Port and afterward Alcalde, has been honored by having his name given to a downtown thoroughfare officially designated as a "walk." He was an associate of two of the town's early day business leaders, Nathan Spear and Jacob Leese. Later he became a brother-in-law of William A. Richardson.

He was a native of Massachusetts and a nephew of William Sturgis, head of the widely-known mercantile firm of Bryant and Sturgis, which then carried on the principal trade with California. He came West as a ship's master, having previously spent several years at sea trading between the East Coast and Honolulu. He was at various times a supercargo and a master.

Hinckley's decision to settle permanently in Yerba Buena was made in 1830. It was then that he signed as master of the bark *Volunteer* with an understanding that after reaching his destination he would turn the vessel over to a representative of the owners then in Northern California.

His landing in Yerba Buena Cove turned the day into a gay occasion, for he had a number of talented musicians in his crew and when the bark dropped anchor they scrambled ashore with bugles, violins and flutes, serenading the startled settlers for hours.

This unexpected entertainment resulted in an enthusiastic welcome for Hinckley himself. After he had shaken hands with a goodly number of strangers, he walked away to gaze upon the little settlement where he had earlier decided to make his home. But for his vision and confidence in the future, he might have been bitterly disappointeed.

As he looked from one side to another, he saw only a few homes, some of adobe and others merely ramshackle shelters put together with rough boards and twisted sheets of metal which obviously had been gathered from abandoned ships. Here and there clothes were fluttering from lines fastened to tree boughs.

He observed only a few stores, actually trading posts, and all about he saw sand dunes of varying heights. Streets were unpaved and some of them were muddy. Yet, when settlers asked him later how he liked the place, he replied with great confidence: "You have a wonderful future here; I am glad I came."

"So are we," they chorused. "We'll all get along fine together."

For some months he traded about the Bay until by good fortune he quickly developed a friendship with Spear and Leese who had the esteem of the townsmen, already having established themselves as store-keepers in Monterey. The three men had come to know each other at a propitious time. Leese had only recently returned from a visit to Los Angeles where he was told by shipping men trading along the coast that with Spear he should open a store and commission house in Yerba Buena. The partners, discussing the idea, agreed that it was a good one, yet they feared that such an addition to their business would be more than two men could handle successfully by themselves. They realized that they would need a partner, but who?

Not long after meeting Hinckley they agreed that he was the man they wanted and he readily accepted their offer.

The new venture soon was yielding large profits. They invested shrewdly in ships and merchandise, once selling two schooners, the *Isabel* and the *Nicholas,* to John Sutter.

Another of Hinckley's good friends was Alcalde Guerrero, from whom he received title to two large lots on the block bounded by Montgomery and Kearny, Clay and Washington Streets. Hinckley shared the land grant with his partner Spear and, having taken the northern half for himself, he erected an adobe home. He was rewarded with more land after assisting Guerrero in landing two unwieldy cannon from the bark *Don Quixoto.*

Shortly after, in spite of his influential associates, Hinckley was accused of smuggling but finally succeeded in completely exonerating himself.

Apparently he did not suffer from the experience for, a short time later, he was appointed Captain of the Port. In 1844, fourteen years after his arrival, he was elected Alcalde. He already had married Doña Susana Martinez, regarded as one of the most beautiful women in the town. A sister had become Richardson's wife, establishing the relationship between the two pioneers.

One of Hinckley's first acts as Alcalde was to build a little bridge across the neck of the Jackson Street Lagoon which enabled people to reach Clark's Point without being obliged to walk completely around the pond. It was the town's first street improvement and the new executive was warmly praised.

Hinckley's career, however, was short lived. He was taken seriously ill in June, 1846 and died soon afterward at the age of 39; yet in his sixteen years in Yerba Buena, he had acquired sufficient popularity to have his memory perpetuated by the street which still bears his name.

Montgomery
The
Flag-Raiser

Montgomery Street 1849

THE CEREMONY WAS brief and simple yet it had nation-wide significance.

It occurred promptly at eight o'clock in the morning on July 9, 1846 when the little settlement of Yerba Buena officially became American territory.

No more than 20 civilians looked on as Commander John B. Montgomery hoisted the Stars and Stripes over the Plaza and formally took the town from the Mexican government.

A short time before, the U.S.S. sloop-of-war *Portsmouth* with Montgomery in command had slipped into San Francisco Bay. The skipper was well prepared to execute the orders he had received from Commodore Sloat. He hoped that he could do so without trouble.

After the *Portsmouth* had dropped anchor, Montgomery and a company of 70 men took to small boats and rowed to a landing place later to become the corner of Clay and Montgomery Streets.

As they scrambled ashore they anxiously scanned the sand dunes and the 30 little houses that sheltered the 200 inhabitants of the town. Minutes later on Montgomery's orders a fife and drum corps broke into a patriotic air and the party marched in double file on the red-tiled adobe custom house on the Plaza.

If the Commander had anticipated resistance, he was agreeably surprised. The few settlers merely watched curiously and waved friendly greetings.

At the Plaza, Montgomery looked about for Sub-Prefect Guerrero to formally demand the town's surrender. Guerrero was not there nor was any official representative of the Mexican regime.

Montgomery made inquiries and was told that Guerrero, to spare himself embarrassment, had already left for his rancho, ordering the

Mexican flag lowered before he departed. The Americans, seeing the bare pole, hastily hoisted their own flag.

Now Montgomery stepped forward and after a few words of introduction read Commodore Sloat's proclamation and his own orders. The *Portsmouth's* cannon roared a 21-gun salute, the little knot of spectators cheered, and the ceremony was over. Thus, a new chapter was written into the history of America.

It was part of a campaign to make all of Northern California U.S. territory. Two days before, Montgomery had taken Monterey. And, following his annexation of Yerba Buena, the American flag was ordered flown in Sacramento, Sonoma, San Jose and all other inhabited places in Northern California. As Soule reports in his "Annals," the flag "was generally beheld with tranquility if not with applause."

Montgomery remained about the Bay for a little more than five months until he was satisfied that all was well.

Later, his once-fond memories of the town were dimmed by sorrow. In December of 1846 two of his sons, both naval officers, started from Yerba Buena bound for Sacramento. The naval cutter they sailed in disappeared and, though Bay and river waters were searched for days, nothing was seen of the boat and crew again.

The Plaza where the ceremony took place was named for Montgomery's ship and some time later one of the town's principal streets took his name. It was then a shoreline of the Bay. On stormy days water splashed over and beyond it, forming a small lagoon at the base of what were then known as Montgomery Cliffs. Always slushy, with deep mud holes, it often was a burial ground for horses and mules that sank in the slimy morass as their owners hurriedly removed packs of merchandise. Businessmen constantly called for some improvement and when the narrow thoroughfare was paved with planks there was general rejoicing.

With the coming of the Gold Rush the street became the financial center of the town, as it still is today. One visitor in the early days, a French writer, called it the Rue Honore of San Francisco. Perhaps he had not heard of the duels and bloodshed which either started or took place on the street.

One such encounter brought about the death of George T. Hunt, a well-known lawyer.

Hunt, sitting in Montgomery Street's Metropolitan Theater, inadvertently put his feet on the chair in front of him just as Numa Hubert from New Orleans was about to take the seat. Words followed and Hubert demanded a duel to avenge his honor. Hubert won the duel but it was said that his adversary's death haunted him through life.

Four years later a few careless words in the Bank Exchange, the town's most popular bar, led to another fatal encounter on the same street. The victim was State Senator W. J. Ferguson, a brilliant orator, who was drinking with a group of friends. Talking glibly, he chanced to make an off-color comment about a young woman, not knowing that one of her close friends, George Pendleton Johnston of Kentucky, was within hearing distance. In the duel that followed Ferguson fell. Johnston was tried under an anti-dueling law that he himself had sponsored and was acquitted, largely on evidence that Ferguson, before his death, had refused to submit to an operation that might have saved his life.

On this same street, at another time, James King of William, editor of *The Bulletin,* was shot and killed by James P. Casey who paid with his life at the hands of the Vigilantes.

This violent way of life, however, did not impress General William T. Sherman as much as the physical condition of the street. Long after his visit there he described Montgomery Street as "the worst bog and succession of mudholes masquerading as a street in the United States in 1849."

Stockton

The Conquering Hero Comes Home

Commodore Robert F. Stockton

ON A WARM, sunny morning late in August of 1846 Commodore Robert F. Stockton sailed into San Francisco Bay aboard the frigate *Congress* and, to his great surprise, found himself the center of a gay celebration in his honor. Men, women and children came rushing to the shore to greet him.

They had heard, though only vaguely, of his brilliant victories in the South over rebellious natives, who were bitterly resentful of American authority. So Stockton was being hailed as a hero.

The colorful scene is vividly described by Frank Soule in his "Annals of San Francisco":

"The entire population of that place (Yerba Buena) and of the adjacent country gave him a formal reception — men, women and children marching in procession to low-water mark to meet him — and addressing him in terms of the most exalted praise and ardent devotion. His triumphant advent was celebrated with a banquet and ball, and the wildest demonstration of joy and satisfaction. The industrious, sober and peacefully disposed part of the inhabitants were glad to be relieved from the domination of the cruel and plundering chiefs and governors, who alternately ravaged the country, contended with each other, and oppressed the people. They soon perceived the advantages of security of life and property, which they never had enjoyed until the flag of the United States was floating on their soil."

The people probably did not know the masterful strategy that brought victory: how he had tricked the enemy into believing that his forces greatly outnumbered theirs although the situation was the exact reverse.

Stockton had first set foot on California soil on July 15, 1846 at Monterey, where he landed from the *Congress*. Eight days later he had assumed command of the Pacific Squadron, replacing Commodore Sloat who was in poor health and obliged to leave at once for the East.

From Sloat and from his own perceptive observations, Stockton soon realized the complexity of the task he had assumed. To his credit he lost no time in formulating his plans.

California, with settlements far apart and little means of communication, was in a state of extreme disorder. Sloat's occupation of Monterey and other coastal points had angered the natives and many were in open rebellion. The Bear Flag incident had added anger and dissension.

In addition, hostile Indians increased the gravity of the situation. Most of them supported the Californios in their hostility to the United States.

Under these circumstances, Stockton recognized the need for quick and effective action, not only to protect Americans already in California but also the immigrant parties known to be on their way. He feared that the Californios, left to concentrate their forces, well might succeed in repossessing those places where the American flag had been raised. He chose to concentrate on dividing the enemy and putting him on the defensive.

There still were other vexing problems. British agents were about, receiving large land grants from the Mexicans who believed that in this way they might forestall or even completely thwart American occupation.

Stockton fully realized the weakness of his forces. He had less than 350 untrained men, mostly sailors and marines unprepared for duty on land. Pitted against him would be more than 2,000 of the enemy; hard and experienced riders. He determined to try a bluffing game — it was his only recourse.

First he issued a hard-hitting proclamation. "I find myself," he wrote, "in possession of the ports of Monterey and San Francisco with daily reports of scenes of rapine, blood and murder. . . . I must therefore and will, as soon as I can, adopt such measures as may seem necessary to bring these criminals to justice . . .

"I cannot therefore," he continued, "confine my operations to the quiet and undisturbed possession of the defenseless ports of Monterey and San Francisco whilst the people elsewhere are suffering from lawless violence . . .

"The inhabitants are tired and disgusted with this constant succession of military usurpers and this insecurity of life and property. They invoke my protection . . . I require all officers, civil and military, and all other persons to remain quiet at their respective homes and stations, and to obey the orders they may receive from me or by my authority, and if they do no injury or violence to my authority, none will be done."

With this ultimatum, Stockton went into action. Fremont and a party were dispatched to San Diego aboard the sloop-of-war *Cyane* while

Stockton and his men set out for San Pedro, taking possession of Santa Barbara on the way.

Reaching his destination, he learned that Generals Castro and Pico were awaiting him with more than 2,000 men. He looked at his own scant force and shrugged his shoulders. "Victory or death," he told himself, preparing for the inevitable clash. He would have to rely on strategy and try to trick the enemy into believing itself far outnumbered.

In the brief time available, he drilled his men as best he could. A few days later, peering through his glasses, he observed two of Castro's men in the distance, approaching with a white flag. Was this a ruse, he wondered, or some move toward conciliation? There was no time to guess or wait.

Stockton quickly barked his orders: his men were to fall into line at once, march in formation through a copse of trees a short space away, about face and continue the operation to give the appearance of an almost endless line.

They were still marching when Castro's emissaries arrived, observed the maneuver, and, of course, greatly over-estimated the size of Stockton's little force. And they were equally surprised when they saw the Commodore's only mortar, poised for action in a way that suggested it was only one of many.

They handed Stockton Castro's note which suggested a truce under conditions the American deemed wholly unacceptable. Stockton so advised his callers, who hastened back with exaggerated reports of what they regarded as their adversary's overpowering strength.

After Castro had dispatched a second detail with the same result, Stockton chose to launch a sudden offensive before Castro should discover the sparsity of the American forces. He started for a point near Los Angeles, knowing that spies would be watching his difficult march over more than 30 miles of difficult rugged country.

The expected clash, however, did not occur. Castro and his officers, deceived by Stockton's clever ruse, broke camp and fled to Sonora for refuge with their disorganized troops. Not until some time later did Stockton learn just how greatly the enemy outnumbered him in artillery pieces as well as men.

Stockton was soon joined by Fremont and together they took possession of Los Angeles. A number of important Mexican officers, including Pico, surrendered but to demonstrate the American spirit of friendliness, Stockton refused to take them prisoners, allowing them freedom on their promise of loyalty.

The promise was soon broken but, even then, no penalties were imposed.

Stockton then proclaimed California a territory of the United States and turned his attention to organizing a civil government. He named officials to function in civil capacities, and drafted rules of conduct, assuming authority as both commander-in-chief and governor. Little more than a month had passed since his operations began, yet much of the insurrection had been overcome and California was now in American hands. Soule says of that achievement:

"In establishing a local government for California, Commodore Stockton displayed the discretion, abilities, discrimination and judgment of the skilful statesman, as conspicuously as he had exhibited on the field the prudence, enterprise and valor of the soldier.

"The march of Stockton upon the capital of California, though it was accomplished without a battle, or the loss of a single man, was nevertheless performed under circumstances of great difficulty as well as danger. . . .

"The moral effect of Stockton's march on Ciudad de los Angeles upon the minds of the Californians was equivalent to a triumphant victory, and the effusion of streams of blood. It broke down the spirit of resistance, destroyed all confidence in the course of capacity of the California generals, and inspired the inhabitants with terror of an enemy who moved with such celerity and boldness. Stockton's humane conduct reconciled the people to the change of government."

Stockton, camped near Los Angeles, was still enjoying the fruits of victory when he was advised that the United States was at war with Mexico. After assuring himself that the southern area, including Santa Barbara, was well protected, he proceeded north to Monterey. There word awaited him of an Indian uprising at Sutter's Fort.

He hurried to Yerba Buena, intending to mobilize forces there to counter the attack but it was not necessary, for he learned that the reports were incorrect and that all was peaceful. He lingered by the Bay long enough to meet Indian chiefs and to receive their promises of friendly relations. This done, he returned to Monterey.

The town by San Francisco Bay was to see him often, however, always welcoming him with adulation, pride and high respect.

Fremont

The
Maverick

General John Charles Fremont

DESPITE HIS REPUTATION as "the great pathfinder" of the wild and rugged West, General John Charles Fremont, bold and courageous, is regarded by many writers as one of the most controversial figures in the history of the country. He was ruthless, undisciplined, strong-willed and in every sense a maverick.

He was a man who thoroughly lacked diplomacy. He paid no heed to wanton killings by his men before and after the Bear Flag revolt in Sonoma. He turned friends into enemies and occasionally brought serious embarrassment to his government. Nevertheless, he did become a United States Senator from California and once ran unsuccessfully for President.

While most of his expeditions were intended to be solely for exploration and scientific study, he frequently assumed military authority. Many credit him for valuable contributions to the transition of California from Mexican to American rule and for subduing rebellious natives. One historian praises him for "finding everything west of the Rocky Mountains."

Perhaps his severest critic was Zoeth Eldredge, one of the State's foremost historians, who insisted that in no way did Fremont deserve such credit. Sparing no words, Eldredge had this to say of the man:

"The unpleasant facts of history are pushed aside and forgotten. We see only the picturesque figure of the hero of romance and we hail him as pathfinder, explorer, conqueror. We give his name to our streets, cities and towns and hold festivals in his honor. . . . This is wrong. The people should be taught the truth. John C. Fremont is not a hero of California. . . . Liberal quotations from original documents show how events have been misrepresented in order to build up an unmerited reputation."

A far different view is expressed by Frank Soule in his "Annals of San Francisco."

"Colonel John C. Fremont," he wrote, "is generally considered the conqueror of California where his exploits, undertaken with so small a force and against such superior numbers, place him on a par with the famous heroes of the days of chivalry."

It was ironic that a man of Fremont's grim determination and independence should have fallen victim of a resentful father-in-law. So bitterly did Senator Thomas H. Benton of Missouri protest the marriage of his sixteen-year-old daughter to the American soldier that he used his influence at least once — and perhaps more often — to have Fremont sent on exploring missions into far-away, untamed and dangerous regions.

This was his form of retribution and with strong political power gained by 31 years in Congress he was successful in overcoming the protests of his son-in-law.

Biographers differ as to how many times the Senator actually was responsible for Fremont's hazardous assignments into unexplored terrain. Some insist that the two men were reconciled after the first expedition; that those following came solely because of Fremont's strength, ability and resourcefulness. Others are certain that the breach was not healed for many years; that Benton was unrelenting in a desire to keep his daughter and her husband apart.

Fremont, born in Savannah, Georgia in 1813, and graduated from Charleston College, began his military career as a professor of mathematics in the Navy. He transferred to the Army, was commissioned a second lieutenant, and assigned to a regiment of topographical engineers.

He was in Washington in this capacity when he met the young and attractive Jessie Benton, then attending an exclusive private school. They fell in love and were soon married, despite the vigorous objections of the Benton family. The Senator angrily ordered his new son-in-law to leave the house and never return. Jessie with defiance looked at her father and quoted from the Book of Ruth: "Whither Thou goest I will go." Now, if the Senator had not succeeded in preventing the marriage, at least he could separate the couple — and he did.

Shortly after the wedding, Fremont received his first traveling orders — at Benton's instigation — to explore a wild region of the Far West, including an area in which Benton knew there were scalping Indians. The bride, of course, remained at home with her parents. It was on this expedition that Fremont climbed the second highest mountain in the Wind River Range, which later was named Fremont Peak.

He had returned home only a short time when he received orders in 1844 to survey the mouth of the Columbia River in the Northwest. During this assignment he sent back valuable data to Washington on the Great Salt Lake area, the Great Basin and the Sierra. That year he was elevated to a captaincy.

If Fremont believed that he might spend some time with his young wife after this mission was accomplished, he was sorely disappointed. There was talk of an imminent war with Mexico and in 1845 he was sent again to the Far West in the belief he might render valuable aid in the conquest of California. He is credited with having helped materially in bringing the territory under American domination and, in fact, later served there as military and civil governor.

It was during his military operations in California that the Bear Flag Revolt occurred on June 15, 1846, an historic incident for which he was widely criticized. Although the extent of his personal participation remains in doubt, the maneuver was carried out by men who had been under his command and resulted in the arrest of General Vallejo, a close friend of Fremont, and a number of others, including Salvador Vallejo, the General's brother, and Jacob Leese of Yerba Buena. They were taken under guard to Sutter's Fort and held prisoners during the short life of the "California Republic."

Fremont's troubles increased after the arrival of General Stephen Kearny and his forces in California. Fremont, who liked his independence, refused to recognize the General's authority and flatly declined to obey his orders. At Kearny's direction, Fremont was arrested and sent to Washington for court-martial.

To the surprise of many, his father-in-law, Senator Benton, hurried to his defense, accusing Kearny of persecution. Nevertheless, Fremont was found guilty and ordered dismissed from the service. The sentence would have been imposed but for the intercession of President Polk. Fremont promptly resigned his commission.

He made two more trips to the West, one at his own expense in which he led a civilian party in an effort to find a feasible route over the mountains to California.

In 1849 he settled for a time near Mariposa and bought a large estate which included valuable gold mines. A year later he was elected to the United States Senate. San Francisco had always attracted him and he spent much time there on government business and with friends.

Despite the demands of his new office, his wife now joined him, practically for the first time since their marriage. Recalling her delight, she recorded in her memoirs years afterward: "Not until 1849 could I share life with him — pioneer life in the new found El Dorado."

Their eldest child, a son, was born in California and was named for his father.

In 1854 the Fremonts moved to New York and two years later he was nominated as the Republican candidate for President but was defeated.

At the outbreak of the Civil War he chose to support the Union cause, though born a Southerner. The government, recognizing his past services and his knowledge of military affairs, commissioned him a major general. He was given command of the entire Western Department with headquarters in St. Louis. Later he was transferred to West Virginia.

When the war was over, Fremont resigned his commission and was retired by Congress with full rank.

He was again nominated for President but withdrew.

Back in civilian life, Fremont became interested in promoting a southern railroad across the continent. With his wife he traveled extensively through Europe and was hailed as an American military hero. In Denmark the couple was formally received by the King and Queen. Germany and Austria also honored him.

From 1878 to 1879 he served as Governor of the Arizona Territory and during that period his wife contributed greatly to the advancement of schools in the region. A gifted author, she also did considerable lucrative writing.

They then returned to New York where Fremont engaged in the practice of law until illness compelled him to retire. In the hope of regaining his health, the family moved to California. There they enjoyed a quiet life until the fall of 1890 when they decided on a short vacation trip to New York to visit friends and relatives. Soon after their arrival Fremont was overcome by heat and died October 30.

Since he left no property, Congress voted the widow a special pension equal to the pay of a retired major general.

Soon afterward a group of grateful California women, eager to show their appreciation of what General Fremont had done for the state, presented the widow with a home and an orange grove.

Bryant

San Francisco's First Author

From the head of Clay Street, 1849

EDWIN BRYANT MAY have won his place in early San Francisco history as a politician or as an author — or maybe both. Whether his name was given to a street for his service as Alcalde or because he wrote the first book on the early settlement, glorifying its beauty and the hospitality of its people, has never been determined. At all events, the book "What I Saw in California," was widely read throughout the country and was subsequently translated into foreign languages. It also rendered invaluable service to pioneers crossing the plains to California, for Bryant indicated the best routes and warned against dangers on the way.

A native of Massachusetts, he came West by the Overland Route with a wagon train, leaving Independence, Missouri somewhat ahead of the ill-fated Donner Party. It was a long hazardous trip, beset with difficulties which ended only when the travelers approached Sutter's Fort and were met by couriers with a note from Sutter offering food and shelter. Their scant baggage was carried to the Fort by Sutter's men and on arrival the tired little band received a rousing welcome. It was their first taste of western hospitality.

After resting for a few days Bryant packed his belongings intending to start at once for Yerba Buena. But, shortly before his departure messengers brought the alarming news that a band of hostile Walla Walla Indians had appeared some miles away, intending to attack the Fort and avenge the murder of a tribesman there two years before. If they could not take the Fort itself, the Indians warned, they would drive off all of the cattle and do other damage.

Bryant stayed to help resist the attack. New defenses were thrown up and the twelve pieces of artillery guarding the Fort were readied for immediate action. Two days later the tenseness subsided; spies hurried back with news that the Indian party was very small and that its members were friendly rather than hostile.

When Bryant finally arrived in Yerba Buena he received a cordial welcome from William Leidesdorff, who invited him into his home. The newcomer was fascinated by what he saw about him. As he chronicled later in his book:

"The morning was beautiful; not a ripple disturbed the placid and glossy surface of the Bay and harbor in which were anchored fully 30 large vessels consisting of whalemen, merchantmen and the U.S. sloop-of-war *Portsmouth*. Besides these there were numerous small craft giving to the harbor a commercial air of which the large cities of the Atlantic Coast would feel vain.

"We were received with every mark of respectful attention and cordial hospitality by Mr. Leidesdorff," he wrote on. "That afternoon I walked to one of the elevated hills in the vicinity of the town from which I had a view of the entrance of the Bay of San Francisco. A thick fog hung over the ocean outside of the Bay. The deep roar of the eternally restless waves as they broke one after another upon the rock-bound shore could be heard with great distinction although some five or six miles distant."

Bryant decided that he would remain in California for a time at least but first he chose to serve in Fremont's forces to help in the military effort. He was commissioned a lieutenant.

Later he settled in Yerba Buena, went into business, and took a part in the town's affairs. On November 22, 1847 he was appointed Alcalde, succeeding Bartlett, and became the second such executive under American rule.

Bryant assumed his new duties with a strong desire to contribute to the development of the community. At a time when very few had confidence in the future of the western coast, he recognized the town's potential as an important commercial center and devoted himself to encouraging it. He worked hard for harbor improvements as the only way to increase trade.

The impoverished condition of the town treasury worried him and to raise funds he promoted the sale of lots along the waterfront, which also proved of material help to the settlers.

His term expired before the gold discovery and he went back to his home in Massachusetts. He remained there for about a year before returning to San Francisco, again traveling the Overland Route.

On his return he was amazed by the growth and development that had taken place.

"I found San Francisco visibly improved," he wrote in his book. "Wherever the Anglo-Saxon race plants themselves progress is certain to be displayed in some form or other.

"On my return I found that an American population had flowed into it. Lots that had been considered valueless were selling at high prices; new homes had been built; commercial houses had been established and a newspaper was being published. The little village of 200 when I first arrived is becoming a town of importance. Ships freighted with cargoes are entering the port and landing their merchandise to be disposed of on shore instead of the former mode of vending them afloat. There is a prevailing air of enterprise and energy."

As added evidence of progress, he noted that Kearny had established a semi-monthly mail service between San Francisco and San Diego. The mail was carried by two soldiers riding horseback.

He remained in San Francisco for several years, acquired considerable property and took an active interest in business and civic affairs. But the East beckoned him again. He sold his holdings, bade goodby to his friends, and left, never to return.

At the outbreak of the Civil War he enlisted in a California Battalion, serving until the end of the conflict. Then he settled in Louisville, Kentucky, joined a newspaper staff, and wrote his book which was soon sold as an accepted standard authority in the field he covered.

In 1869 he was fatally injured in a fall.

Years later, in 1875, a man named Andrew J. Bryant became San Francisco's fourteenth mayor, a circumstance leading some to believe that it was for him that Bryant Street was named. Early authoritites, however, agree that the honor went to his earlier, unrelated namesake.

Hyde

The Philadelphia Lawyer

George Hyde

THOUGH HE WAS practicing law in Philadelphia in 1842 and knew practically nothing of the Far West, George Hyde was obsessed with a strong desire to have California become a possession of the United States. He foresaw the coming war with Mexico and had implicit faith in American victory.

So eager was Hyde to play a part in bringing the western territory under the Stars and Stripes that he closed his office and volunteered his services to the Navy. In time he not only saw his hopes materialize but became the third Alcalde of Yerba Buena under American rule.

He was born in Philadelphia August 22, 1819, a descendant of English nobility and the fourth of his line to bear the name of George. For years the family had been wealthy, with property passing from one generation to the next. His grandfather had founded a large publishing house.

George Hyde III, his father, had died at the age of 28, leaving an estate that provided more than enough for the boy's education. After completing grade schools, young George was sent with his brother to Mount St. Mary's College in Emittsburg, Maryland.

Since he had no financial problems, he laid his plans for long post-graduate studies, giving little thought to a career. His mother remarried while he was still in college, however, and a year later found herself in serious financial difficulties. George was told by the executor of the estate that he must choose at once between a business career and a profession. He decided to study law.

At 20 he was graduated with honors from Mount St. Mary's and left at once for Philadelphia to begin his law studies. On July 18, 1842 he was admitted to the Bar. He opened a small law office in his native city and with a fair practice developing he decided to marry.

His bride was Ellen McCoy, of a distinguished Philadelphia family. They were to become the parents of six children.

Life for the young couple might have continued happily in their home city had not Hyde become so seriously concerned over growing tensions between the United States and Mexico. Why he should be so disturbed over the fate of California was something that he could not explain, yet he resolved to do what he could in behalf of the distant land known to him only through reading.

His opportunity, as he saw it, came when it was announced that Commodore Robert F. Stockton had been appointed to take command of Pacific waters. The young attorney applied for a position under Stockton and was elated to be named the Commodore's secretary aboard the *U.S.S. Congress.*

His wife returned to live with her parents and Hyde sailed from the East Coast October 29, 1845. The voyage was so difficult that the *Congress* did not drop anchor in Monterey Bay until nine months later, on July 14, 1846. Just a week before, Commodore John D. Sloat had raised the flag of the United States over Monterey and claimed it in behalf of his government.

Hyde, now satisfied that California was in American hands, requested discharge from service as had been promised him before his departure from the East. Leaving Monterey, he headed directly north for what was then Yerba Buena, arriving in the middle of August. The town, which then had a population of 200, became his permanent home. He sent for his wife and on her arrival they established a modest residence on Clay Street near Dupont. Their home became known as "the Sazarac."

Conditions in the little settlement were turbulent. Captain Montgomery, who had arrived aboard the sloop of war *Portsmouth,* was trying to restore order and to establish a civil government. He asked Hyde to become the Alcalde but the offer was refused and Lieutenant Bartlett was appointed in his stead.

As a lawyer, Hyde busied himself trying to settle titles under old land grants, many of which were in dispute. The task was far more difficult than he had expected, for the former Mexican officials, angered by American occupation, flatly refused to provide needed information.

Hyde was therefore obliged to hunt through great stacks of yellowed documents to uncover what he needed at the cost of much time and patience. When disputes were settled, Montgomery authorized the Alcalde to grant a 50 vara lot to any person who applied.

Hyde's services in clearing land titles and in proposing a form of government for the town brought him into prominence. When Bartlett, the Alcalde, was taken prisoner by an angry group of Californios and held for several months while on a business trip, Hyde was named to serve until his return.

He assumed his duties with such understanding that people began to speak of him as a likely candidate for permanent office. After Bartlett had returned and concluded his term in February, 1847, Edwin Bryant was chosen to succeed him. He served only four months and Hyde was made Alcalde in June, 1847. The appointment came while Hyde was away on a business errand in San Jose. Knowing nothing of his selection, he returned home to find himself the chief executive.

He soon was obliged to transact all of his official business in his own law office, since the Alcalde's headquarters in the old adobe Custom House on the Plaza had been taken over by a company of Marines ordered ashore to defend the town.

This situation later saved him from embarrassment while he was presiding at a trial — one of an Alcalde's many official duties. *The Star,* with which he was unfriendly, had openly accused him of smoking in the courtroom.

In reply, he simply explained that the courtroom was his own private office where he could do as he pleased, though he was careful to say that he never smoked during formal sessions.

The Hydes built an attractive new home on a grassy flat that most people considered to be far out of town. It was on the corner of Post, Market and Montgomery Streets, close to where the Mechanic's Institute now stands.

George Hyde left office in April, 1848 and resumed his law practice until 1852 when he retired with sufficient means to live a quiet, peaceful life until his death on August 16, 1890.

Stevenson

San Francisco's
First Mason

Colonel Jonathan Stevenson

MANY BELIEVE THAT Stevenson Street honors the memory of the famous author, Robert Louis Stevenson, who loved San Francisco and did much of his writing in the City.

Actually, the narrow downtown thoroughfare is named for Colonel Jonathan Drake Stevenson, a soldier, lawmaker and the first Grand Master of the Masonic Order in California.

Before coming West, Stevenson had spent busy years in New York City where he was born on New Year's Day, 1880. He was proud to be the grandson of a soldier who had fought in the Revolution and the son of a shipmaster who for years had been in the service of New York's revenue department.

In young manhood he had evidenced extraordinary business acumen, which came to the attention of Governor D. D. Tompkins of his native state. A close friendship developed and when the Governor engaged in an enterprise to run steamers from Staten Island to Manhattan, he appointed Stevenson as his agent. It was an association that led to advancement. When Tompkins was elected Vice-President of the United States, he promptly selected Stevenson to be his private secretary.

In Washington Stevenson quickly made friends with important men in high places and won their confidence. They held him in high regard, to such an extent that on one occasion William L. Marcy, who became Secretary of State, wrote to a member of the Cabinet:

"I will say to you with great cheerfulness, that I consider Stevenson a warm and devoted friend to me and to the Democratic Party and its principles. . . . I have corresponded with him and I have found him to be strictly faithful to truth, perfectly honorable. He never seems to me to think of himself when his friends or his party are in danger."

Soon after reaching his majority, young Stevenson became a member of a military company in New York. Five years later he joined with Colonel W. W. Tompkins in forming a distinguished group of citizen soldiers that became known as the Tompkins Blues. He was in command of a regiment when he resigned in 1840 with the reputation of being one of the finest tacticians in his state.

Six years afterward he was elected a member of the New York State Legislature. While on a business trip to Washington he met President Polk who offered him the command of a volunteer regiment, with the rank of colonel, to serve in California. The war with Mexico already had started. Stevenson readily accepted, with the understanding that it would be his responsibility to recruit his men.

This he did with such caution that some of Polk's severe critics grasped the opportunity to raise a bitter political issue. They charged that politics were responsible for Stevenson's rejection of some volunteers. A few of those he had refused threatened to take legal action, claiming that their reputations had been damaged.

The controversy continued up to the hour the Colonel had set to board one of the three transports that would take his regiment, 750 strong, to California. It was then he learned of a plot carefully conceived by his antagonists: if he could be served with papers for legal action before his departure, it would be possible to detain him, perhaps indefinitely, and he well might lose his command.

Stevenson, however, was equal to the situation. Hurriedly boarding one of the transports, he issued orders to sail as quickly as possible and directed that no person should be allowed aboard unless he were a member of the regiment. Soon the sheriff approached the ship in a launch, intending to board it until an officer in charge announced that he had instructions to shoot any unauthorized person setting foot on the deck. The sheriff withdrew but early the next morning complained to the Mayor. A squad of policemen was dispatched to the transport with orders to arrest the Colonel. The vessel with Stevenson aboard already was at sea.

Stevenson arrived in San Francisco March 7, 1847. Awaiting him were orders from General Kearny for the dispersion of his forces to various parts of the state — to San Francisco, Monterey, Sonoma and Santa Barbara.

The regiment had become known as the Seventh New York Infantry. Stevenson had his troubles with it, not only aboard the transport but after landing. Despite all of the precautions he had taken in selecting volunteers, a number of his men proved to be former Australian convicts known as Sydney Ducks, ruffians who at times became unmanageable.

The Colonel soon endeared himself personally to the native population however, maintaining order with a firm hand, yet acting always justly. His men also adored him and he had won the respect of his superiors.

In October, 1848 the regiment was mustered out. With a few officers and enlisted men from his outfit, Stevenson went into the mining country. A group of miners in the Mokelumne Hill district, in the heart of the Mother Lode, implored him to draft a code of regulations for those working at the mines. His proposals were accepted without change and became the basis for the regulation of mining claims in later years. In fact, he was selected to supervise enforcement of his code.

Somewhat later he moved to San Francisco and entered into partnership with Dr. William C. Parker, the former assistant surgeon of the regiment. They engaged in real estate transactions there and in Santa Cruz and were the first to sell large-sized lots which netted considerable profit. Before long they acquired wealth. They were the first to construct a home with lathes and plaster, and also the first to erect buildings on pile foundations over the swampy shores of the Bay. Later Dr. Parker withdrew from the firm after Stevenson had bought him out.

His eccentric style of dress made him a familiar figure about the town, always wearing a long-tailed coat and a peculiar cap, covered with black oilcloth above the visor. With his young and vivacious wife, who had come from Australia, he presided over an English-styled country home near Mission Dolores.

About this time a new interest came to demand much of his time and effort: Freemasonry. He had been a prominent member of the fraternity in New York, and was thought of immediately when the creation of a Masonic grand lodge in California was initially proposed in New York. Peter Lassen, long active in Masonry in the eastern state, was sent to confer with Stevenson, who readily agreed to render all possible assistance.

Lassen then traveled to Missouri to obtain the needed charter. In 1848 the California Grand Lodge was officially created and Stevenson was honored by election as its first Grand Master. He was installed with fitting ceremonies by Charles Gilman, a past Grand Master of Maryland, who had come to California expressly for the occasion.

In his inaugural address, Stevenson called on his brother Masons to stand firmly together and to remain steadfast behind the Masonic creed. "As a member of this Order," he declared, "no man can be a stranger among his brethren; no man can be in sickness or affliction without someone ministering to his wants and contributing to his comfort."

The first Masonic Hall in San Francisco was erected in 1849 under Stevenson's supervision.

At the time there were many in want in San Francisco and other parts of California. A cholera epidemic added to the need for extensive relief activities. As the highest Mason in the State, Stevenson put Masonic principles into action, rendering great assistance, and sometimes defraying costs out of his own pocket.

In 1851 business in San Francisco began to decline and Stevenson, like many others, felt the financial pressure. He was heavily in debt; his creditors were demanding money. Concerned with their welfare as well as his own, he promptly assigned all of his assets to those to whom he was indebted. As a mark of confidence and respect, they permitted him to continue with his business.

He liquidated his assets as profitably as he could, eventually paying all of his creditors' claims, both in interest and in principal. If he had been less prompt and conscientious, he might have sold his properties a few years later at enormous profit.

As time passed he regained his fortune and lived a comfortable life, devoting much of his time to public welfare and to his individual efforts in behalf of the sick, the distressed and the needy. It was said that no one in want ever left him emptyhanded.

He is remembered today not only by the street named for him but by a conspicuous place in history among the early leaders of his adopted State and by the many who have followed him in the ranks of Masonry in California.

Folsom

The Soldier of Fortune

Joseph L. Folsom

CAPTAIN JOSEPH L. FOLSOM was a soldier with a sharp eye for business.

He served his country well but he also looked out for himself. Soon after he had changed his uniform for civilian attire, in the early months of 1850, he was on his way to amassing a fortune.

Some criticized his daring business ventures yet the city gave his name to a downtown street and he was further honored when a Northern California town became officially known as Folsom.

Tall and lean with dark sideburns and mustache, Folsom prided himself on his ancestry. He was born on May 19, 1817 in the little town of Meredith, New Hampshire where his maternal grandfather had settled after engaging in encounters with Indians and later fighting in the Revolution. He claimed kinship with Brigadier General Nathan Folsom, also a veteran of the War for Independence, who had represented New Hampshire in the Continental Congress.

Captain Folsom was one of several children in a family of moderate circumstances. When his father died, friends advised that the estate be liquidated and the family move to Northfield, New Hampshire, where they could live close to relatives.

There Joseph received his schooling. From an early age thoughts of a military career intrigued him, and he was honored with an appointment to West Point from Franklin Pierce, then a member of Congress and later President of the United States.

In June, 1840, at the age of twenty-three, young Folsom was graduated with the rank of brevet second lieutenant. He was assigned to Florida where he came under the command of General Worth in a campaign against the Seminoles.

With peace restored, he led a party of Indians to a new home in western territory, after which he was sent to an area in the upper Mississippi as a member of the Fifth Infantry. By this time he had been promoted to the full rank of second lieutenant.

In 1844, only four years after leaving the Academy, he was summoned to West Point to teach infantry tactics. The distinction was accorded him in recognition of his familiarity with the subject.

Folsom was not too happy as an instructor, preferring active military service. However he contented himself as best he could until the war with Mexico became imminent. He then requested release from the classroom to return to the field. This was denied, no doubt because of his value to the Academy. A second request some time later received a similar response.

The War began and Folsom chaffed for action. He renewed his application, only to be turned down a third time — probably a fortunate decision for the young soldier, since his old regiment which he would have rejoined suffered very heavy losses in the battle at Molino del Rey.

However, Folsom still was determined to engage in fighting. When he learned that a regiment of New York volunteers under the command of Colonel Stevenson was being prepared to leave for California, he again pressed his application for transfer, this time expressing a strong desire to join the Stevenson contingent.

The two men had never met, but Stevenson, learning of the request, decided that Folsom would be the ideal man to serve in the quartermaster's department as a staff officer.

When this news reached Folsom he was far from pleased. In fact, he bluntly refused to accept the assignment unless his rank was elevated to that of captain. Stevenson looked askance at such an ultimatum.

Much bickering followed. Folsom was finally offered a first lieutenancy which he reluctantly accepted and, on the day of the regiment's departure, he was advanced to the rank he had requested.

The voyage to the West was long and uncomfortable. It was not until March, 1847 that the regiment reached San Francisco Bay. There orders awaited for the establishment of an army supply depot on the bay shore. Folsom was put in charge with authority to select a suitable site and function for his department over the entire Pacific Coast.

He was gratified at receiving so important an assignment. First he traveled throughout the area, looking for the most strategic location — finally deciding in favor of San Francisco. His duties included the handling of all funds collected in the port during the war with Mexico, as well as all disbursements for the civil and military governments of the State. In effect, he had the distinction of being the first American collector to serve in California.

Folsom held this important post until the summer of 1849 when he took temporary leave from active service and left California for the

East. It was then that the soldier turned businessman and fortune hunter.

He already knew — in fact, it was common knowledge — that the colorful pioneer, William A. Leidesdorff, had left no will when he died in May, 1848 and that the value of the estate had increased many fold because of the Gold Rush. A squabble over its distribution was under way and Folsom saw a chance for enormous personal profit. He journeyed to Jamaica where at extremely low cost he bought the rights of a number of claimants.

Returning to California after seven months absence, he managed to convert his rights into a ranch of 35,500 acres where the town of Folsom was later established. He is said to have paid less than $75,000 or about $2 an acre for this land. His purchases also included 309 lots which he later sold for $607,000. With these profits he made still further investments.

His transaction with the Leidesdorff claimants brought severe criticism from many quarters but Folsom insisted that he had done no wrong; that he acted legitimately and well within his rights. He even offered to put the issue before the courts, but this was never done.

Moneymaking now was in his blood and he continued to invest shrewdly, having implicit faith in the future of the city. Some said that he was buying recklessly, especially land that was only sand dunes, but Folsom's judgment was vindicated when his fortune not only doubled but even trebled. He became one of the wealthiest men in the community, where he remained until his death in 1855.

Bartlett

The Yankee
Alcalde

Lieutenant Washington A. Bartlett

To LIEUTENANT WASHINGTON A. BARTLETT belongs the credit for officially naming San Francisco. He did so in a formal proclamation on January 30, 1847 near the close of his term as the first U.S. citizen to serve as Alcalde in the town by San Francisco Bay.

Bartlett, a United States naval officer aboard the U.S.S. *Plymouth,* had reached the little settlement in August, 1846, soon after the town came under the authority of the United States. His commander, Captain John B. Montgomery, ordered him ashore with instructions to assume the duties of Alcalde, which he did on August 14.

It was a wise choice. Bartlett, often described as "a gallant looking man," spoke Spanish well and had demonstrated administrative ability. He was warmly welcomed by settlers and natives alike, with promises of friendship and support.

Bartlett had not been in office long when he encountered serious confusion arising from the community's name, Yerba Buena. While the inhabitants used this designation, nearly everyone in other parts of California referred to the place as San Francisco, because of its location on the Bay.

On his own authority, Bartlett decided early one winter morning that he would remedy the situation before going out of office. He penned his proclamation, signed it, and when Sam Brannan called at the Alcalde's office later that day in search of news, Bartlett handed him the document and told him to publish it.

In the next issue of Brannan's *California Star* subscribers read the following notice over the Alcalde's signature:

"Whereas the local name of Yerba Buena as applied to the settlement or town of San Francisco, is unknown beyond the district; and has been applied from the local name of the cove, on which the town is built;

"Therefore to prevent confusion and mistakes in public documents, and that the town may have the advantage of the same name given on the public map,

"It is hereby ordained that the name of San Francisco shall hereafter be used in all official communications, or records appertaining to the town."

It was as simple as that and those who read the lines under the brief title of "An Ordinance" were less interested than they were in adjoining items about crime and business. The name of Yerba Buena passed into history.

Bartlett, related to one of the signers of the Declaration of Independence, was born in Maine on September 3, 1812. At an early age he moved with his family to New York City where he received a good education. He had specialized in naval and legal subjects and was well versed in both, which no doubt influenced Montgomery to select him, over a number of other well-qualified officers, to assume the duties of Alcalde.

From the start he faced perplexing problems. He had trouble with Sam Brannan who recently had arrived with his Mormon party. The latter did not respect authority and it was some time before he would recognize Bartlett's position.

There were many other difficulties including disputes over land grants and boundaries. Some of these he held in abeyance, for he had been instructed to prepare for an election to select the town's officials in a democratic way.

This he set for September 15. It was a memorable occasion since it marked the community's first election. The Custom House, popularly known as "Old Adobe," was selected as the voting place. Polls would be open from 11 in the morning until two p.m. When they closed at that hour everyone who so desired had cast his ballot.

Three inspectors had been appointed — Don Francisco de Haro, William H. Davis and Frank Ward — and they looked on with close attention. Since few more than a hundred ballots had been cast, counting was by no means difficult and was quickly done.

Bartlett, with 66 votes, was the winner over two other candidates. One of them, Nathan Spear, received only a single vote, undoubtedly his own. Other town officials were also chosen.

One of the Alcalde's first acts was to appoint Erasmus Burnham to serve as Sheriff and Chief Constable.

The town at this time had not been surveyed, and no boundaries had been set. Bartlett sent for Jasper O'Farrell, an engineer, and commissioned him to make this first official survey. The few streets he charted included California, Clay, Montgomery, Washington, Bartlett (which later became Pacific) and Howard (afterward renamed Sacramento).

Bartlett governed with a strong hand yet with understanding especially for those less fortunate than himself. He had not been in office long when an unscrupulous group of speculators cornered the bread and flour market, compelling the underprivileged to pay what were called famine prices. Protesting this outrage without result, Bartlett took matters into his own hands and obtained control of a large quantity of flour which he offered a unusually low prices, until all in need were adequately supplied.

His humanitarian concerns were further demonstrated when news came of the Donner Party tragedy. Calling together a group of charitably-minded people, he collected clothing and provisions, together with a considerable amount of money, to send to the survivors.

Once Bartlett's dedication to public welfare cost him his liberty for more than a month. It was at a time when the town was suffering from a shortage of meat. The Alcalde set out alone for a large rancho near San Jose intending to relieve the situation. On the way he was seized by a band of lawless natives known as irregulars and held prisoner. Bartlett tried to reason with them, explaining his mission but they refused to heed his pleas. In his absence George Hyde, who succeeded Bartlett in office, served as temporary Alcalde.

Bartlett's early schooling in legal matters served him well when he was sued for breach of contract by a merchant from whom he had arranged to buy materials for the town. Believing that he had been imposed upon, Bartlett refused to recognize the agreement and was hauled into court. Facing the judge he declared that he would not proceed with the trial unless the plaintiff agreed that the loser should pay the costs of the suit. This condition the merchant refused to accept and the case was dismissed.

Throughout his term of office Bartlett was held in high regard. His wife joined him and they took part in what social life existed. The marriage of their daughter to a multi-millionaire Cuban, Señor Ovido, caused much excitement.

On retiring from office, Bartlett resumed his naval duties for a time and was given command of a ship that made important surveys along the Pacific Coast. San Francisco continued as his home until his death.

Kearny

Leader of the Army of the West

Major General Stephen Watts Kearny

BRILLIANT MILITARY OPERATIONS in California and New Mexico won lasting fame for Major General Stephen Watts Kearny.

Early San Franciscans, many of whom knew him well, showed their esteem by giving his name to an important street. Yet there now are some who believe that the honor was bestowed on Dennis Kearney, the haranguing sandlot orator whose chief concern was that "the Chinese must go." Actually, he did not appear until long after the General's western campaigns. There also is a difference in the two names, the racist agitator having always signed himself "Kearney" with an additional "e" before the last letter.

General Kearny was nearly six feet tall, every inch a soldier. He was a man of imposing figure and military bearing. with features finely-set and a pleasing smile. Those who knew him said he was mild-mannered and understanding, with no egotism despite his high rank and unusual accomplishments. On the field and in public life alike, he insisted on obedience to his commands and would tolerate no carelessness or indifference to duty.

He was born in Newark, New Jersey in 1794 and completed his early education there. He was attending Columbia University in New York City when the War of 1812 broke out.

He left the University without receiving his diploma, enlisted, and received a commission as first lieutenant at the age of 18. He was assigned to the Thirteenth Infantry under Captain John E. Wood. For bravery in the battle of Queenstown Heights he received a special citation and six months later he became a captain. His advancement continued steadily until he finally attained the rank of Major General following his successful operations in the Far West.

His first years of military service after the War were devoted chiefly to Indian fighting. He particpated in a campaign against the Comanches, following an expedition under General Atkinson into Yellowstone. Later he assumed command of the Third Military Department based in St. Louis and in the next few years undertook various missions to subdue hostile Indian tribes.

The year 1846 found him in command of Fort Leavenworth. War with Mexico appeared to be unavoidable and the War Department was eager to take necessary steps in anticipation of armed conflict. Accordingly, Kearny was given orders to lead an expedition into New Mexico and California: the occupation of these territories was regarded as of paramount importance of the Nation.

Kearny mustered close to 1,600 men and provided them with adequate weapons. They started out June 26, 1846, dubbed "the Army of the West." Little more than two weeks later they were in Santa Fe, having met little or no resistance. The native forces had retreated and Kearny raised his flag to a salute of 13 guns.

Then, in pursuance of orders for the humane treatment of native inhabitants, he called them together and offered friendly assurance that in no way would they suffer. He promised the establishment of civil government to protect life and property.

When these responsibilities had been met, the General turned his attention to the long march into Northern California. It began September 25, 1846. The expedition had traveled less than two weeks when Kearny encountered Kit Carson and a small party of men who gave word that the conquest of California had been successfully accomplished.

General Kearny had his orders and he was not one to disregard them. Moreover, Carson advised that serious trouble with hostile Californios was to be expected; in fact, there already had been some skirmishes. With some reluctance, Carson agreed to accompany the General and his forces since he was fairly well familiar with the country.

The trek was far more difficult than expected, though the Indians they encountered were friendly. On the way came the first word of impending trouble.

It came from a small party of Mexicans who were leading a herd of wild horses southward. Vaguely these men spoke of an uprising "somewhere northward" by Californios who angrily resisted California rule. A courier with the group was taken prisoner. In his pouch Kearny found secret messages which not only confirmed the insurrection but also stated that Americans had been expelled from various places — particularly Los Angeles and Santa Barbara.

Kearny warned his men of a likely clash, checked his ammunition, and resumed the march in the direction of the enemy. The confrontation came at daybreak on the morning of December 6, 1846 as they approached an Indian village known as San Pascual where hostile riders on fast horses waited the arrival of the Americans, who were led by Captain Abraham Johnston.

With two lieutenants Kearny rode close behind, followed by fully 50 mounted men and more than 100 foot soldiers. With them were a number of howitzers, dragged by mules.

At first sight of the enemy, Kearny realized that he was badly outnumbered. There was no alternative but to risk himself and his men in a desperate try to force his way along the route that they were following.

The Californios closed in. Kearny gave the order for a forward thrust. Soon men were struggling with each other in ferocious and bloody hand-to-hand combat.

First Captain Johnston fell to the ground, a bullet in his head. Others followed; some dead, some seriously wounded. Cannon roared and the attacking Californios suddenly turned, spurred their mounts, and were off.

"Follow them," cried Kearny and with his men he hurried in pursuit. The second encounter came sooner than they had expected, for the retreating forces turned abruptly and charged again. There was a second battle — fiercer and more costly than the first. It lasted less than ten minutes but in that time sixteen men, including three of Kearny's highest officers, were killed.

The General himself was wounded along with 15 others. Most of them were victims of lances which the enemy used more skillfully than firearms.

There could be no countercharge. The attackers rode off in safety, leaving a bloody field behind. Kearny, unable to lift himself from the ground, considered his dilemma, fearing that a third attack might come at any time.

Captain Henry Turner, who now assumed command, turned his attention first to the wounded and then proceeded to reorganize the broken ranks.

Soon afterward, by good fortune, Lieutenant Edward Beale appeared with Kit Carson, eager to render help. Their daring dash for relief brought the needed reinforcements.

The lost battle of San Pascual was by no means the last engagement for Kearny in California. After recovering from his wounds, he moved south with reenforcements sent him by Commodore Stockton and battled rebellious groups at several points.

Finally, in March, 1847, he received orders from President James K. Polk designating him as military and civil Governor of California. He took charge at once, selecting Monterey for the capital; then proceeded with the appointment of Alcaldes and other officials in various places. Much confusion developed over claims to property held by the various Missions in Northern California. These were disputes that he could not settle quickly; he simply ordered that such lands should continue in religious hands as before the American occupation.

As Governor he took a keen interest in the affairs of San Francisco and did much to help its people. One of his first acts was to grant the town title to hundreds of water lots which soon were surveyed and sold at public auction, adding considerably to an almost empty treasury. The lots were mostly located east of Sansome Street, in a part of the one-time Yerba Buena Cove which became mud flats when the tide was out.

He also was having trouble with General Fremont, a clash over authority that would lead to the latter's court-martial.

In the middle of May, Kearny announced that he was ready to give up his post in California and leave for St. Louis. He left May 31, after turning over his affairs to Colonel Mason.

On his way he came upon the bodies of some members of the ill-fated Donner party and gave them such burial as he could.

By August he was back at Fort Leavenworth pressing mutiny charges against Fremont and preparing the evidence that he would present later in Washington.

Kearny's elevation to the rank of Major General in recognition of his courage at San Pascual and his long services in the West came in July, 1848.

Three months later, on October 31, 1848, he died in St. Louis.

O'Farrell

Surveyor with Vision

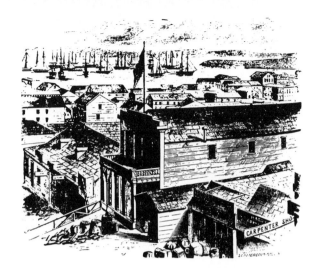

Clay Street, opposite Portsmouth Square

EARLY IN 1847 a group of angry San Franciscans cried out that lynching was what young Jasper O'Farrell deserved — and some of them rushed to his lodgings determined to do just that. Fortunately the young Irish engineer had been forewarned and saved himself by fleeing to Sausalito, where he rented a fast horse and rode to Sonoma, where he took refuge.

The irate citizens had just seen his new maps, the first extensive and formal drawings of the little town, and they complained bitterly that he had made Market Street far too wide. Property owners along that thoroughfare were the most critical; they declared that they would lose too much of their land.

O'Farrell, however, had foresight, envisioning a street that would become the busiest and most important in a thriving city. In fact, he mapped it to parallel what then was Mission Road.

The mapmaking assignment was probably furthest from O'Farrell's mind when he left his native Dublin for America. Since he was well-schooled in civil engineering, he had no fear of unemployment in the new land and set out boldly in search of work when he arrived in New York.

Wherever he went people told him of greater opportunities for engineers in the virgin West. Lacking funds to buy his passage, he found a job as a cooper aboard a whaler and set out for California. His ship landed in Yerba Buena cove in 1843.

Soon after his arrival he was attracted by the large cattle ranches on Bodega Bay, and forgetting his interest in engineering for the moment, he went there and found work. With his earnings he bought acreage, cheap at the time, and engaged in cattle raising for himself. He still yearned for a chance to follow his own profession, however, and the opportunity came when he was offered work surveying old Spanish and Mexican land grants.

During one of these expeditions he unwittingly became an eyewitness to the fatal shooting of the twin sons of Francisco de Haro, and their uncle, Jose Reyes Berryessa, by men under Fremont's command.

The tragedy became a subject of angry criticism and prolonged investigation, so protracted that ten years later O'Farrell issued a public statement detailing what he branded as wanton murder.

After completion of his surveying assignments, he moved to Yerba Buena. It was a fortunate move for O'Farrell. Just at this time Washington Bartlett, the Alcalde, decided that a detailed map of the town was badly needed, a map that would show existing streets and designate future ones. Bartlett knew that some years before, in 1839, a rough and incomplete survey had been made by Jean Jacques Vioget, a young Swiss sailor and surveyor, but it failed to meet the present requirements of an expanding community. What the Alcalde really wanted was a new and complete layout of the town.

Whether O'Farrell applied for the assignment or was sent for by Bartlett is not known. The fact remains that they did meet and that the Alcalde was impressed by the 26-year-old Irish engineer with the long, thin nose, dark bushy hair and unkempt beard. When their meeting ended, O'Farrell was instructed to proceed at once.

He had not progressed far when Bartlett was succeeded by Edwin Bryant who not only approved of the undertaking but wanted it expanded to include land then under water. The increasing number of ships arriving in the Bay and the need for wharves and docking facilities convinced him that Bay fill was of paramount importance.

Though the town was now in American hands, Mexican law was still respected, giving the Governor control over disposition of lands a fixed number of feet below the high water mark. Sensing a need for change, Bryant appealed to Governor Kearny who in March of 1847 rescinded the old requirement, granting San Francisco full rights to beach and water property lying between points then known as Rincon and Fort Montgomery. By this significant action, O'Farrell faced a much larger task; his map would now require an expansion of town limits and call for far more imagination and technical skill.

Kearny's proclamation caused great excitement. "I do hereby grant, convey and release to the town of San Francisco," it read, "the people or corporate authorities thereof, all the rights, title and interests of the government of the United States and the territory of California in and to the beach and water lots on the east front of said town, included between the points known as the Rincon and Fort Montgomery . . . provided the said ground hereby ceded shall be divided into lots and sold by public auction to the highest bidder. . . ."

O'Farrell was busy at his drawing board when the auction took place on July 20, continuing for three days amid active bidding. In all, some 450 lots, completely covered by water, were sold at prices ranging from $50 to $100 each. Seven years later less desirable water lots were being sold for from $8,000 to $15,000 apiece.

The map the young engineer finally presented for the Alcalde's approval called for radical changes in the contour of the town. He had taken topographical difficulties into account and, in a measure, had twisted its entire layout. His drawings covered an area of one-and-a-half square miles, fronting the cove and extending three-quarters of a mile north to south and two miles east to west.

He designated Market Street to cut diagonally across a checkerboard pattern of other streets, altering their angles slightly so they would meet the main thoroughfare at right angles. The move came to be called "the O'Farrell twist." It was a radical departure from Vioget's earlier crude survey. It reflected vision and confidence in the town's expansion and its future. Streets, he insisted, should be from 75 to 80 feet in width.

In designating what he considered principal streets, O'Farrell also named them, choosing to honor prominent pioneers he had come to know.

To his surprise, property owners along Market Street were in an uproar, insisting that its width was not only absurd but unnecessary, since it would give the city privately-owned land. Indignation meetings were called and one became so heated that an angry crowd demanded that the engineer be lynched.

O'Farrell could not understand the logic of the protests, especially since huge sand dunes blocked the street, one of them close to where the Palace Hotel was later built.

Tempers gradually cooled and the map was accepted, though ridicule continued for a considerable time.

Actually, adoption of the map was a godsend for the town. Word soon spread that the town by the Bay had outgrown its swaddling clothes and had tremendous future. Officials in Washington announced that duty would be lifted on goods brought into the harbor on vessels flying the American flag. Before long, four Army transports, carrying fully a thousand men, arrived in the Bay. The men had volunteered on the promise that they would be permitted to remain in the West after completing their service.

The population grew steadily and San Francisco prospered. Many of O'Farrell's former critics were now making money simply by using his map as a guide for their investments.

As the work of young O'Farrell continued to gain approval, the aldermen, in a gesture of appreciation, named a street in his honor.

The development of O'Farrell Street was slow at the start but increased and on this street, east of Larkin, many distinguished pioneers built their homes. One of them was Raphael Weill, who became the owner of one of the largest downtown department stores, The White House, an early-day member of the Board of Education, and a civic leader. And it was on this same street that two enterprising restauranteurs, Joseph Malfanti and Henry G. Utzeit, opened an eating place that attracted epicures from all parts of the world. It was called Delmonico's and its meals, advertised as "unequalled dinners" cost exactly one dollar.

Brannan

"The Paul Revere
of the
Gold Rush"

Sam Brannan

SAM BRANNAN, ONE of San Francisco's earliest and most colorful pioneers, has been called "the Paul Revere of the Gold Rush." On a bright day in 1848 he ran excitedly through Portsmouth Square with a bottle, which had originally held quinine, in one hand and his battered, wide-brimmed hat in the other.

"Gold, gold, gold — from the American River," he shouted over and over, holding up his small container of glistening yellow dust and tiny nuggets.

Within hours excitement was running high. The rush to the Mother Lode began soon afterward.

Some historians, however, point to a striking difference between Sam Brannan and the earlier revolutionary who rode his horse to alarm the colonists that the British were coming. Brannan, they say, deliberately withheld his announcement of the gold discovery for weeks until he had feathered his own nest — and that he did so very successfully. The story is that, having received secret word of the gold find at Sutter's Mill, he anticipated a stampede of fortune hunters and shrewdly kept the information to himself until he had over-stocked his store in Sutter's Fort with every sort of goods that miners would need — picks, axes, tents and other equipment. The store soon did a landoffice business and Brannan reaped a fortune.

Be that as it may, Brannan did rise to a position of high esteem in San Francisco, recognized as one of the settlement's richest, most successful and most influential citizens. He was a rugged individualist and he usually had his own way.

A native of Maine, he had spent much of his early years in eastern states, moving about as an itinerant printer. Once he published a small weekly called *The New York Messenger*.

In 1842 he joined the Mormon Church, became a dedicated supporter of its gospel and a close associate of Brigham Young. After much discussion between the two, it was decided that Brannan should take a Mormon party to the Pacific Coast to establish a colony outside of United States jurisdiction, while Young would lead a much larger number to Utah which he regarded as a "promised land."

Brannan's party, some 200 strong, set out for California aboard the ship *Brooklyn*. The larger group, prepared for a long overland trek, left Nauvoo, Illinois in mid-February, 1846.

It was a disappointed band of Mormons that put into Yerba Buena cove aboard the *Brooklyn* one afternoon in 1846, expecting to land on foreign soil. For, after 178 days at sea, one of the first sights to meet their eyes was an American flag fluttering over the old Custom House at Portsmouth Square. Brannan, the most irate, flung his hat on the deck, exclaiming, "There's that damned rag again." Only a few weeks before, California had become American territory.

When the last of the 200 emigrants had come ashore, it was estimated that the town's population had nearly doubled.

For a short time Brannan assumed his rightful place as leader of the Mormons. He preached regular Sunday morning services, summoning his followers by loudly ringing a handbell. Despite his disappointment, he was impressed by his new surroundings and believed that Young and his people should abandon their plans for settling in the Salt Lake area and move to California instead.

After seeing that his charges were well-housed in tents and adobe huts, Brannan hurried overland to meet Young and to press his proposal. He told the Mormon leader of California's climate and rich soil. But Young was obdurate, insisting that he disliked the idea of a religious colony being located in a seaport and did not believe the Mormons should live in a "competitive atmosphere."

Brannan returned alone to Yerba Buena. He no longer felt concern for his group, whose members soon were left to shift for themselves. Later, during the Gold Rush, some of them became quite prosperous but Young's continued pleas for the payment of tithes fell on deaf ears. When Brannan received an angry letter from Young demanding "the Lord's share of your earnings," Brannan bluntly answered that he would only honor a message signed by the Lord.

Young, however, was not so easily dissuaded from pressing his claims. Twice he sent emissaries to California to demand tithes but each time they were intercepted by Brannan's bodyguards and forced to return home empty handed.

About this time, some of Brannan's co-religionists turned against him with bitter accusations of misappropriating church funds. Others said the charges were a reprisal by a group in the *Brooklyn* party excommunicated by Brannan for "licentious conduct." He was tried before a jury, the first in California, and promptly acquitted. Later he resigned from the church.

While this conflict was going on, Brannan busied himself with many plans for his own advancement. Having shrewdly put a small printing press and necessary supplies aboard the *Brooklyn,* he established the town's first newspaper, *The California Star,* which made its initial appearance on January 9, 1847. It was the second newspaper in all of California.

A few weeks later *The Star* printed its first big "scoop" — Alcalde Bartlett had officially changed the name of Yerba Buena to San Francisco. No one seemed to care.

The paper soon began to publish the rich opportunities awaiting settlers in the Bay area. Hundreds of extra copies were sent to Missouri and other states and Brannan assumed the role of a one-man chamber of commerce.

Before long he found time to open a store in Sutter's Fort which he left in capable hands, returning to undertake the organization of a bank. Still later he would form a telegraph company and an express firm, enterprises that were to make him the wealthiest man in the town and one of the richest in the entire state. His fortune was estimated at $5,000,000. He had invested heavily in mining.

For more than 20 years he was recognized as a leader in the town's affairs, not only because of his business success but for his eagerness to help others as well, as he did in sharing his considerable knowledge of agriculture with those interested in farming.

He became the principal organizer of the first Vigilante Committee on June 9, 1851 after John Jenkins, a one-time Australian convict known as "The Miscreant," had been caught stealing a safe from the shipping office of George W. Virgin. Jenkins' career ended on the gallows.

Brannan already had established a reputation as a vigorous fighter for justice. On one occasion he was called to Sutter's Fort to act as judge in the trial of a bellicose character, Charles Pickett, who attacked those who disagreed with him and in turn was accused of being "a debaucher of squaws." Pickett, owner of a trading post, had just killed a man and claimed self-defense.

The trial was at its height when "Judge" Brannan stepped down from the improvised bench to make a vigorous plea for the prosecution. "You can't do that," Pickett protested angrily. "You're the judge."

"I know it," Brannan shot back, "but I'm also the prosecuting attorney."

Brannan showed his courage and sense of justice again after the Hounds, a merciless band of ruffians and criminals, had plundered the tents of a group of Mexican-Americans and totally wrecked their property.

The town was furious and, as usual, Brannan took the lead. He called on the Alcalde, Dr. T. M. Leavenworth, demanding action. When Leavenworth said there was nothing he could do, Brannan demanded: "Then issue a proclamation calling for men of courage to meet me this afternoon in the Plaza."

Hours later close to 300 men gathered, listened to his tirade against the Hounds, and helped collect money for the relief of the victims. Then Brannan called on the men to volunteer as special deputies. Everyone responded. Armed with muskets and other weapons, they started in pursuit of the hoodlums and drove them from the town. Some fled on foot into the interior; others took to the Bay in small boats. Twenty were intercepted near Stockton with one of their leaders, named Roberts, and brought back to Yerba Buena. There they were held in the brig of the warship *Warren* anchored in the Bay while awaiting trial. All of them were convicted and sent to prison. The Hounds no longer were a menace.

Brannan was equally vigorous more than a year later after J. C. Jansen, a popular merchant, had been slugged and robbed in his store in broad daylight. Two men were arrested and when an angry mob tried to storm the jail, the prisoners were moved to safer cells.

Anger was running high when a proclamation appeared urging that the pair be lynched. Those who read it recognized Brannan's handwriting. Calmer minds proposed that a jury be impaneled to try the men. Brannan was obdurate. "We are the mayor and the recorder," he shouted to the crowd. "We are the hangman and the law."

This time, however, he was outvoted. The prisoners were brought to trial before a jury, convicted, and sentenced to fourteen years in prison. Brannan still insisted that his proposal should have been carried out. Perhaps that is why Josiah Boyce, in his biography of Brannan wrote:

"Mr. Sam Brannan, the lion-hearted, a man always in love with shedding the blood of the wicked."

The street named for Brannan originally extended for only two blocks and some of it was under water. There in the early days, Claus Spreckels built the town's first sugar refinery. Over its muddy ground walked many Chinese emigrants embarking from Pacific Mail steamships docked at the foot of the street.

Brannan, the man of wealth and influence, who so vigorously led the cause of justice, came to an ignoble end. He took to drink when his investments began to fail; finally lost his entire fortune and became a drunkard. In disgust he wandered into Mexico and became involved in a colonizing scheme that soon collapsed. Penniless and without friends, he returned to California and died in Escondido, San Diego County on May 5, 1889.

Townsend

The Roving
Medic

Dr. John Townsend

FATE PROVIDED NO immunity to Dr. John Townsend, San Francisco's first practicing physician.

After ministering day and night to victims of the cholera epidemic in 1850, he and his wife fell victims to the scourge of the dreaded plague.

Though medicine was his chosen profession, he followed a strangely shifting career. Of extremely restless temperament, he was never satisfied to remain long in any single place or occupation. He turned from doctor to soldier, to miner, trader, and real estate investor; and finally to public office. He served the city as Alcalde and once was President of the town council. He was really a soldier of fortune but as a medical man he was known for his devotion to the welfare of his patients.

He reached San Francisco early in 1845, traveling West over the difficult Overland Route from the family home in Fayette County, Pennsylvania, where his father, an Englishman, was a pioneer.

After receiving his medical degree from Lexington Medical College, Dr. Townsend had chosen to wander about rather than confine his practice to his home community. He moved over a wide course, settling for short periods in other parts of Pennsylvania, in Indiana, Ohio and in Missouri.

He had returned home for a visit to find his family bent on going West, a plan that appealed to his own roving spirit. He packed his belongings and started for Missouri in May, 1844 with his wife and brother-in-law. There they joined the Stevens party in the hazardous journey to California.

With long delays in preparations, they did not start until early winter snow and rain were falling. Traveling in such weather was even more difficult than they had expected, especially the hard push through the mountains.

The Townsend wagon broke down at Donner Lake where he and a few other stalled travelers saved themselves and their companions from starvation by trapping coyotes and wolves. Others in the Stevens group were stopped at the Yuba River; some pressed on to their destination, arriving in greater number than they had started with, for the stork had followed the pioneers across the plains and mountains.

When Townsend and his family finally reached Sutter's Fort, the goal of all overland travelers, they found California in chaotic condition. Townsend soon joined the American forces to help in the conflict with the natives and served with credit in the Micheltorena campaign. He then moved to Monterey to resume medical practice.

By this time the Yerba Buena settlement had grown to the point where it needed a physician. Learning of this, he moved north and looked about for an advantageous situation. He found a small lot on California Street between Montgomery and Sansome, the present site of the Merchants Exchange Building, and erected a little wooden house that served both as a medical office and as a family residence.

Up to that time when settlers became ill they had to rely on family remedies or the judgment of a drug store clerk. They were elated at the coming of an experienced doctor. Townsend's presence quickly became known and his little office was always crowded.

Before long he became a member of the school board that guided the affairs of the town's first public school and in April, 1848 he was appointed Alcalde to succeed George Hyde, over whose administration there had been considerable dissatisfaction.

Even before his term as Alcalde expired, Dr. Townsend was stricken again with wanderlust. The Gold Rush had begun and he could not resist a powerful urge to join the prospectors. Mining was not to his liking, however; calloused hands were not for a medical man and he returned home, convinced that he would rather gather wealth more slowly in an easier occupation.

Soon he became bored again; his practice was not exciting and he knew that others were profiting in real estate. He talked things over one night with a patient, Cornelius de Boom, a recent arrival from Antwerp who was trying his hand in property investment. Together they formed a partnership and undertook to settle a portion of the Potrero. The venture was unsuccessful because of the distance from the main settlement and Townsend again returned to medicine.

By this time agitation had started for a town physician who would serve the needy at the treasury's expense. Fortunately, Dr. T. R. Palmer had arrived and on Townsend's recommendation he was selected as the first to fill the position.

Turning over his practice to the new arrival, Townsend, his wife and new-born son moved to a ranch of nearly 200 acres that he had purchased close to San Jose. For a few months he was content in his new surroundings but, as before, he again craved a change of scenery.

The family moved again, this time north to Santa Clara where their contentment was suddenly interrupted by the first cases of cholera.

The malady spread, with frequent deaths. Dr. Townsend unhesitatingly threw himself into the crisis, traveling miles by day and night to treat the sufferers. He even made frequent visits to San Francisco, assisting Dr. Palmer, with little or no thought of his own well-being.

One night he felt ill and soon realized that he had fallen victim of the plague he had been fighting. Hours later his wife was stricken. In a short time both were dead, leaving their small son to be cared for and reared by neighbors.

Mason

Gold Rush
Governor

Rush for the gold regions

COLONEL RICHARD BARNES MASON, the fourth civil and military governor of California, was totally unprepared for what he saw in San Francisco when he arrived in the early morning of June 20, 1848.

In his Monterey office he had been receiving reports about the gold discovery five months before. With them came frequent but inadequate mention of a rush from San Francisco to the Mother Lode. Finally, Mason decided to see for himself.

To his amazement he found the city inhabited mostly by women and children; only a scattering of men remained. Many shops were closed, business appeared to have come almost to a standstill, and ships lay at anchor deserted by their crews. Inquiring about, he was told that nearly the entire male population had taken to the mines and their return depended largely on their luck.

With his aides, he started for Sutter's Fort, still eager to learn what had taken place. On the way he passed abandoned homes, neglected farms and mills.

At Sutter's Fort he found a widely contrasting scene. The place was booming and bustling with activity. Fortune hunters, with packs on their backs and their arms filled with provisions, were moving impatiently from boats that had taken them up the river to the gold fields. The few small stores were crowded and hotel rooms, renting at $100 a month, were at a premium.

Mason moved further into the area, where he was told by prospectors that a daily yield of $100 in gold dust and nuggets was not unusual. He then went to Sutter's Mill where he listened as James Marshall related his own story of the original discovery and escorted him to the tailrace.

Before his tour was interrupted by a call to return at once to Monterey, Mason learned that fully 4,000 men were mining with pick and shovel, with an average daily yield of close to $50,000.

Mason considered demanding fees or rent from the miners, many of whom were prospecting on goverment land, but he realized the difficulties that would result from such procedures and finally abandoned the idea. What surprised him most, aside from the Gold Rush, was the honesty of the miners themselves. Carrying small fortunes in their pockets, they were going about without molestation; crime was rare and mostly trivial. The few who occasionally were caught in thefts were hanged without trial.

Mason reported his observations to Washington in lengthy documents and these, together with reports from Thomas Larkin and a few others, started the westward trek to the gold fields.

Like his predecessor, General Kearny, Mason spent most of his adult life in the military. He claimed Fairfax County in Virginia as his birthplace and spoke proudly of his grandfather, George Mason, who had been a friend of George Washington and had authored the state's original Bill of Rights.

At the age of 20, Richard Mason changed his civilian clothes for an Army uniform. He was commissioned a second lieutenant in 1817 and moved up through the ranks until he became a full colonel in 1846. Two years later he won the rank of brevet brigadier-general in recognition of his services in California.

He had served in the Hawk War in 1832 and in other engagements before orders called him to California. He reached San Francisco in February, 1849 and soon assumed the duties of civil and military governor from his predecessor, General Kearny.

Almost from the start he found himself confronted with many difficulties largely brought on by the Gold Rush, but he succeeded in bringing about a fairly well-functioning government, despite lack of help from Washington. Disputes over land titles brought no end of trouble. Realizing that such issues called for legal knowledge, Mason wisely selected Henry W. Halleck to serve as Secretary of State.

Halleck, a lawyer of recognized ability, delved deeply into the problem and his reports, defining grants and the laws relating to them, did much to allay trouble among those who held grants to property.

Another cause of Mason's worry was the growing number of soldiers and sailors who were deserting to try their luck at mining. He once threatened to dispatch mounted men to effect their return but realized that this would be a useless move since most of the cavalry had already left the ranks to become miners. In this predicament he merely satisfied himself with a proclamation calling on the people to help in apprehending deserters. There was not much cooperation.

At one time, when desertions were reaching an alarming rate, it was found necessary to impose severe punishments on those who were caught. In one instance a cavalry private narrowly escaped an unusually severe penalty: he was sentenced to forfeit all pay, have his thigh branded with the letter "D," and receive 50 lashes on his bare back after his head had been completely shaved. When calmer officers interceded, pointing out the soldier's youth, he was spared the branding and the lash in return for dishonorable discharge from the service.

Mason was able to ease a troublesome situation that arose over regulations requiring the payment of customs duties in coin. After several protest meetings had been called, he agreed to a compromise whereby duties might first be paid in gold dust, provided they were redeemed with coin within six months, or half in 90 days.

As Governor of the territory, Mason's authority was never questioned for he was a determined man, always firm, who made it clear that his word was final. He had a high regard for law enforcement and insisted that legal procedures be followed to the letter.

Never was this better demonstrated than on an occasion when two murderers were taken to the gallows under sentence by the court. Before a large and angry crowd, nooses were slipped over the heads of the condemned men and the ropes thrown over a protruding beam. Through careless handling, the knots opened and the pair dropped to the ground little the worse for their experience.

The hangman was about to repeat his performance when a priest who had taken the confessions of the two, stepped quickly forward.

"Get away," he called to the executioner. "The sentence of the court has been imposed and these men deserve their liberty."

The crowd protested and after an angry exchange it was finally decided that Governor Mason should decide the issue. The prisoners' lawyer hurried with the sheriff to Mason's office and told him what had occurred.

The Governor listened attentively, shook his head, and jumped to his feet. "These men," he said firmly, "have been sentenced to be hanged until they are dead. When that's been done, we can discuss the failure of the first try." Further argument was futile.

Mason's term of office was short lived. In May, 1849 he asked to be relieved and as soon as he had turned over his affairs to Bennet Riley he left for the East. There he was given other assignments which he filled until his death July 25, 1850, the year that California was granted statehood. He was then 55 years of age and with his demise the career of a brilliant soldier passed into history, with San Francisco's Fort Mason and a downtown street remaining to honor his memory.

John Augustus Sutter

Sutter

Victim of The Lust for Gold

IF JOHN AUGUSTUS SUTTER had not decided in 1839 to colonize an expansive area of California's rich Sacramento Valley and if he had not by chance hired an itinerant contractor named James W. Marshall to build a mill, the great Gold Rush and the development of the Far West might not have occurred until years later. But all through history coincidences have played strange roles in the affairs of men and, no doubt, always will.

Ironically, Sutter and Marshall, responsible for the gold discovery in January, 1848, failed to reap the fortune that was theirs. Both had carefully connived to keep their find a secret for as long as possible but were betrayed by a woman who had overheard their whispered talk and could not restrain her tongue. Sutter died almost penniless and Marshall had to content himself with a claim to fame rather than riches.

Sutter's life was colorful, adventuresome — and disastrous. Born in Germany, he spent his young manhood in Switzerland, living extravagantly. He probably would have remained there but for a business failure in Berne that brought him face to face with a debtor's cell. He chose a hurried flight to America, leaving his wife and five children behind.

After staying for a time in St. Louis, he traveled overland and joined a trapping party into Vancouver. His intention was to proceed from there to Yerba Buena but no ships then were sailing south. His only recourse was to take passage on the brig *Clementine* which finally reached his destination by way of Sitka, Alaska and the Sandwich Islands. Fourteen months had passed since he had left Missouri.

Sutter was in his middle thirties when he set foot on California soil July 1, 1839. He was greeted by the Yerba Buena settlers with some suspicion, perhaps because of his arrogant manner and his boastful claim to having been a captain in the famous Swiss Guard.

Long before his arrival he had dreamed of establishing a large settlement on the shores of San Francisco Bay, which he would call New Helvetia ruled as an independent principality. Those who listened, now that he had reached the Bay, shook their heads and said the plan was foolhardy. But Sutter was not to be so easily discouraged. He lingered to sell his wares, for he had accumulated considerable saleable merchandise in Sitka and in the Islands. During this time, he decided to change the course of the project he had in mind.

While in the Northwest he had heard much of the rich, fertile lands in the Sacramento Valley. There, he thought, might be an even better place to start his empire.

California was still under Mexican rule, so he went to the authorities and asked for land. At that time the government looked upon settlement by foreigners with disfavor but Sutter finally succeeded in winning the support of those in office. He swore his loyalty to the Mexican government and in due time received a grant to a tremendous stretch of land — nearly 50,000 acres — in the valley of his choice. But he still needed money to pursue the project.

He continued for a time to trade around the Bay and when he had accumulated sufficient funds he purchased three small boats for a voyage up the Sacramento River. With him he took eight Kanakas, a 14-year-old Indian boy, a few native sailors, and a bulldog.

His reception was far from what he had anticipated. As he pulled ashore in a rowboat, he was met with warlike cries from a crowd of Indians. Sutter, however, could handle such situations. He extended a friendly hand, smiled, distributed gifts, and informed the Chief as best he could that the tribe would always be welcome on his newly-acquired lands.

Though Sutter was thoroughly pleased with his new surrounding, the boat crews thought otherwise. They demanded that he return with them to Yerba Buena. Sutter had no intention of doing so. After unloading his provisions, he told the dissidents that they could go back in one of his three vessels. Some did, but those who remained quickly helped him to select a location for the center of his settlement. The site was not far from the point where the Sacramento and American Rivers meet.

Then he carefully picked a homesite and with his helpers erected an adobe structure that would provide a degree of comfort and shelter.

He soon gave the area the name of Nuevo Helvetia and from the start ruled it with an iron hand. He shed his arrogance to treat the Indians graciously and they became his friends. Some of them he hired to hunt and trap. Others helped him erect new buildings, a little store, and a blockhouse that became known as Sutter's Fort.

Word of his undertaking gradually spread. Before long he was being joined by hunters and by sailors who had left their ships at Yerba Buena after torturous voyages around the Horn. Meanwhile, acting solely on his own authority, he lay claim to a wide expanse surrounding the spacious property that had been granted him. No one bothered to dispute his rights.

From time to time he heard vague rumors about gold; a few traders said that Indians had shown them tiny nuggets but he showed no interest. He seemed content to rule his little empire and to busy himself with improving it.

By now he was investing recklessly and running into debt. Nevertheless, he could not resist an opportunity to buy the holdings of the Russian-American Fur Company at Fort Ross, some 50 miles north of San Francisco Bay. The Russian government had ordered the enterprise abandoned and Sutter found that he could buy the properties for $30,000 — which he did not have. He settled for a down payment of $2,000, assuming a burden that it would be impossible for him to meet, despite the later discovery of gold on his land grant.

In January, 1848, after close to nine years of work on Nuevo Helvetia, Sutter decided to build a mill on a fork of the American River, located some 60 miles from the present city of Sacramento. Marshall, who had wandered into the area in search of work, was hired. The project was still in its early stages when Marshall concluded that it would be necessary to cut a tailrace to divert a portion of the river's current. This was done and before long he discovered a few tiny, sparkling particles of what looked like gold in the tailrace.

Trying his utmost to evade the eyes of nearby workmen, he gathered a few particles and hastened to Sutter's home, some distance away. The date has been officially set as January 24 but at this point historians differ as to what actually occurred.

One version has it that Sutter scoffed at the idea of gold, insisted that the specimens were worthless, and threw them away with no desire to even have them assayed. Only later, according to this story, was he induced to send a small nugget to Isaac Humphrey, a mining man in San Francisco, who not only found it to be pure gold but hastened to Sutter's Fort and struck a rich pocket with little effort.

The other version, by far the most plausible and the one generally accepted, is that Sutter realized at once the value of the find and decided with Marshall that they must keep the discovery secret as long as they could. What they did not know, however, was that Sutter's cook, a Mrs. Wimmer, had overheard their low-voiced conversation and soon confided what she knew to a few people about the place.

Strangely, the news was slow to spread, for it was not until March, more than two months later, that the secret became public property. Sam Brannan's sensational announcement in Yerba Buena spread like wildfire. Before long the word was being relayed not only along the coast but eastward as well. The stampede was soon to start.

It began first on San Franciso Bay. Sailors deserted their ships, shop clerks left their jobs, the doors of stores were locked and nailed up. Within weeks the town was practically deserted as almost every man able to travel hurried north to hunt for gold and fortune.

By May more than 2,000 men were scrambling over the hillsides with picks and shovels, staking claims and digging. It little mattered that the property belonged to Sutter. No one even stopped to think of this in the mad scramble for what lay beneath the surface.

The influx continued in ever-greater numbers. Fortune hunters came from Mexico, from Central and South America, and from Europe. It appeared that men from everywhere were rushing into Northern California.

Through it all, Sutter looked on, a helpless victim of the horde. His crops were trampled, his cattle slaughtered and his buildings ruthlessly torn to pieces. Even the mill was pulled apart in the mad rush for lumber.

Sutter posted notices demanding that miners come to him for permits. They were ignored and when in desperation he asked that he be paid ten per cent of the gold mined, the newcomers merely laughed. Some even accused him of trying to conceal richer fields and on one occasion there were violent threats of lynching.

Misfortunes piled up. Shortly before the gold discovery he had sent for his wife and family, convinced that now they could live happily together. But this was not to be. On their arrival, Mrs. Sutter and the children saw only utter desolation and the home they had anticipated a shambles. The wife fell ill and died. A son was killed trying to defend what remained of the property from an Indian mob.

Sutter, a broken and disillusioned man, left the Valley for the Bay. His land grant had been contested and he prepared to sue the government not only to recover the full loss of property but to settle his claim to the land. The suit dragged on for years while Sutter did his best to earn a meager living. He ultimately lost the suit.

Hoping that Congress might do what the courts had refused, he went to Washington and filed a petition. It was still pending when he died almost penniless.

For his part — quite different from what he had envisioned — in the development of the West, a San Francisco street and a Northern California county bear his name.

Burnett

The Poorman's
Advocate

Peter Hardeman Burnett

PETER HARDEMAN BURNETT who became California's first
civil Governor, and later was appointed a Justice of the State's highest
court, came up the hard way. From early boyhood through much of
his adult life he had known extreme poverty, which gave him thorough
understanding of the problems of the poor.

This experience was reflected in all of his executive and judicial
acts; he was determined that those in want should receive the full protection and benefits of the law.

Unlike many others, Burnett made no effort to conceal his early
struggles against privation. He often recalled a time in Oregon when
his shoes fell to pieces and he was obliged to attend public meetings
barefooted because he had no money to buy new ones. He was then
dividing his time between a meager law practice and his farm which
together did not yield enough to provide for his wife and six children.
He would tell of a day when a friendly neighbor saved them from going
without food by leading him to a wheat field where a few potatoes were
growing without cultivation.

He was born November 15, 1807 in Nashville, Tennessee. His father
was a contractor who had erected a number of frame buildings when
the city was still a small village. His forbears on both sides were
Virginians.

His fourth birthday had just passed when the family moved to a
farm in Williamson County and later to Howard County in Missouri,
where they experienced all of the rigors of pioneer life. Five years afterward they moved again, this time near Liberty in the same state. There
the father took up 160 acres of new land, trying desperately to make
them produce enough for family wants — but with little success. They
subsisted mostly on wild game that he trapped or shot.

In his memoirs, written in later years, Peter Burnett told much of family privations but said nothing of his education. Presumably, he attended small public schools. His training in the law came long afterward.

He was 19 when he returned to Tennessee with an uncle, obtaining his first job in a Bolivar hotel. His wage was $100 a year and his tips no doubt were few. He went about in tattered clothes, a cause of great humiliation he admitted in later life, for he feared that he would be ridiculed.

After six months at the hotel he found a better job in a store owned and operated by a Methodist minister. Hopefully, the pay was better, for it was at this time that he married. He was then 21 years of age; his bride was five years his junior.

Frugality helped him to buy the store in 1829, its owner accepting notes for a large balance due him. Somehow, as a young businessman, Burnett found time to study law in spare hours and people came to him for advice which he gave gratuitously.

Probably because of financial worries it was decided about this time that his wife should join her parents in Liberty, Missouri. He would stay in Tennessee until he could dispose of the store. It was a difficult and time consuming task and not until 1832 was Burnett able to join his wife. Even then, he was still faced with poverty.

In his new home he divided his time between a newspaper called *The Far West* and a store where he worked for $400 a year; yet he did manage to continue his law studies and finally was admitted to the bar.

Considering himself unprepared to venture into active practice, he chose to engage in a mercantile business with a partner, John Thornton, but the venture failed, leaving Burnett heavily in debt.

A brighter turn did not come until 1838. That year the Mormons were expelled from Missouri, bringing litigation over land and property. Burnett grasped the opportunity, opened a law office, and for the first time in his life prospects grew brighter. Two years later, his ability having won recognition, he was appointed District Attorney. The pay was poor, however, and he finally decided to move to Oregon.

The family by now had been increased by five children and Burnett hoped that in new and developing country there might be better chances for success for his growing family. They settled in Fort Vancouver where he became interested in politics. He was elected to the Oregon Legislature and in 1844 became a Justice of the territory's Supreme Court, a position which enabled him to play an important role in improving existing laws.

Public service brought more honor than money, so he undertook to increase his income by developing a law practice and by farming. Again he found himself in desperate financial need. It was then that he was compelled to go about without shoes, an embarrassing predicament, yet he did not hesitate to attend public meetings because he considered this his duty. Despite all hardships, he often spoke of Fort Vancouver as "the happiest community" he had ever seen.

The long struggle against adversity had not eased and there seemed little chance of improvement when word reached Oregon of the gold discovery and the rush to the mines. Burnett weighed the situation, concluding that there might be new opportunities in California; certainly he could expect nothing worse.

Leaving his family behind, he traveled south and, on reaching San Francisco, prepared at once to try his luck at mining. He had not yet left for the gold fields when he received a letter appointing him to the Supreme Court of Oregon. He felt obligated to decline since he had already declared his intention of becoming a resident of another state.

For a time he prospected on the Yuba River with little success; then went to Sutter's Fort where he became a business agent for Sutter, a position that paid him well.

Later he decided to move to San Francisco and try his luck again at law. It was a wise move, probably the best he had ever made, for there was need for legal talent and for men who could meet the political needs of the territory. Burnett grasped his opportunity, accepted responsibilities, and drafted a number of proposals for a type of provisional government that would be just and practical until California achieved Statehood.

For this work he received wide acclaim and when General Bennet Riley resigned as Military Governor following the drafting of a new State Constitution, Burnett was elected to succeed him. He sent for his family and prepared to meet the many problems involved in establishing order in the territory.

When his term ended he resumed the practice of law but with definite aspirations for a place on the Supreme Court. It did not come until January 13, 1857 when he was appointed to fill a vacancy. He served with distinction until October 1858 when he retired. His opinions have been regarded as of unusually high quality.

Now, with plenty of time and without financial worries, he devoted himself to writing, much of it on political and religious themes. In 1878 he wrote his memoirs, recalling his long struggles and reflecting his high sense of duty and of integrity.

He died in San Francisco May 17, 1895 and was buried in the Catholic cemetery in Santa Clara.

Prominent people gathered for the final rites, paying tribute to a citizen who had perservered through life and finally had succeeded in gaining two high places in his adopted state.

Burnett holds the distinction of being one of only three Supreme Court Justices for whom San Francisco streets are named.

John W. Geary

Geary
The First
Postmaster

APRIL 1, 1849 was a joyous day for the people of San Francisco. Their first postmaster had just arrived from Pennsylvania and announced that he would assume his new duties as quickly as he could. For months his coming had been eagerly awaited for the town was badly in need of efficient mail service.

The newcomer was a young man of marked ability named John W. Geary. He had brought large amounts of mail with him and had found much more awaiting distribution.

After locating living quarters for himself, his wife and baby, Geary set out to find a suitable place for the town's first postoffice. He rented a little store at Montgomery and Washington Streets. He had no experience in the work he was about to undertake and now wondered how to proceed. No facilities were at hand. However, as he eyed the creaky wooden floor a plan of operation soon evolved.

Resourceful by nature, Geary took a piece of chalk and carefully drew 26 little squares on the flooring, one for each letter in the alphabet. Then he began to distribute letters, packages and newspapers; simply dropping them into the proper areas. Before long he was ready for business.

Delivery was equally simple. During business hours he would remove a pane of glass from the only window and hand mail to those who came and gave their names.

Geary's assignment had come as a reward for valiant service to his country in the war with Mexico. Long before he had donned a uniform, however, he had proved his mettle and established himself as a man of high principle and capability. Born in Pennsylvania's Westmoreland County, his schooling had been interrupted when his father died, leaving many debts. Determined to liquidate them, he became a school teacher.

When all of the bills were paid, he continued to work and save until he could attend Jefferson College in Canonsburg, where he studied civil engineering.

For a time he moved through several states, working at different jobs. Then, at the outbreak of the Mexican War in 1846, he readily answered the call for volunteers. He became colonel of a regiment that fought under General Scott at Vera Cruz, where he distinguished himself for military skill and bravery. In one engagement he was wounded. In another he led his men up the heights of Chapultepec in a brilliant and successful engagement.

When peace came he marched with a detachment of 400 men from Mexico City to Pittsburg, a distance of 3,000 miles.

His military achievements were highly praised and on January 22, 1849 President Polk gave him what appeared to be suitable recognition — appointment as postmaster of San Francisco. Some days later Geary sailed with his wife and child aboard the *Falcon*. They reached their destination on April first after perilous encounters with a band of ruffians bent on robbery and murder.

Geary made friends quickly in his new home and won the confidence of the townsfolk. They liked his cordial manner and respected him for the way in which he handlied his postal duties. Before long he came to be regarded as a leading citizen.

The little store, meanwhile, had proved itself inadequate for the volume of business he was handling, and Geary moved the postoffice to larger quarters. He worked long hours, with little help for men were demanding high wages and his budget was sparse.

All was going well when Geary received unofficial word from Washington that a shift of top officials had taken place and a new postmaster had been named to succeed him. Shocked and disappointed, he promptly resigned and decided to become a merchant. With William Vorhees and O. P. Sutton he formed a partnership, establishing a firm in the auction and commission business. They did well and Geary invested heavily in real estate. With the Gold Rush under way property was being sold at absurdly low prices.

In August 1849, only months after Geary's arrival, an election was called to fill the highest office in the town. Apparently Geary was unaware of the esteem in which he was held, for his nomination came as a complete surprise. His first inclination was to decline but friends prevailed on him to accept the honor and he was chosen the sixth and last American Alcalde.

Geary assumed the high office at a time the town was near chaos. Government was disorganized and inefficient. Crime was rampant, with no facilities for enforcing law and order. Robberies were common occurrences and two murders in a single day were not unusual. It was not an easy task to bring about stability and a sense of order.

As Alcalde of a town of 20,000, Geary was not only mayor but sheriff and recorder, coroner and magistrate as well. On his shoulders fell almost the entire burden of city government.

However, he did have the support of the best elements and in a surprisingly short time a change took place. A relentless foe of crime and corruption, Geary went before the town council, pleading for help. "You are now," he said frankly on his first appearance, "without a single requisite for the protection of property or the maintenance of order."

Recognizing the need for prompt action, the Councilmen voted to appropriate funds to purchase the brig *Euphemia,* which had been abandoned in the Bay after its crew had deserted for the mines. It was converted into a jail, the town's first, and for four years it served that purpose.

He also was authorized to appoint the first peace officers. One of his selections was Malachi Fallon, a one-time Tammany politician, who had served as warden of New York's Tombs after a long career as a saloonkeeper. Fallon later became city marshal.

Then Geary, as a further measure toward strict law enforcement, organized a chain gang for those convicted of serious crimes. Weighted heavily with balls and chains, they were put to work on street improvements.

In May of 1850, a year after Geary took office, the first city charter was adopted. It became time to elect a mayor under the new system. Geary was the man to whom everyone looked and he was chosen by a heavy vote to serve a one-year term.

Even before the year had passed, people marveled at the changes he had brought about. Order had been restored. Crime was greatly reduced. Now house dwellers did not bother to lock their doors and merchants often left unpacked goods on the streets overnight.

Word of the mayor's accomplishments in the community spread throughout the state and he was hailed as one of California's ablest government officials. Soon he was being called on by other towns for help and counsel. Always he came forward, sharing his concern for the public good with others.

When his term of office came to an end, Geary felt that he had done his duty. During the lawless period his wife had returned to Pennsylvania with their two children — the youngest born in San Francisco — and Geary was anxious to join them.

He left San Francisco on February 1, 1852 but before his departure he had decided to leave a suitable gift to the community.

His present was the land on which Union Square now stands. This he formally deeded to San Francisco and the City Council passed a resolution making it public property for all time. He never returned.

Geary's public service did not end with his departure from San Francisco. Soon after the outbreak of the Civil War he joined the Union forces with the rank of colonel and was with General Sherman in the historic March to the Sea.

In the early stages of the war Geary was badly worried by reports that California might join the Confederacy. Although far away and heavily burdened with military duties, he developed a steady correspondence with the Rev. Thomas Starr King of San Francisco, who was fighting valiantly to keep the state in the Union. Geary gave the vigorous Unitarian minister much worthwhile counsel and suggested leading citizens who might become strong allies in the cause.

When the War ended, he retired with the rank of major general and moved to Kansas, where he later was elected Governor. He probably would have remained there but, when his wife died suddenly, Geary chose to have their children reared by relatives in Pennsylvania.

In that state, too, he served as Governor. He died in 1873.

Gough

The House of Mystery

Mammy Pleasant

ONLY A FEW San Francisco streets still hold memories of strange, eccentric early-day characters who lived on them in days gone by. Octavia is one, for at the corner of Bush Street stood the celebrated "Bell House of Mystery," dominated by the uncanny Mammy Pleasant, the center of many a fantastic legend of pioneer days.

Contrary to lingering belief that Octavia Street received its name at a Latinate designation of its location eight blocks east of Divisadero, it was named in honor of a woman, Miss Octavia Gough. Her brother, Charles, was a member of a commission to lay out streets west of Larkin on what would be known as the Western Addition and availed himself of the opportunity to honor his devoted sister by perpetuating her name.

The street gained its notoriety, however, from its association with another woman. For many years, she cast a weird spell over the household of a wealthy Scot, Thomas Bell. Just how she did it no one ever knew but no one ever doubted that many a wealthy home would be wrecked were she to tell what she knew of the capers of the city's most respected men.

Mammy Pleasant's real name was Mary Ellen. Her mother was a free northern Negro; her father a Cherokee Indian. Dark skinned, with high cheek bones, thin lips and one blue eye, she had arrived in San Francisco in the early 'fifties from New Orleans with her husband, John.

It was common knowledge that she had been a procurer in her early western days. Rich men tipped their hats to her. She knew their secrets but she never told.

Apparently her reputation as a cook had preceded her, for on her arrival in San Francisco she was met at the wharf by an excited group of men, bargaining for her services. She demanded — and received — $500 a month, more than double the pay of others and she was firm in her price. Dishwashing she flatly refused to do, nor would she wash clothes, which compelled her employers to send out their laundry, at a cost of $20 for a dozen pieces.

For a few years her services were in great demand. Her husband, meanwhile, had gone his own way. Finally she decided to go into business for herself. She opened a boarding house and often boasted that such leading figures as Broderick, Terry and Sharon ate at her table.

In spite of her lust for money, she was deeply concerned with the plight of southern Negroes and decided to do something to help them. She closed the boarding house after a time and traveled through the Deep South helping many of the deprived black people flee to Canada.

It was shortly after her return to San Francisco that she met Bell, a partner in a firm that represented the Rothschilds, and a man of no little influence in the community. From the start she exercised a mysterious power over him, by what means no one seemed to know. She introduced him to a woman friend, Teresa Glingman of New York, and romance soon developed. Bell let Teresa take his name and established the home that for years was known as the "House of Mystery."

Mammy Pleasant, originally engaged as a housekeeper, ruled the place. She was tyrannical and, when she pressed for the marriage of her employer to his mistress, Bell evidently had reason for not refusing.

She sent for a priest and stood by as a witness to the wedding but the ceremony had a strange affect on the relations of bride and groom. While they had lived together happily in their unwed state, arguments started soon after the nuptials.

One night there was a violent quarrel and the new Mrs. Bell fled with the family jewels. Bell had his bride arrested but through Mammy's efforts a truce was effected — they were to divide the house and for years husband and wife lived apart in separate rooms.

Again Mammy exerted her exotic power over the man who hired her. She induced him to offer his wife $50,000 for each child she would bear him. The estrangement obviously ended, as they had six children — three boys and an equal number of daughters.

Years later tragedy descended on the "House of Mystery." One night Bell, then advanced in years, fell to his death from a third-story balcony.

How it happened remained a mystery but many had their own theories — perhaps because Mammy's familiar red shawl was found close to the body. The police took no action but the housekeeper continued to hold sway over the household for many years after Bell's strange death.

In the end she and Mrs. Bell came to violent disagreement. Mammy packed her belongings and moved away. She finally died penniless at the age of 92.

All that she knew of the Bells and of many others went with her to the grave. The house became something of a landmark and for years legend insisted that it was haunted.

Davidson

"California's
Most Remarkable
Man"

Professor George B. Davidson

As A SCIENTIST, specializing in astronomy, geodetics and geography, Professor George B. Davidson probably received more decorations than any other scholar of his time.

During his long residence in San Francisco and his work on the University of California campus he received awards from 35 scientific institutions throughout Europe and the United States. World famous universities conferred honorary degrees on him and he was decorated by foreign rulers.

San Francisco showed its appreciation of his attainments in two ways; not only as an avenue designated in his honor but Mt. Davidson was named for him. Some biographers say that he was "the most remakable man who ever lived in California."

During his long career he published more than 300 books and papers — covering a wide variety of subjects ranging from the stars, to London's sewers, to the temperature of the waters of the Golden Gate. Two of his books reflect his great interest in California — "Discovery of San Francisco Bay" written in 1907; and "The Origin and Meaning of the Name California," published three years later.

He served the federal government in various ways, adding much to the store of scientific knowledge. The University of California benefitted by his accomplishments, as did many scientific bodies.

Once he accompanied James Lick, the eccentric pioneer-philanthropist, to gaze at the stars through a telescope. Fascinated by what he saw and by Davidson's explanations, Lick later became the donor of the observatory on Mt. Hamilton that bears his name.

Many have called George Davidson a self-made scientist. Though he received a good education in his early years and won several degrees, he pressed on constantly to broaden his knowledge and explore new fields.

He was born in Nottingham, England on May 9, 1825. At seven he was brought by his parents to America. They settled in Philadelphia, where the boy received his early education. By the age of 17 he had acquired so extensive a knowledge of astronomy that he was hired as a computer and observer at Girard College in his home city.

He worked there for eight years until his thorough knowledge of his subjects attracted the attention of those in charge of the United States Coast Survey. He already had carried on intensive studies in geodetics, the science of measuring portions of the earth's surface by triangulation and astronomical observations. A man of such learning was needed for important work on the western coast.

Davidson, then 25 years of age, was selected. Heading an expedition, he arrived in California in 1850 and decided with little hesitation that San Francisco would be his permanent home, though for years his government work would take him to distant places.

He was called on to establish exact geographical locations in the West, to settle the boundary lines between the United States and Canada, and the borders between California and Nevada. Similar services were rendered to the territory of Alaska.

This work continued for several years and it was during one of his business visits to San Francisco in 1858 that he married Ellinor Fauntelroy. She was the youngest daughter of Robert H. Fauntelroy of Virginia and a granddaughter of Robert Owen, a noted Scottish educator and philanthropist who founded one of the world's first communes at New Harmony, Indiana. To the Davidsons were born three children, two sons and a daughter.

In pursuit of his astronomical and other scientific interests he traveled to many foreign countries, through Europe and into China, Egypt and India. He observed two total solar eclipses and a transit of Mercury. In 1874 he made a special trip to Japan to see the transit of the planet Venus. Universities and scientific societies in many countries invited him to lecture and for technical discussions.

In 1879 he built his own observatory, the first in California, in San Francisco. He soon found it to be far too small. Then, knowing of Lick's interest in astronomy since childhood, he sent for the millionaire and persuaded him to provide funds for the Mt. Hamilton Observatory which he took an active part in planning.

Nine years before, Davidson had been appointed an honorary professor of astronomy, geodetics and geography by the University of California, a post he filled until 1905 when he assumed emeritus status.

During this period he was also made a member of the University's Board of Regents on which he served until 1884, combining the responsibilities of a Regent with his duties as an instructor.

Death ended his career in 1911.

The widow and their eldest son, Thomas, a scientist and an inventor, continued to occupy the old-fashioned four-story family residence that the Professor had built in the early 'nineties on Washington Street, a dwelling that for years had been the scene of important conferences with men high in the world of science.

After Thomas' death Mrs. Davidson chose to live alone and in seclusion, cooking her own meals and caring for herself.

Years later neighbors became alarmed after they had failed to see her about for days. The police were called and Mrs. Davidson was found dead in bed, the victim of a heart attack.

In her will she asked that the house be demolished if her heirs did not desire to live there. It was torn down a year later and a valuable collection of scientific papers, trophies and souvenirs was divided between the University and the Academy of Sciences, of which Davidson once had been president.

Russ

The Pioneer Landlord

Russ's Garden

THE FIRST HOME that J. C. Christian Russ set up in San Francisco in March of 1847 was anything but pretentious. Yet it had walls and roof, sufficient at least to provide shelter for his family of twelve until better accommodations could be procured.

Lumber was scarce and expensive. There were no "For Rent" signs in sight. Russ, a resourceful jeweler who had been practically wiped out in the East when his shop was looted, simply did the most expedient thing. Since the ship which had brought them on the long voyage from New York was to be abandoned in the Bay, he hired a few seamen to detach the cabin and haul it to a sandlot.

The lot was at Bush and Montgomery Streets, then popularly referred to as "the suburbs." High hills of sand obscured their view from what was considered the heart of town. But Russ and his brood were content. At least they had a place to live.

They were never to know that many years afterward a tall and busy office structure, named for him, would stand on the site of their crude and humble residence.

Russ had foresight. Though the Gold Rush was yet to come, he was confident that the little settlement was destined to grow into a busy seaport. Moreover he had a sense of thrift and he was not afraid of work.

While Russ was still contemplating a new business venture, he became a landlord. He combed the beach on the little cove, gathering up loose lumber. With it he built a small cottage close to his own ramshackle home. Finding a tenant was no problem. That was only a beginning.

With more lumber obtained in the same way and some that was purchased second hand, he put up a second and then a third shack. Months later he owned more than thirty little cottages which rented as fast as they could be completed. Russ was on his way to a new start in his adopted town.

Migrating to the West was furthest from the minds of Russ and his wife in the Fall of 1846. They were happy and contented where they were and though Russ' jewelry store was not a heavy money-maker, it provided enough to meet the needs of a large and growing family.

Perhaps life would have continued in its routine way if Russ had not closed his shop earlier than usual one evening to view a torchlight procession in honor of General Jackson. Returning to the store early the next morning, he stood aghast at what he saw. The front door was lying across the pavement and the store stripped of almost everything of value. To make matters worse, he had no insurance.

For several days he pondered his loss. He had a little money in the bank, but it was not enough to restock the looted shop. He considered looking for a job as a clerk but the idea was not appealing.

"I'm just too disgusted to stay around here any longer," he told his wife one morning. "Why don't we all go West where there should be opportunities for men like me?"

His proposal met with approval, not only from his wife but also from their two eldest sons who had been thinking of volunteering for the Mexican War.

In a short time the family had booked passage on a ship named the *Loo Choo* and was packing what could be taken along. The boys enlisted with permission to join a regiment when they arrived in California.

A few months after their arrival in San Francisco, Russ decided to try his hand again at the only business he really understood. He opened a little jewelry shop, with an office for assaying. Though his stock was small at first, people came to buy and before long he was doing well.

As time passed, Russ became wealthy. Besides his business, he invested prudently in real estate. He built a small hotel, the Russ House, not far from the place where the ship cabin once had stood.

Long before this the family had abandoned that cabin for a better home but eventually Russ began to look about for an even larger and more luxurious place to live. Fond of the suburbs, he bought a sizeable piece of land in what people called "the wilderness." It was at Sixth and Harrison Streets. Some ridiculed him for building in such an isolated area, but there, with profits from his jewelry store, he erected a home that people of the time called a mansion. Around it he laid out expansive gardens with arbors and similar attractions.

The thought came to him: Why not let others share in the beauty of his new home and its flower-covered surroundings? His wife agreed and the place soon took on the name of Russ Gardens.

Russ not only threw his gates open wide but invited nationality and other ethnic groups to celebrate their holidays there. Soon Russ Gardens echoed on Sundays with German songs or Swiss yodeling; and sometimes with the exotic music of Chinese fiddlers.

Typical of these festivities is one recorded under the date of 1853 by Frank Soule in his "Annals of San Francisco":

"May Day was celebrated by a large number of our German citizens in the cheerful and imposing style observed in Fatherland. The Turner Gesang Verein (Gymnastic Musical Union) took the most active part in the festivities. Dressed in loose brown linen coats and pantaloons, proper for their exercises, they marched with banners flying, and musical instruments sounding, to the gardens of Mr. Russ. There somewhere about eighteen hundred persons of German blood participated in the different enjoyments of the day. They leaped, balanced and twirled; danced, sang, drank, smoked and made merry, as only such an enthusiastic race of mortals could. . . . "Das Deutsche Vaterland" was chanted in the most raptuous manner, and for the moment the different performers seemed to forget their native local distinctions and the very land that now gave them shelter, to become in heart and spirit only members of the one comman brotherhood of Germans."

Russ by now had made a name for himself in the community. Its leading citizens were his close associates and he became one of the most popular members of one of the town's highly respected social clubs, The Old Friends, known for its popular breakfasts.

His sons, too, had attained success. One of them, Henry, was a well-known athlete.

Though many years now have passed since the deaths of Russ and his family, his name still is well remembered, not only by the downtown building but by a street designated in his honor.

Davis

Cabin Boy
on a Horse

William Heath Davis, Jr.

ONE MORNING IN the summer of 1833 an 11-year-old cabin boy scrambled down the Jacob's ladder of the American trading bark *Volunteer,* rowed into Yerba Buena cove, and came ashore. He looked about, eager to explore his new surroundings.

As he moved slowly along the water's edge, he caught sight of the thick adobe walls of the Presidio and was curious to see what might be inside. He feared that plodding over sand dunes might be difficult, for his sea legs were still somewhat wobbly.

He was relieved, therefore, to see a man approaching and, when the two met, the boy explained his situation. The stranger smiled and dropped a friendly hand on the young shoulder. "Don't you worry," he said reassuringly. "You can ride my horse; he's over there just a little ways."

"Thank you, sir," the lad replied. "But who are you?"

"My name's Candelutio Miremontes. Come along with me."

The youngster was soon on his way and after visiting the military post he rode on. He had gone only a short distance when he came to a large potato patch. It interested him and dismounting he walked around it, fascinated by something he had never seen before. Some hours later he returned the horse and rowed back to his ship, tired but happy.

The cabin boy's name was William Heath Davis, Jr. Long after, he was to become one of the town's most prosperous merchants.

Through Davis' busy business career the horseback ride remained vivid in his memory. He would recall the story to visitors and, time permitting, he would walk with them to the corner of Kearny and Washington Streets to point out just where he had seen potatoes growing.

No doubt young Davis' liking for the sea was inherited from his father, a shipmaster from Boston who had sailed the seas for years before settling in what then were called the Sandwich Islands. There he married the daughter of another Boston sea captain, Oliver Holmes, who had married a native Hawaiian and called the Islands his home for many years, once serving as Governor of Oahu.

William Heath Davis, Jr. was born in the Sandwich Islands in 1822. In the family tradition, he followed the sea for a number of years, the memorable visit to the potato patch taking place on his second visit to Yerba Buena. The first was on the previous year when the boy arrived aboard the bark *Louisa*. His third trip in 1838 was the last for some time. He had decided to settle by San Francisco Bay.

His uncle, Nathan Spear, had recommended a business career, suggesting he start as a clerk in Spear's large mercantile store. Young Davis accepted the offer and ultimately became manager of the business. But, four years later, the sea called again, and he left the store to ship out on the *Don Quixoto* as supercargo. In this capacity he made a number of trips to the Islands, as well as up and down the coast.

Smuggling was at its height during this period, largely because of excessive duty. In later years Davis often recalled the devious means sea captains took to evade the Mexican customs collectors. Since customs were paid only at Monterey, some skippers would land the most valuable portions of their cargoes at an obscure spot on the coast, check the remainder at Monterey and return to pick up what had been left behind.

One of his favorite stories involved an experience aboard his own ship, the *Don Quixoto:* A customs collector was invited into a stateroom and locked in after he had been well supplied with liquor, cigars and a promise of $20 to be paid the next morning. With the customs officer well out of sight, crews worked throughout the night unloading cargo and delivering it to its consignees. If the collector on awakening noticed that the ship was lighter than the night before, he kept the information to himself.

Davis tired of seafaring in 1845 and decided to return to business, making Yerba Buena his home. This time, profiting by the experience offered by his uncle, he opened his own business and prospered. His profits were invested in shipping operations and eventually he became a wealthy shipowner. After some time, he bought his uncle's business and merged it with his.

In the meantime he had married Maria de Jesus Estudillo, the attractive daughter of Joaquin Estudillo, owner of extensive acreage in what is now San Leandro.

He took an active interest in community affairs and was elected a member of the town council.

In 1849 Davis undertook to erect the second brick building in the town, selecting a location at the northwest corner of Montgomery and California Streets. Bricks and cement were brought from Boston for the impressive four-story building. On its completion in 1851 he leased it to the federal government to be used as a custom house. Unfortunately, it was swept by fire only months after its occupancy.

Before engaging in this venture, Davis' interests had turned to schools and education. Soon after American occupation of the territory, *The California Star* had begun to agitate for a public school, pointing out that children were without adequate means of education. There had been a private school housed in a shanty on the west side of Dupont Street near Broadway. It was headed by J. D. Marston who, along with several trustees, abandoned their duties to hurry to the mines during the Gold Rush. With the school closed, the need for public facilities became acute. As evidence of its concern, *The Star* offered the town a lot and magnanimously added a gift of $50.

The issue came before the town council which authorized the erection of a suitable building with proper equipment and the hiring of a teacher. Open April 3, 1848 on the west side of the Plaza, the building also served as a town hall, courthouse and jail.

Davis was elected a trustee, serving with Dr. John Townsend and other prominent men.

As time passed Davis suffered serious business reverses. Discouraged and in poor health, he went to live with his married daughter, Mrs. Edwin H. Clough in Hayward. But he was not idle.

Friends urged him to write his memoirs, but Davis chose rather to relate the development of the State as he had seen it. The result was a book which he titled "Sixty Years in California." It was well accepted as a valuable contribution to the history of the State.

In the last years of his life he moved back to San Francisco and was present during the earthquake and fire of April, 1906 which destroyed much of the city. He died three years later on April 19, 1909 at the age of 87.

In 1968, fifty-nine years after his death, prominent businessmen who had known Davis in his later years appeared before San Francisco's Board of Supervisors in City Hall. They were incensed over a move to change the name of the street that honored him. A popular State Senator, Eugene McAteer, had died and it was agreed that a street should bear his name. Just why Davis Street was chosen for the change was not disclosed but friends of the one-time popular merchant were adamant in their protests.

The move was finally dropped after much discussion when it was agreed instead that the name of the late Senator should be given to a new public school.

Green

Man with a
Past

Clay and Kearny Streets, June, 1854

OCTOBER 29, 1850 was an uproariously happy day in San Francisco — but not for Talbot H. Green.

This was the day Californians received the news that the State had been admitted into the Union. The celebration knew no bounds. Business was suspended; the entire State went wild with excitement.

For Green, however, the day brought the first of a series of staggering blows which were to finally topple him from his place as a beloved leader of his community.

Green had been a favorite in San Francisco, rated as one of its most important and respected citizens. He had come West from Pennsylvania with one of the early immigrant parties and had settled first in Monterey, where he had risen rapidly in the business of Thomas Larkin, more than sufficient reference for any man.

On Larkin's recommendation Green was admitted into the San Francisco mercantile firm of Howard & Mellus, one of the city's principal concerns. There also he advanced rapidly and a brilliant future lay ahead.

Though of plain appearance, he had ingratiating ways, a warm personality and a brilliant mind. In a very short time he was recognized as everybody's friend. He had an open purse for those in want; widows and orphans benefitted by his generosity. When serious business disputes arose, men came to Green asking him to arbitrate. His time was theirs; he always refused fees for his services.

He already had assumed an important part in civic affairs, serving on the town council and as a member of a state commission formed to investigate charges of mismanagement against Alcalde Leavenworth.

When the legislature met in anticipation of California's statehood, friends pleaded with him to accept the nomination for United States senator. He could have had it for the asking but Green said that he was too busy. He even spurned nomination to be the city's mayor, though such prominent friends as Larkin and Brannan urged him to accept.

Was modesty the reason for Green's desire to avoid the public spotlight? After all, when Green announced his forthcoming marriage to Mrs. Allan Montgomery, an attractive widow, leading citizens decided to make the wedding a public celebration. But Green declined; he insisted on a private ceremony with Frank Turk, the assistant alcalde, performing the civil rites.

Such was Talbot Green's place in the community on that first Admission Day. As was to be expected, he was a leader in the procession. But, then, as the marchers dispersed slowly at the Plaza, Green unexpectedly met his Waterloo.

He had scarcely stepped away from his companions when a woman pushed her way through the crowd and extended her hand to him, exclaiming: "Why Mr. Geddis, is it possible that you are here in California?"

With no show of emotion, Green took her hand and gave her a friendly smile. "You must be mistaken, madam," he said calmly. "My name is Green — Talbot Green." And he started to walk away.

The woman followed with an angry look on her face. "Certainly I am not mistaken," she retorted with a show of temper. "I cannot be mistaken. I've known you all your life — and I've known your wife, your sister and your children."

Again Green insisted that she was in error and turned away, pale and trembling. The exchange, however, had been overheard by bystanders who had no reason to hold their tongues. Rumors quickly spread but people shook their heads and said that Green's reputation was unimpeachable. Larkin and his associates brushed the accusations aside, pointing out that such cases of mistaken identity were not unusual — even though on occasion a person mourned as dead in an eastern city had been met walking a downtown San Francisco street.

The incident had nearly been forgotten when the Democrats assembled some time later to nominate a mayor and other city officials. Green was their choice for mayor. However, there had been prolonged bickering over the selection of minor candidates and the nomination of a standard bearer was deferred for several days — too long a time for Green.

On the morning set for the resumed session a weekly newspaper, regarded as an irresponsible 'scandal sheet,' appeared with an article that created an instant sensation. Without mention of a name, it stated that the man about to be nominated for mayor was living under an alias; that he had changed his identity after disappearing from Pennsylvania with a large sum of money entrusted to him by a bank in Gettysburg.

In no time the town was buzzing with excitement. Larkin, Brannan and Howard, Green's closest friends, immediately called on him, assured him of their confidence and loyalty, and pleaded that he confide in them.

"Talbot, we'll stand by you," said Larkin, speaking for the group. "Only tell us the truth."

Without hesitation, Green declared himself a victim of unfortunate error.

"Then let's go to the editor of this paper and demand to know where he got his information," Larkin proposed. Green readily acquiesced.

The editor had no hesitation in naming his informant and the group went to interview the man. "Did you authorize that story?" Larkin demanded. They waited anxiously for his answer.

The other nodded. "Of course I did," he said bluntly. "And Mr. Geddis knows it's true."

Green looked the stranger squarely in the eyes, showing no emotion. "You're badly mistaken, sir," he said softly. "I'm not the man you think I am. This is a case of mistaken identity — and I can prove it."

The other smiled. "Paul, what nonsense you're talking now," he said without a show of malice. "We've known each other since childhood. Now that you're rich why don't you acknowledge the truth in front of these gentlemen; then go home like an honest man, pay the money back to the bank, and do the right thing by your wife and children."

If Green was moved he did not show it. "Can't you see a difference between me and the man you take me to be?" he inquired.

"Not a particle," was the answer, "except what few changes I'd expect after ten years had passed."

With that the meeting ended. The party started for Larkin's office, with Green's friends still far from convinced, such was their loyalty; yet with some reluctance they feared that the accusations must be true.

It was a sad, dejected group that walked into Larkin's place. Once more Green's friends assured him of their friendship and begged him to admit the truth. "If money's in your way," said Brannan, "we'll give you what you need to pay the bank. Isn't that fair enough?"

Trembling, Green struggled for an answers. Tears were now streaming down his face. "No—it's not—true," he stammered. Then, regaining his control, he declared that he intended to prove his innocence and easily could.

The group soon broke up and each man went his way, with no plans for further conversation.

Early the next morning Green called on his close friend, John McGlynn, to tell him what had happened. He also announced that he had booked passage to leave for Panama on the following day en route to Pennsylvania. There he hoped to obtain legal proof of the falsity of the accusations. He concluded with a strange request.

"I want you, Mac," he asked, "to get me the nomination for mayor this morning. I will then address a letter to you declining it and thanking the convention for the honor."

Apparently McGlynn showed some surprise, for Green continued: "If you will do that, it will give me the opportunity of denouncing this scandal."

This McGlynn promised to do but it proved impossible. When the convention got under way another squabble developed over nominations for lesser offices and again selection of a mayoralty candidate was deferred.

Meanwhile words of Green's intended departure had reached his friends and a farewell party was hurriedly arranged. It took place in Larkin's office. Champagne flowed freely as one man after another toasted the departing friend. Festivities were drawing to a close when Larkin got on a table, raised his glass, and offered this toast: "May the most honest men among us always remain as honest as we believe Talbot Green to be."

Again the party drank. Green climbed to the table top and tried to speak. But emotion overcame him and he broke into hysterical weeping, unable to speak a word.

Shortly afterward, he was escorted to the wharf by his friends. They all shook hands, helped Green aboard, and stood by waving until the ship began to move. The others, with what has been described as a "sickening feeling" turned away and returned to their own affairs.

Through channels of their own, the disappointed friends undertook to learn Green's fate. News came irregularly and with some confusion and contradictions. They heard first that Green and his wife had reconciled and that they had bought a farm on the Susquehanna River, planning to retire to a quiet life.

Long afterward word came that Green was in Texas, busy in land speculations, operating under the name of Paul Geddes. To his associates there he had confided his intention of returning to San Francisco to go into business with Sam Brannan, all of which was news to his former friend.

Bit by bit details of Green's past life came to light. It was learned that he had been entrusted by the bank with $7,000 in notes to be redeemed and returned in gold. With the notes in his pocket, he was enticed into a gambling game and lost everything he had. In despair, he decided to change his name, abandon his family, and go West.

He did return to San Francisco some years later but he was a broken man, shunning his former associates, who, in turn, shunned him.

His stay was short but he returned again on several occasions. His reception was always the same.

However, no one ever moved to change the name of the street that honored him. No doubt people felt that he had suffered enough and chose not to add to his disgrace.

Howard

The Pioneer
Philanthropist

William D. M. Howard

SOME HISTORIANS HAVE given William D. M. Howard the distinction of being "the most public spirited man in early San Francisco." Other pioneers have been cited as civic leaders but Howard, in the judgment of those chronicling the early days, deserves special recognition.

He was a merchant with a deep concern for the welfare and advancement of his community. Philanthropies were a part of his daily life. And he had a strong sense for justice, once saving two innocent men from the gallows when lynch law threatened to override the courts.

Like many of the time, his beginning was humble. He started as a cabin boy on a sailing ship determined to spend his life at sea.

When he was still in his early teens, he left his native Boston where he was born in 1818, to take his first job aboard the sailing ship *California*. At 20 he was ready to become a supercargo on Boston vessels that came West to trade up and down the Pacific Coast. He became a first mate and in this capacity sailed to Yerba Buena.

Howard saw business opportunities in the little settlement and decided to remain. He first became the buying agent for a Boston firm dealing in hides and tallow and then, after gaining some experience, decided to engage in business for himself. Fortunately, he met a clever merchant, Henry Mellus, and they formed a partnership, dealing in general merchandise. Howard saw the need for additional capital and went back to Massachusetts to raise it. He was successful and returned to devote his energies to the newly-formed business. Soon they were making money.

They had not been in business long when a unique opportunity arose. They had learned that valuable properties of the rich Hudson Bay Company were to be sold. With some of their earnings, augmented by borrowed funds, they made the purchase which yielded enormous profits.

The firm expanded rapidly. With the coming of the Gold Rush trade boomed and Howard became a wealthy man.

He recognized his responsibility to the community and became involved in all of its affairs, offering his services in every civic undertaking. Before long he had won recognition as an able, dependable leader. He was called on to preside at public meetings and to direct activities to suppress the lawless, especially the Hounds, who then were terrorizing the townspeople.

In July, 1847 the town alcalde, George Hyde, found government burdens more than he could carry by himself. He appealed to Governor Mason who ordered an election to select six councilmen to share the problems. "There is wanted in San Francisco," Mason said in his call, "an efficient town government, more so than in the power of an alcalde to put in force. There may be soon expected a large number of whalers in your bay and a large increase in your population. . . . I therefore desire that you call a town meeting for the election of six persons who when elected shall constitute the town council, and who in conjunction with the alcalde shall constitute the town authorities until the end of the year 1848."

The election took place little more than a month later, and Howard was chosen as one of the six members of the council. After a year he was reelected to serve another term.

During those times his popularity increased steadily in response to his constant concern for all the people, manifested by his opposition to increased taxes and what he regarded as unreasonably high salaries for town officials.

He was firm in his convictions and on occasion found himself compelled to oppose popular demands when he believed that he was in the right. Once he joined a small group of colleagues in demanding a fair trial for two men accused of robbery and threatened with lynching by an angry mob eager for blood.

Over the raucous cries of fully 3,000 infuriated men, Howard pleaded that the law must take its course. He called for establishment of a committee to see that the court would take fair and prompt action, and to guarantee the protection of the accused until they had been tried.

Over heated objections, he finally won his way and was named chairman of the group. In the end the two accused men were found to be innocent and the real culprits were apprehended soon afterward.

He became a member of the committee of fourteen that organized the first Vigilantes. And, when the town demanded fire protection, it was Howard who formed the first fire company and sent East for the first fire engine, which he presented as his gift.

With similar pride and generosity he met the requirements of a growing town as they developed. When the need for the first public school became apparent, he came forward, and offered a building of his own rent-free. In addition, since there were no funds available to hire teachers, Howard paid their salaries out of his own pocket until the necessary school taxes could be levied. It was the same when a cholera epidemic broke out and the town found itself without a hospital or funds to provide one. Again Howard turned over one of his own buildings for this purpose, refused to accept a cent for rent, and even furnished some of the equipment. He also organized a militia company and personally met some of the expenses.

On one occasion a group of churchmen called on him, complaining that they had no place to worship. "Don't worry," he told them. "You can have a lot I own on Natoma Street."

With some hired help and the volunteer services of a few carpenters in the group, a church was soon erected. It took the name of Howard Presbyterian Church in honor of the donor.

Howard built his own home on a rancho some distance from the town. Over its wide pasturage grazed the first herd of pedigreed cattle in California. Sections of the cities of Burlingame, Hillsborough and San Mateo stand on some of this land today.

The street the pioneers named for Howard was unique in two respects — its unusual paving and the characters that it attracted. One of them, a beautiful young woman, was known as "Floating Annie." She worked in a high class millinery shop and was often seen moving quickly over the narrow blocks going to and from her work with what onlookers described as "the grace of a fairy."

The first paving was an experiment that soon proved faulty and had to be abandoned. First a solid bed of rock was laid with a heavy coating of tar. Over this heavy wooden blocks were set, effecting what appeared to be a firm and substantial foundation. During the summer people said that it was "working like a charm" but they had not anticipated the winter rains. After the first heavy downpour, which continued through an entire day and night, the wooden blocks swelled, popped out of place, and made the street impassable. In the end they were taken up and sold for kindling.

For the most part Howard Street in the early days was inhabited by people of Irish birth or parentage. All were ardent Irish sympathizers and it was said that every saloon had "Free Ireland celebrations" every night throughout the year.

Coleman

Leader of the Vigilantes

Hanging of Jenkins on the Plaza

WILLIAM T. COLEMAN was a staunch believer in law and order — up to a certain point.

That point was reached twice in the early days of San Francisco when Coleman realized that he could not resist angry demands for lynch law and agreed to join Vigilante Committees.

The first time was in 1851; the next five years later when this man who had argued most to uphold the courts became the head of the Vigilantes.

In that capacity Coleman assumed something of a high and dignified position. He sometimes rode in a carriage while others walked. At The Oriental, a restaurant and recreation center where those highest in the town's affairs gathered for meals and talk, Coleman had the undisputed right to preside at the head of a table reserved for men. He was usually flanked by Dr. Beverley Cole, who held the title of physician to the Vigilantes, and Isaac Bluxome, a prominent businessman, who served as secretary of both Committees.

Coleman was a successful merchant and banker. His name was honored by a street. Soon after his arrival in California from Kentucky in 1849 he had opened a store in Placerville, which then was called Hangtown because the first lynching in the state had taken place there.

Later he went into business in Sacramento and finally moved south to San Francisco where he opened a large mercantile business and eventually expanded into banking.

But it is for his leadership of the Vigilantes that Coleman is best remembered. In casting his role with them despite his firm belief in legal justice, he was not a turncoat. Actually he had capitulated because he believed that this was the expedient thing to do.

In 1851 and 1856 he agreed to participate in lynchings only when he became convinced that there was no other way to avert widespread rioting that would result in bloodshed and loss to private property.

Coleman, tall and of imposing figure, first came to the fore as a Vigilante early in February, 1851 when an angry crowd threatened to hang two men on trial for assaulting a merchant and looting his safe. Believing the pair might be released, the mob was bent on taking the law into its own hands.

Amid cries of "Hang them," Coleman stepped forward boldly and urged the irate men to disperse so the trial could proceed in an orderly way. No one heeded him. Hoping to avert serious trouble, Coleman then proposed a compromise. He asked that a committee be selected to name an impartial judge and jury to take over the trial. There was reluctant agreement and Coleman became a member of the group. The accused men were acquitted.

The committee then agreed to perpetuate itself but a short time later when a man named Lewis was arrested as an arsonist, Sam Brannan took matters into his own hands and issued a call for a meeting in his office. There the first Vigilante Committee came into being with Brannan as its president and Coleman a member — though some said he had joined only in the hope of influencing the others against violence when the next crisis occurred.

They did not have long to wait. Soon afterward a man named Jenkins was caught stealing a safe. He was seized by Committee members, rushed to Brannan's office, and found guilty after witnesses had been heard.

Again there came a cry for hanging and once more Coleman called for law and order, pleading for delay until tempers cooled. No one paid attention to his words. Jenkins was taken to the Plaza and hanged. His execution brought little criticism, especially since the names of the 150 men signed to the Vigilante constitution were those of highly respected citizens.

The committee gained new members rapidly and finally numbered 700. In the months that followed it dealt with close to a hundred offenders in all types of crimes. Three were hanged.

Apparently lynch law was having some effect. Crime was gradually declining but the Vigilantes still were unwilling to disband; they chose to maintain formal organization in the event its services were needed.

Four years passed during which the group slowly disintegrated. Then, suddenly, violence flared again. The United States Marshal, the highly respected William R. Richardson, was shot down in cold blood by a notorious gambler, Charles Cora. The Marshal was not related to William A. Richardson, the founder of Yerba Buena.

Again Brannan rallied his men, urging Cora be hanged without a trial. Once more Coleman interceded, pleading for the law as he had four years before. He might not have won his point if Brannan hadn't been jailed on charges of inciting a riot.

Cora was tried and the jury disagreed. Another murder, not long afterward, stirred the Vigilantes to immediate action. The victim was James King of William, owner and editor of *The Bulletin,* who was shot and killed by James P. Casey, a member of the Board of Supervisors, after King published stories identifying Casey as a former Sing Sing convict.

The murder created a sensation. Irate crowds gathered about the jail bent on lynching and demanding custody of Casey. Once more Coleman protested and his plea was supported by Mayor Van Ness in an emergency call for order. But no one was in a mood to temporize.

Coleman, recently returned from a trip abroad, was surrounded by an excited crowd which urged him to become the leader of the Vigilantes or form a new committee. He initially refused but during the tumultuous hour which followed he changed his mind, realizing, as he had before, that only summary justice could avert uncontrolled violence.

Close to 2,000 men responded to his call and signed their names as members of what became known as the Second Vigilante Committee. The number continued to increase and three days later everyone knew what was about to happen. A building on Sacramento Street was rented, cannon were set on the roof, gunnysacks were filled with sand and placed to form an eight-foot wall around the structure. Because of its appearance and use, it became known as Fort Gunnybags.

The call for action came early on Sunday morning. Coleman had organized his men in military fashion. When the command was given, an army of more than 2500 angry determined men started the march to the jail.

A cannon was mounted facing the jail doors and a demand was made for Casey. He was dragged out quickly by a jailer who realized the futility of resistance.

The prisoner was lifted into a carriage, driven to Vigilante headquarters and hanged on an improvised gallows. Half an hour later Cora, awaiting a new trial, received similar treatment. The wanton murders of two influential citizens had been avenged but the Vigilantes did not disband.

Notorious gamblers, grafters and other undesirable characters were brought before trial groups selected by Coleman and his aides. On conviction they were ordered banished from the town. In some cases the Vigilantes paid for their transportation.

If the Committee looked favorably on its work, Governor Johnson did not. He signed a proclamation declaring that a state of insurrection existed. The Vigilantes were in a quandry but finally concluded that, since they had rid the town of murderers and undesirables, the time had come to disband. A Fourth of July celebration brought their activities to an end.

Coleman returned to his business affairs and to entertaining in his beautiful home on Taylor Street atop Nob Hill, a white villa in Roman style with a walled garden. Near it the family of Senator George Hearst lived for a time.

Only once, long after the disbanding of the Vigilantes, was Coleman called on for help. He was living quietly in his mansion when Dennis Kearney's sandlot speeches against the Chinese threatened to incite serious rioting. Angry men were overheard planning to set fire to the lumber yards near the water's edge. The police chief, fearing trouble, recalled the activities of the Committee, and sent for Coleman.

Years had passed and those who had been most active now were in retirement, content to leave law enforcement in the hands of the authorities. However, they responded to Coleman's summons, organizing this time not as Vigilantes but as The Citizen's Committee. They armed themselves with ax handles and soon became known as "Coleman's Pick-Ax Brigade." The need to use these weapons never arose. Evidently their presence and their past was sufficient warning, and the trouble soon subsided.

Brenham

The Fearless
Mayor

Charles J. Brenham

CHARLES J. BRENHAM, who became San Francisco's second mayor in May, 1851, was only of average physique and strength, but he was a fearless man. When he faced emergencies his own safety was of no concern. A vigorous supporter of the power of right over might, he did what he believed to be his duty and always emerged the victor.

Never was Mayor Brenham's rare courage better demonstrated than on an afternoon some months after he had taken office. He was at his desk when word came that an infuriated mob was gathered in and around the large store of Alsop and Company, determined to hang a man who had been caught pilfering merchandise.

Dropping his papers, Brenham hastened to the place to be confronted by more than a thousand angry men. The store was thronged. Toward the rear the thief was being held, his hands tied behind his back. The mob milling outside was demanding action.

"As your mayor I demand that you disperse at once," Brenham shouted over the angry cries of those around him. "The law must take its course."

Not a man moved and from some there came defiant words but the Mayor recognized his duty and stood his ground.

"All right then," he shouted again. "If there be law-abiding men among you, move out. We have courts to handle cases such as this."

Few more than a dozen men began shuffling their way out of the mob, followed by jeers from all the others.

Brenham advanced a few steps, stroked his short, dark beard, and pulled his heavy gold watch from his vest pocket. Looking at the timepiece and then at the crowd, he called out once more, this time louder than before, "I'm giving you just ten minutes to disperse. If you don't, I'll send for the Marshal and everyone of you will go to jail. Remember,

I said ten minutes."

For a few moments there was silence. Some of the rioters exchanged puzzled glances, then began to move. Before the time limit had ended, the crowd was on its way. The Mayor waited until he was certain the trouble was over, then quietly walked back to his office.

Curiously, Brenham had been elected to the town's highest post without seeking the office. He was essentially a steamboat captain who liked his work and had no concern for politics. Yet, once elected, he became absorbed in public life.

Brenham had celebrated his twentieth birthday only a few days before he left his home in Frankfort, Kentucky in the fall of 1837 to become master of a large steamboat. As a youth he had worked as cabin boy on steamers plying the Mississippi between Vicksburg and Crescent City. Curiosity and ambition prompted him to learn much about their operation and occasionally he was allowed to take the wheel.

Nevertheless, seasoned captains reacted with some surprise and much annoyance when they learned that young Brenham had been hired as captain of one of the best steamboats on the river. Evidently there was much talk for when Brenham docked at New Orleans the insurance company notified the ship's owners that they would be obliged to cancel their policy because of the master's youth. Brenham's employers and some friends came forward, vouching for his ability, and the matter was finally dropped.

His next voyage took him to San Francisco where he arrived on August 18, 1849. He was soon hired as captain of the steamer *McKim* which was operating between San Francisco and Sacramento.

A year later one of the most unexpected experiences in Brenham's life occurred. His ship had landed in San Francisco only a few hours before when a group of men representing his party, the Whigs, came aboard and informed him that he had been nominated for mayor. Brenham stared at his callers in amazement.

"Why me?" he inquired. "Politics do not interest me and I'm happy with what I'm doing." The others were insistent, for they believed he possessed the qualities needed for the important post.

"I'll accept then but on one condition," he finally agreed. "I'm earning a good living on this boat and I don't intend to gamble with my job. I'll run for mayor if you'll agree that I will not speak at a single meeting; I won't leave the wheel to campaign. If you'll accept me on these terms, I'll run."

He was unsuccessful despite the vigorous efforts of his supporters. The election went to Colonel Geary but eventually Brenham was to find himself immersed in public life and politics.

Meanwhile, however, he had purchased the steamer *Gold Hunter* with several partners. He was doing well when the Whigs again chose him as their candidate in 1851. Again Brenham declared that he would not campaign but circumstances were to bring about a change of mind. A large company wanted to buy his ship for trade with Mexico. He accepted the profitable offer and, with no ship to occupy his time and attention, decided to engage in vigorous vote-getting for the coming election.

He had a popular opponent, Frank Tilford, who believed that he could easily win. But Brenham, now free from his shipping responsibilities, became a tireless campaigner. Never had the voters seen such electioneering. He spoke at public meetings at least twice every night, and often more. Although inexperienced as an orator, Brenham surprised his listeners by his force of speech and his clear analysis of the city's problems.

People soon rallied behind his candidacy and he was voted into office by a large majority.

He had not anticipated all the problems that would confront him. The day before his inauguration on May 5, 1851, San Francisco was swept by a disastrous fire that caused tremendous losses. The city dropped into low spirit and many frankly voiced a loss of confidence. There were other problems; lawlessness increased almost overnight.

Fortunately for the new mayor, he had the support of conscientious and dedicated officials. Sometimes they disagreed with him but Brenham had the force of his convictions and his leadership was recognized.

It was during these trying times that Brenham was obliged to take his first courageous stand against vigilantes justice. The trial of a man named Lewis, arrested on a charge of arson, had barely started when a throng of angry, impatient men stormed the courtroom, demanding the prisoner be turned over to them for immediate execution.

A riot was well under way when the Mayor was summoned for help. Rather than call for officers of the law, he went himself and without protection cried out to the crowd, demanding that the court be allowed to administer justice in a lawful way. It would have been easy to overpower the man as he stood alone but Brenham held the respect of his fellow-citizens and they obeyed his order, though with much reluctance.

As the end of his term of office approached, Brenham expressed a desire for reelection but the Whigs, encountering political and legal difficulties, decided not to engage in the race. Dr. S. R. Harris became the new mayor.

Brenham went into the banking and exchange business with a partner, Beverley C. Sanders. The firm took the name of Sanders and Brenham and was successful from the start but the former mayor had had a taste of politics and wished to continue in public life.

He became a member of the Whig State Central Committee and

was later chosen to be its president. In November, 1852 he was nominated again for the mayoralty and elected to serve until October of the following year.

Brenham had been in office only a short time when President Fillmore nominated him to be Treasurer of the Mint and Assistant Treasurer of the United States. The position commanded a far greater salary than that of mayor but Brenham was happy in his present office and declined the federal appointment, even though it had been confirmed by the Senate.

Brenham's biographers pay high tribute to the efficient and just manner in which he fulfilled his duties. They point out that his messages on vital issues were masterpieces of writing, evidencing deep understanding of the basic principles of government.

There were instances when he found himself compelled to take issue with the council on important matters. His position was always supported by the people.

His motives were never questioned, nor were his integrity and honesty. As one writer, Frank Soule, said in his "Annals": "No one has ever performed or will ever perfom the duties of an office with more purity of purpose, and with a greater regard for the true interests of the city, than did Mr. Brenham. He retired from the office without the slightest taint or suspicion."

When Brenham stepped out of the Mayor's chair, he had many friends and strong supporters. No doubt he could have sought other public office had he desired but he seemed content to retire into private life. However, he continued a wide interest in public affairs and frequently was called on for counsel. The one time cabin boy on a river steamboat had traveled far and in his memory a street bears his name.

Baker

The
Silver-Tonqued
Orator

Colonel Edward Dickenson Baker

THERE WERE SEVERAL reasons why Colonel Edward Dickenson Baker was highly regarded in the early days of San Francisco.

He was recognized as one of the most brilliant lawyers in the community. People called him their silver-tongued orator. And many envied him for his close friendship with President Lincoln, the two having practiced law together in Springfield, Illinois.

Baker had been given the rare privilege of introducing Lincoln at his first inauguration in 1861 and he became the President's chief advisor on all matters pertaining to the Pacific Coast.

If these achievements were not enough to justify the distinction accorded Baker by his fellow-citizens, there were the tributes he received for his successful efforts to keep California in the Union at the time of the Civil War, when many desired that the State join the Confederacy.

Baker liked to think of himself as a native American although he was born in London on February 24, 1811 and came to the United States with his parents as a child. They settled in Springfield where Baker worked his way through school and law studies.

Before coming to San Francisco in 1851 he had followed a varied career. From his law practice in Illinois, he moved to neighboring states and once worked on the Panama Railroad as a superintendent of construction for a sub-contractor.

As a young man he had served in the Black Hawk War with the rank of major and later in the war with Mexico as a colonel.

He returned to Springfield, became interested in politics, and was elected to Congress in 1845. Three years after his first term had ended, he was returned to Washington. In the House he was an outstanding spokesman against slavery.

As an attorney in San Francisco, Baker won a well-deserved reputation for his ability and gift of oratory. When he addressed a jury or spoke at important public meetings, he was certain to attract a crowd, for people were drawn by his eloquence and sat spellbound.

At one time he surprised his fellow citizens by undertaking the defense of Charles Cora, the notorious gambler and underworld figure who had ruthlessly shot and killed the popular William R. Richardson, an outstanding citizen and a federal official.

Cora's conviction for murder was regarded as a certainty; he had shot an unarmed man without provocation. That Baker, in his high position, should rally to such a man's defense was something few could understand. But Baker insisted that any man, regardless of guilt, was entitled to a fair trial and the best legal talent he could afford.

Cora's mistress, Annabelle Ryan, a former prostitute from New Orleans, paid Baker a fee of $10,000. The lawyer raised a plea of self-defense. His closing argument was a masterpiece of oratory, so convincing that it resulted in a disagreement among the jurors. Baker was said to have accomplished the impossible. It did Cora little good, for he was hanged by a group of Vigilantes before his second trial could take place.

On frequent occasions Baker demonstrated his rare gift of speech in orations on public occasions — whether sad or festive. His eulogy at the funeral of Senator David S. Broderick, who had been killed in one of the city's most dramatic duels, drew tears from the thousands who assembled. He pictured Broderick as a martyr to freedom's cause and his stirring words were said to have done much to strengthen the cause of liberal government and social justice.

At another time he was asked to deliver the key address at the dedication of old Laurel Hill Cemetery. He chose the theme that the departed would enjoy eternal rest amid the trees and shrubbery around their graves. As if addressing those who had passed away, he declaimed in his clear and resonant voice: "The truth peals like thunder in our ears — thou shalt live forever." His speech was published in full and those who had not been present read every word.

In the late 'fifties, he became one of the foremost figures in the organization of the Republican Party in California. So strongly was his influence felt that party members in Oregon invited him to come north as their spokesman. He moved there and in 1860 they elected him to the United States Senate.

Baker, however, continued to keep a close eye on affairs in California and with the approach of the Civil War he became determined to keep the State in the Union. In this effort he soon found himself a bitter opponent of United States Senator William M. Gwin, one of the strongest supporters of the secessionists.

Southern sympathizers had organized into semi-military groups which at times became unruly in their public demonstrations. To Baker's dismay, California authorities merely looked on with no effort to curb disorders. Over Gwin's strong oppostion, he used his political influence to bring about such changes in public officials as were needed to keep the secessionists in line.

Baker was at the height of his career at the outbreak of the Civil War. Moved by patriotism, he impulsively locked up his home in Oregon, enlisted, and with the rank of colonel accepted the command of a regiment of Pennsylvania volunteers which comprised many men who already resided in California and Oregon. He fell in his regiment's first engagement at Ball's Bluff, Virginia on October 21, 1861.

Halleck

Investor in
The Future

Henry W. Halleck

BY 1852 THE RUSH to the gold mines was virtually over, though many prospectors still lingered in the Mother Lode with hopes of striking hidden veins. But the inflation of the earlier period was having serious effect on San Francisco's economy. Worried merchants looked at their dwindling bank accounts, shook their heads, and wondered what could be done.

During this business recession, a self-appointed leader came forward. His name was Henry W. Halleck. He had conceived a daring project which he believed would help materially to end the depression.

Calling a meeting of influential businessmen, he told them that with their financial help he could put the town back on its feet.

"How are you going to do it?" they inquired skeptically and with some levity.

"By restoring confidence," he answered quickly, and this time there was a round of laughter.

When one man asked sarcastically, "And just how do you do that?" Halleck had a ready reply.

"We can restore confidence," he asserted, "by putting up the largest building in this town, an expensive building, and if people see that we're willing to invest a lot of money they'll soon realize that we have faith in the town; they'll have confidence too, and that's what is needed."

"How much will such an expensive building cost?" another man inquired.

Halleck turned to the man at his side, a well-known architect named G. P. Cummings, with whom he already had discussed the plan. "You tell them," said Halleck.

"Three million dollars," the architect blurted.

"Halleck, you're just a stupid fool," one prominent merchant shouted and the others nodded their agreement.

"I disagree," Halleck shot back, trying to hold his temper. "If you won't help me with the financing, I'll find it somewhere else, but I'll tell you once more that you're missing an opportunity. This town simply needs a show of confidence."

"Then get it somewhere else," exclaimed another of his listeners, and the meeting soon broke up.

Halleck was ready to meet the challenge. Working alone, he hurried East and told his story. In the end he succeeded in borrowing large sums from banks, from other financial houses, and even from a few railroads. The logic of his argument and his own confidence had won their backing.

When Halleck returned to San Francisco he was ready to move ahead. He had already selected a site at the corner of Washington and Montgomery Streets. From the gold fields and the mining towns he assembled Chinese coolies by the hundreds. As quickly as they reached the Bay, he and his aides, under Cummings' direction, put them to work using round baskets to scoop up the mud flats.

When the excavation was completed, redwood logs which had been floated across the Bay from Contra Costa County were placed crosswise over the enormous hole, forming what resembled a wooden mat. To this initial covering a second layer of redwood logs was added, and then topped by heavy, thick ship planking.

Onlookers laughed and called the project "Halleck's Folly." They were positive that the builder was doomed for disaster. "That building is going to sink," some said. Others insisted that a strong tide would carry it outside of the Golden Gate and into the Pacific Ocean.

Meanwhile Halleck, with his borrowed funds, had sent far and wide for building materials. He imported cement from England; glass from Belgium, France and Germany. From Philadelphia he bought lumber and 1,747,800 bricks — all loaded on ships traveling around the Horn.

Fourteen months were required to complete what then was regarded as an enormous structure. It was opened to the public a few days before Christmas of 1853. Many who toured its rooms and hallways still insisted that it would collapse. But Halleck was not worried. By profession he was an engineer and he knew that he had built well.

The building was first called the Washington Block, later the Montgomery—or Monkey—Block. It survived the earthquake and fire of 1906, only to be razed in 1958 to make way for several new and modern buildings.

While completion of San Francisco's largest building was the highlight of Halleck's colorful career, it was marked by many public services, so many that it was deemed proper to give his name to a street. A graduate of West Point, he had come to be regarded as an expert on fortifications. In his early Army years he had been called on to provide for the protection of New York Harbor.

He was sent to California in 1847 with the rank of first lieutenant to inspect fortifications along the Pacific Coast. His promotion to a captaincy soon followed.

Richard B. Mason, the Military Governor, appointed him Secretary of State, giving him a place of high importance in the military government.

In the summer of 1849, with California under American rule, it became necessary to draft a Constitution. A convention was called to meet in Monterey on September 3 and Halleck was one of the first to be selected as a delegate. The convention had not progressed far when he became one of the central figures in a highly controversial issue, a dispute over California's boundaries.

Halleck lined up with William Gwin, who had arrived only a short time before from Tennessee with the hope of being elected one of the first United States Senators. They contended that California should consist of all the land acquired from Mexico under the Treaty of Guadalupe Hidalgo — the entire Far West. Rough maps drawn by Halleck disclosed that he envisioned an area embracing all of Nevada and even part of Utah.

Bitter opposition developed, with many contending that so enormous an area could not be properly governed.

In the end Halleck and Gwin were forced to yield. Agreement was reached on the present boundary line traversing the Sierra.

As the convention progressed with Halleck continuing in his important role, the many details of government were formulated. Slavery was forbidden by unanimous vote of the delegates. Halleck personally drafted many sections of the document.

By this time Halleck had come to regard himself as a Californian, enamored of the Western country and intrigued by what he had learned of its early history. In fact, his interest was such that when a group of influential men in 1850 decided that a California Historical Society should be formed, he readily agreed to participate in its organization. He was elected a member of the first board of directors and aided in drafting the constitution which set forth the Society's purpose: "to cultivate the social virtues of its members, to collect and preserve information connected with the early settlement and conquest of the country, and to perpetuate the memory of those whose sagacity, enterprise and love of independence induced them to settle in the wilderness, and become the germ of a new state."

Halleck and his colleagues had laid a sound foundation. The Society gained status from the start and today holds an eminent position in the State, as the recognized source of information in all matters pertaining to Californiana.

His influence in public affairs continued. In 1853 he was appointed chief inspector of California lighthouses and after a time he became a member of the Board of Army Engineers, designated to build new fortifications along the coast.

Late in 1854 he resigned from the Army to accept a partnership in a large law firm, specializing in the field of land titles.

His interests widened. He became president of the San Francisco-San Jose Railroad and a director of the New Almaden silver mines. In 1860 he was honored by an appointment to command the state militia with the rank of major general.

With the outbreak of the Civil War, he was called to Washington and asked to reenter active military service. During the early stages of the conflict he served in the field as well as in Washington. President Lincoln later appointed him to the rank of General of the Army, the highest position in the Union forces. He served in this capacity from 1862 to 1864.

After the war, he returned to San Francisco with his wife. They occupied a large home at Second and Folsom Streets which became the scene of many brilliant social affairs.

Through the remainder of his life Halleck gloried in the success of his downtown building project, satisfied that it had accomplished its purpose. Probably it was well that he did not live to see it demolished.

Alemany
California's First Archbishop

Father Joseph Sadoc Alemany

WITH ALL DUE reverence, a modest young priest faced Pope Pius IX in private audience with a bold request that probably was totally without precedent. It was a Sunday morning — June 18, 1850.

The visitor was Father Joseph Sadoc Alemany. Two weeks before, he had been selected by the Pontiff to become the Bishop of Monterey in far-off California, a new outpost the Church deemed neecssary to combat with spiritual power the vice and lawlessness rampant during the Gold Rush.

While most young clergymen would have accepted the assignment without question, Father Alemany received it with grave doubts — he considered himself inadequate for so monumental a task. Training told him that a Papal order was always final, yet his conscience troubled him and he was at a loss to know what to do.

After much thought, he confided his misgivings to a Cardinal who arranged an audience with Pope Pius. When the two finally met, the padre explained his predicament and was about to ask to be relieved when the Pontiff interrupted him. "You must go to California," the Pope said firmly. "There is no alternative. Where others are drawn by gold, you must go to carry the Cross. God will assist you."

The young priest bowed, then said respectfully, "Holy Father, while it is not my wish to oppose the will of God, I must point out my lack of qualifications for the Bishopric and ask your Holiness for permission to refuse the nomination."

The Pope's response gave Father Alemany all of the assurance that he needed. "I appreciate the prudence that prompts your reply," he asserted, "but it is for me to judge this matter. According to St. Thomas, prudence and obedience are equally necessary virtues and the wish of Christ's Vicar is the will of God for you. Do not ponder over what to say or do for the Lord will direct you at the proper time."

With that the audience ended; there was nothing more to be said. Father Alemany, then in his early thirties, was soon on his way, arriving in California in December, 1850. Three years later he became the first Archbishop of California, headquartered in San Francisco, with jurisdiction extending north to the Oregon border.

He served for 34 years, laying solid foundations for Catholicism on the Pacific Coast and contributing much to the spiritual and social advancement of the entire region.

As he had expected, his assignment was an extremely difficult one, especially in early days when the gold fever with its inherent materialism left people with little if any concern for spiritual duties. In the mining areas might had power over right, but the new prelate rose to his responsibilities with deep dedication and a simplicity that gave strength to his teachings.

His effectiveness is perhaps best epitomized by his biographer, Father John Bernard McGloin, S. J., Professor of History at the University of San Francisco, who concludes his widely-read book, "California's First Archbishop" with this line:

"He was indeed 'a great priest who in his days pleased God'."

Like many others who have had their names carved indelibly in religious history, Archbishop Alemany had humble beginnings. He was born on the Island of Mallorca on July 13, 1814 of poor but God-loving parents. They instilled in their young son a fervent devotion to their faith and to its rites. From childhood he rarely missed the daily recitation of the rosary.

As a boy he already had determined to dedicate his life to religious pursuits and at 16 he entered the Dominican Order in his native town of Vich, taking the holy habit in September, 1830. By good fortune he was assigned to a novice master Father Pedro Vaquer, a Catalan Dominican, who had distinguished himself as a noted preacher of the time.

On the completion of his canonical year of novitiate in 1831, the young man was sent to the town of Tremp on the Spanish mainland for a three-year course in philosophy. From this he went to Genora close to his hometown of Vich for theological training.

Then came a rude and unexpected interruption. Anti-religious forces had risen and by law all friars were expelled from the monastery, causing the young student and his colleagues to flee for refuge. It was a sad day for Alemany when bigotry compelled him to change his religious habit for civilian garb and make a hurried departure.

He found safety at the home relatives not far from Vich until conditions improved and he could move to Rome to resume his studies. Showing unusual aptitude, he advanced rapidly and was ordained when a year below the canonical age. To his great delight he celebrated his first Mass on Easter Sunday, March 26, 1837.

During his years of study he had expressed a keen desire for missionary work. Although his preference lay in the Philippines, his well-demonstrated zealousness was to lead to a still more challenging assignment — America.

With others of his Order, he arrived in New York April 2, 1840 at the end of a difficult 50-day ocean voyage. They left soon for Cincinnati and before long were busy with Dominican missionary work in Ohio, Tennessee and Kentucky.

Father Alemany made friends everywhere and his devotion to the cause won favor with those he met. In 1847 he was chosen master of novices at St. Rose, Kentucky and other important appointments soon followed. He did not know, however, that his work had come to the attention of the American hierarchy and that he was being considered for still more important service, perhaps in California where the church faced desperate needs for leadership.

He was recalled to Rome where his appointment to the bishopric had been discussed and finally agreed upon. No one was as surprised as Father Alemany himself.

Following his unusual audience with Pope Pius, he returned to America and on Sunday, December 8, 1850, as Bishop of Monterey, he offered Mass in St. Francis Church in San Francisco. In his new capacity, his responsibilities embraced all of California, then only sparsely settled. The new Bishop became still more conscious of the grave duties that he had assumed. Cheerfully he reponded to the warm reception he had received and gave thanks to San Francisco's leading Catholics, who not only honored him with a reception but presented him with $1,400 to defray the costs of extensive travel to all parts of his new diocese.

He moved from one end of the state to the other, pausing here and there to settle problems that confronted him. On New Year's Day 1851 he celebrated a Pontifical Mass before a congregation that crowded the mission church. There were many other services of like importance in many sections of the territory.

By 1851 Bishop Alemany was well established in Monterey. There, as elsewhere, he was enthusiastically received and given lodging in the home of a prominent family. But much of his work was carried on in San Francisco, the largest community entrusted to his care, where many of his important decisions were made.

One of his many important achievements occurred early in 1851 when he established the Dominican Convent of St. Catherine in Monterey which had been sanctioned by the vicar general of the Order in Rome. Such advances, however, were not made without obstacles of many kinds, for the Bishop often found himself obliged to clear titles to properties held by the Church.

His untiring labors and the problems still remaining were among the principal items discussed at the First Plenary Council of the American hierarchy which assembled in Baltimore on May 9, 1852. There was general agreement that the Diocese of Monterey covered far too great an area and that a new archdiocese should be created with its site in San Francisco, growing into a bustling community due largely to the Gold Rush.

The proposal met with approval in Rome and in 1853 the new Archbishop Alemany assumed his new duties with less territory but with a rapidly growing population as his responsibility, for his eastern boundary had been set at the Colorado River.

At Midnight Mass on Christmas Eve of 1854, Old St. Mary's was blessed and dedicated as the Cathedral seat of the Archdiocese. Built of wood and granite from China, the church was the largest religious structure in California.

Other churches followed. St. Brigid's at Van Ness Avenue and Broadway was one of them, its site then covering the entire block bounded by Van Ness, Franklin, Broadway and Pacific Avenue. Archbishop Alemany had paid $5,000, a sum which some of his parishioners considered extravagant, for the land, mostly sand dunes fully 15 feet above the street level. The new church, taking the place of a small wooden structure, was dedicated in February, 1865.

Early in 1883, just 30 years after he had become titular head of the California Archdiocese, Rome inquired of Archbishop Alemany as to his choice of a coadjutor with the right of succession. He favored the appointment of Father Patrick William Riordan, one of two priests who had been mentioned for the office, and after a time his selection was approved.

Archbishop Alemany, elated over the coming of a younger man with wide experience, now asked to be relieved. He was beginning to feel the weight of years and, as he wrote to Rome, he was anxious to gratify "a special wish to help in the increase of my Order in Spain."

Permission was granted and Riordan became the new Archbishop of California on December 24, 1884.

The press had much to say in gratitude for the retiring Archbishop's long and effective services. *The Monitor* concluded a long tribute with the words: "Beyond what was needed for the simple necessaries of life, he has not drawn a single dollar from the revenues of the Archdiocese in exchange for his long labor and now that he returns to seek an asylum for his chosen Order in his old age, he does so in poverty as perfect as when he first took his habit. . . ."

After receiving a fitting farewell, Archbishop Alemany left San Francisco May 24, 1885. He visited Rome, then went to Viterbo and later moved on to Valencia with new and ambitious projects engaging his attention. But his sight was failing and his health was poor.

On the Feast of the Epiphany on January 6, 1888 he suffered a cerebral hemorrhage while hearing confessions. He recovered sufficiently to offer Mass several times before his condition began to decline alarmingly.

He died Saturday, April 14, 1888 in Valencia. In fulfillment of a wish expressed for many years, his remains were interred in his native town of Vich with all of the honors of the Church and San Francisco gratefully named a busy boulevard for him.

Garrison

He Gave His
Pay Away

Cornelius K. Garrison

CORNELIUS K. GARRISON, who became San Francisco's fourth mayor on October 1, 1853 only six months after his arrival in this city, puzzled his associates in City Hall. Throughout his term of office he steadfastly refused to draw his salary. Month after month he was told that his pay warrant was ready but each time Garrison brushed the word aside with the simple request: "Keep it for me; I'll draw my money when I want it."

The answer to public curiosity did not come until his one-year term had expired. Only then did the Mayor call for the large amount of accumulated money due him — but he did not keep a cent of it for himself. He divided his earnings between Catholic and Protestant orphanages, the Ladies Relief Society, the Mercantile Library Association and a number of churches of different denominations. It was his way of showing his love for the people of the city he had adopted after years of moving about the United States and Canada.

Garrison had been a successful businessman, despite several unlucky ventures. His early years were spent at sea as a cabin boy, much to the embarrassment of his proud mother who considered this occupation demeaning to the family.

He was born March 1, 1809 on the family farm on the banks of the Hudson near West Point, a home established by his forebears more than 125 years before on their arrival from Holland. On both sides of his family, he was the descendant of some of the earliest settlers of New Amsterdam, which later became New York.

His mother had urged a career as an architect for Cornelius, the second child of a family of five sons and two daughters. But when the boy was thirteen, his father, once an affluent financier, suffered sudden reverses that necessitated an immediate change in the family's way of life. In consequence, the boys began at once to seek ways to support themselves. Young Cornelius' choice of work threw his mother into hysterics. Always independent, he ignored her protests and shipped out as a cabin boy on the only ship then trading along the Hudson River.

His mother, proud of her heritage, felt the humiliation of what she considered degrading work for any of her sons. "What would the Kingslands, the Buskerks and the Schuylers think if it ever reached their ears that my son was a cabin boy," she sobbed, as she continued naming other influential members of her Dutch family. Her protests, however, were to no avail.

After three years he finally responded to his mother's repeated urgings, and quit his job to enroll in a New York school to study architecture and building trades. These courses kept him at his books and drawing boards for the next three years.

Again bidding his family farewell, he started for the Northwest, settling in Canada. He was only nineteen but his schooling had prepared him for a successful career in shipbuilding on the Great Lakes. He had completed four steamers when a flattering offer came from the Upper Canada Company to become its general supervisor. He readily accepted. He spent nearly six years at his work and undoubtedly would have remained but for border tension developing between the United States and Britain. Always patriotic, Garrison decided to return to his own country before trouble became serious. He settled in Mississippi and invested in a steamer. Unfortunately, it sank in the River with a valuable cargo of 1,200 tons of cotton and other goods.

He was looking for a way to recoup his losses when word came of the California gold discovery. He developed a bold new plan. Instead of digging for gold, he decided to establish a commercial business in Panama at an intermediate point between the Atlantic coast and California. The venture proved financially successful and, undoubtedly, Garrison would have continued with it but for an excellent offer from the Nicaraguan Steamship Company to become its principal agent on the Pacific Coast with headquarters in San Francisco. He was still preparing for the move when two large eastern insurance companies, learning of his new berth, appointed him to act as their agent in conjunction with his other affairs. The total financial offers made him were a staggering sum in those years.

At this time the Nicaraguan Steamship Company was in desperate financial straits and its principals feared for its survival. Garrison fully realized the chance he was taking but felt confident of his ability to reestablish the firm's business in the West. With amazing resourcefulness he succeeded in putting the company back on a firm footing and actually increased its business.

He won the respect of San Francisco's leading businessmen. Almost immediately they recognized his ability and integrity and he quickly assumed an important place in public affairs. To his astonishment, he was visited by a delegation of prominent citizens only months after his arrival and asked to become a candidate for mayor. He was elected by a flattering vote.

His inaugural address, delivered early in October, 1853, is recorded by historians as "'a model of plain, unpretending common sense . . . a message that would challenge any paper of its kind in sound business ideas and financial responsibilities. It contained the germs of what became some years afterward the cry for reform in the administration."

Revealing himself as a strict moralist at a time when vice was generally accepted as a necessary evil, Garrison denounced saloons and gambling in public places. Taking many of his listeners by surprise, he cried out against Sunday theatricals — something that no city official had ever done.

"A man to be great must be good," he asserted. "The city and its people must observe the dictates of morality and if it is their ambition to rise to high summits of human glory, it is to be hoped that the right thinking portion of our community will lend their example and influence to terminate those habits and customs which are inclined to further destroy the best impulses of our nature. No nobler sight can greet the eye of man than can be witnessed from the hilltops, a people the most industrious and enterprising upon the face of the globe, resting as here they can rest in the midst of plentitude and peace from the labors of the week."

A great outburst of applause greeted his words yet there were those who had listened with tongue in cheek, believing that the time was not ripe for the reforms demanded by the new mayor. Many were to be surprised later when under Garrison's determined leadership, new ordinances were passed restricting gambling and other forms of vice.

He went still further in launching a new era of better living for the community, especially for the poor.

Education was another of his concerns. On one occasion when unnecessary red tape threatened to tie up funds for erection of badly needed schools, Garrison advanced the money out of his own pocket.

Toward the Negro community he displayed an interest surprising for the time when only few thought of social justice. Realizing that there was no school for Negro children, he arranged for one and when criticism came from certain quarters he had a quick explanation. "They eventually will became citizens and enjoy the same rights that we have," he declared. "The way to prepare them is through education."

Philanthropy was another of his virtues. He contributed liberally to every charitable cause and in late 1853 when word came of a serious epidemic in New Orleans, Garrison called together a group of former

Louisianans to head a city-wide relief organization.

Because of Garrison's kindly manner and humanitarian impulses there were those who on occasion dared to attempt unscrupulous schemes for profit. Such a situation developed when a notorious speculator and his henchman sought to benefit by depreciating a valuable strip of waterfront property. One night they were boldly laying a line of heavy piles for a considerable distance, seriously obstructing navigation and imperiling the use of the harbor. Informed of these goings-on, Garrison hastened to the scene and found the police unwilling to interfere because of the political influence of the perpetrators.

Garrison brushed the officers aside and not only demanded that the work be stopped but that every pile be removed. There were no more such incidents.

In 1859 Garrison returned to New York and became successful in financial undertakings for the next decade. But his love for San Francisco remained with him and he decided to spend the remainder of his life there.

A week before his departure from the East, he received a message signed by the leading business and professional men of the city inviting him to be their guest at a welcome home banquet set for August 10, 1869. He accepted. The affair proved to be a large and enthusiastic gathering of prominent citizens.

Responding to the warm welcoming words of the toastmaster, Garrison spoke with deep emotion concluding with these words:

"Gentlemen, my heart is too full of gratitude to permit me from doing aught else but beg you to accept the poverty of my language to express my full feelings of gratitude."

Donahue

"Father of
California
Industry"

Peter Donahue

A MASSIVE AND impressive monument of bronze and stone stands at the gore of Market, Bush and Battery Streets in San Francisco as a lasting tribute to Peter Donahue, often referred to by historians as "the father of California industry."

Indeed, the career of Peter Donahue was a living example of what pioneer San Francisco offered to men with skill, determination and imagination.

He was already a skilled and experienced mechanic when he arrived in San Francisco in June, 1849 as the chief engineer of the steamer *Oregon,* which had sailed from Panama. He had served his apprenticeship on the East Coast, to which he and his two brothers had immigrated from Glasgow, Scotland, where Peter was born January 11, 1822.

He was a self-made man with little schooling. While in his early teens he worked first in a cotton mill, then in a locomotive works, and finally in a machine shop in Patterson, New Jersey — a job for which he received $1.50 a day.

In 1847 Peter Donahue was hired as assistant engineer of a new steamer constructed in New York for the Peruvian government. It became the first vessel built in America to sail through the Straits of Magellan. He had barely landed in Calloa, Peru when word came of the gold discovery in California and he lost no time in booking passage to San Francisco aboard the *Oregon.*

Once in the West he hastened to the mining country, working placer diggings at Auburn but with so little success that he decided to return to San Francisco and pursue his trade.

With his scant savings he opened a little blacksmith and boiler-making shop on Montgomery Street near Jackson. Soon his brothers, James and Michael joined him. The shop was the beginning of the

Union Iron Works which eventually became the Bethlehem Shipbuilding Corporation of today.

Aware of an abundance of scrapped machinery, stoves and like materials, ruined in frequent fires, he bought it at salvage prices, then melted and molded it into cast iron for which there was a great unfilled need. The product sold for one dollar a pound and in little time he was doing a thriving business.

Then, sensing a need for cooking ranges, he designed, with his brothers' help, a model that was made completely from surplus boiler plates. He also built the first printing press produced in California. On it was published the newspaper announcing California's admission to the Union.

Before long new opportunities came. The plant produced the first quartz mill and the first locomotive ever made in San Francisco. It made machinery for the *Saginaw,* the first warship built on the Pacific Coast and engaged in extensive ship repairs.

As important as these accomplishments were, Peter Donahue was not content. His imagination was still at work as he carefully studied community needs with a view toward using his skills to meet them. He turned his attention first to street lighting; for, in 1850, there were only a few oil lamps along Merchant Street and the cost was borne by property owners.

He was convinced the time had come for a gas plant, not only to illuminate the streets but to serve householders who had to depend on kerosene lamps and candles. His brothers shared his enthusiasm though none of them knew anything about gas. However, they could study and they did.

Late in 1852 they received a permit from the City Council to erect a gas plant, install lamps and lay pipes. For street lighting they would charge 32½ cents a lamp per night. Service to private consumers would come later.

They organized the San Francisco Gas Company, the first of its kind in the West, with a plant on property bounded by First and Fremont, Howard and Natoma Streets. Tidewater on the Fremont border permitted the easy landing of coal imported from Australia but they had no pipes and no money to purchase them. Peter went East, borrowed funds, and arranged with a Philadelphia manfacturer to provide the necessary piping. By 1854 the new concern had 237 customers and the number was growing steadily. The little company was destined to become today's Pacific Gas & Electric Company, one of the largest distributors of gas and electric power in the country.

With the gas operation successfully under way, Peter Donahue turned his attention to transportation. The California Steam Navigation Company then ran the only line of river steamers and he saw an opportunity for competition. He established his own line, operating two small steamers, the *Goliath* and the *Herman,* and offered passage at reduced fares.

This, however, was no help to transportation within the city. Donahue envisoned street cars to meet the problem. He organized the Omnibus Street Railroad in 1861, obtained a franchise and became the president of the city's first street car line. Cars ran from South Park off Third Street to North Beach by way of Montgomery, passing in front of his first blacksmith shop.

Donahue then reasoned that if he could construct a street railway he could start a railroad. In 1863 he became one of the builders of the San Francisco and San Jose Railroad which was acquired by the Southern Pacific seven years later.

Success moved him to look further. Scarcely was the new line operating well than he began construction of a railroad through Marin and Sonoma Counties to end at Healdsburg. Serving growing territory that had badly lacked transportation facilities, the road became the nucleus of the Northwestern Pacific which was finally completed in 1871.

He had many more accomplishments. One was a government contract to build the monitor *Comanche.* The ship's frames were fabricated in New Jersey to Donahue's design and sent to San Francisco aboard the steamer *Aquila,* sailing around the Horn. Late in 1863 the vessel arrived safely in the western port only to sink during a heavy storm.

With an agreement still to be fulfilled, Donahue sent to New York for divers and recovered the ship's cargo from the bottom of the Bay. Then the *Comanche,* similar in design to the famous U.S.S. *Monitor* in the Civil War naval battle, was assembled under Donahue's personal direction and successfully launched in 1860. Though it was designed to protect the Pacific Coast, it was never in battle. In 1899 the *Comanche* was consigned to be sold for junk and its hull became a coal barge.

In addition to all of these activities, Donahue found time for civic duties. He involved himself not only in organizations furthering mechanical industries but also in personally encouraging young men with mechanical aspirations. He became one of the first trustees of Mechanic's Institute, a director of the Hibernia Savings and Loan Society, the National Gold Bank and the State Investment and Insurance Company. For a year he served as president of the Society of California Pioneers and was credited with having made a large financial contribution to the Bank of California when it faced a financial crisis.

For his service on the staff of the commanding general of the California National Guard he received the title of colonel.

It was a sad day in San Francisco when Peter Donahue died on November 26, 1881. To preserve his memory his son, James Mervyn Donahue, decided to erect a monument six years after his father's death.

Douglas Tilden, the city's distinguished sculptor, was engaged to design a fitting memorial. The result was a monumental work consisting of an enormous lever press handled by three sinewy mechanics, their bodies bare except for leather aprons around their loins. Two others hold a heavy metal plate ready to be punched. In front are medallions of Peter and his son while at the rear stand symbols of the trade — the anvil, the propellor and the locomotive driving wheel. The main facade bears this inscription:

Dedicated to Mechanics

By James Mervyn Donahue

In Memory of his Father, Peter Donahue.

The formal unveiling of the monument in May, 1901 was an historic event with crowds of people in attendance. Irving M. Scott, then president of the Union Iron Works, formally presented the huge memorial to the city and it was accepted in the name of San Francisco by Mayor James D. Phelan.

Lick

The Eccentric
Philanthropist

James Lick

THE FAMOUS LICK OBSERVATORY atop Mt. Hamilton carries on its donor's lifelong desire to study the secrets of the stars.

As a poor farm boy near Stumpstown in a picturesque Pennsylvania valley, James Lick often spent long night hours sitting alone astride a hand-hewn fence, his bare feet dangling, his eyes fixed on the moon and stars, eager to know more about them. Books were scarce and there was little that he could learn about astronomy.

Many years later, after he had accumulated millions in San Francisco's early days, he bequeathed $700,000 for the erection of the Observatory, hoping that there scientists would learn from the skies what he had always wanted to know. The gift, however, was only one of his many public benefactions, for though he lived frugally, denying himself even the most common luxuries, he wanted others to have the comforts that he never personally enjoyed.

In many ways Lick was an eccentric recluse, a man of many paradoxes. Crude in manner and illiterate, he has been called a Midas, for his ventures, mostly in real estate, turned to a fabulous fortune.

In San Francisco he built the finest, most luxurious hotel in the city at that time, yet he insisted on occupying its only dingy, sparsely furnished room. Before his death he bequeathed more than $3,000,000 for a trade school, a home for the elderly, a public bath house, and a symbolic statue.

He died a bachelor though there was one sad romance in his early life and to his only heir, resulting from that ill-fated love affair, he left half-a-million dollars.

Born in a humble cabin August 25, 1796, James Lick faced hardships from his earliest days but they served to develop a man of strong character, determined to conquer any obstacle that came his way.

His paternal grandfather, William Luk, had come to America several years before the Revolution, fleeing from his native Germany in quest of freedom. He served in the War with honor, enduring hardships at Valley Forge. On September 15, 1765 a son, John, was born. The latter as a young man, moved to Stumpstown near Fredericksburg and changed his name to Lick. He became a successful carpenter and cabinetmaker, trades that he later taught to his son, James, who was born in 1796.

James was approaching manhood when he fell in love with the daughter of the town's most prosperous miller. The young couple asked for her father's blessing but met with an angry rebuff. "You're only a poor carpenter," the father told Lick. "If you can own a mill as good as mine, come back and I'll give my consent."

It was a challenge that took Lick to many parts of the world, determined to amass a fortune and return to claim the girl he loved.

At twenty-one he left Fredericksburg for Baltimore where he became an expert piano maker, a trade that he followed successfully for thirty years. When he learned that many of the pianos he was making were being shipped to South America, he took decisive action, sailing to Buenos Aires where he established his own piano factory with almost immediate financial success.

Four years later he started for Europe in search of new markets. The factory was left in capable hands and for months Lick toured the capitals of the continent.

His return trip home almost ended in disaster. After a stormy voyage, his ship was seized by officers of a Brazilian war vessel and he was taken prisoner with all of the other passengers. For a time he feared for his life but finally he succeeded in escaping and returned, badly shaken, to resume charge of his factory.

He was accumulating money rapidly when new threats of war induced him to sell his business and return to America, taking with him a large quantity of hides which he sold at enormous profit. Only days after his arrival in Pennsylvania he was told of great opportunities in California and wanderlust took him westward.

He landed in California early in January of 1848, bringing with him $30,000 in gold, his work bench and his tools. The latter were never used again, for he was to amass a fortune in other ways.

Seventeen days after his arrival gold was discovered. The rush to the mines soon started and San Francisco was fast being deserted. Lick quickly saw his opportunity for profit — but not with pick and shovel. Word of his wealth had spread and fortune hunters were offering him real estate at give-away prices. So eager were they to sell that Lick's initial investment of $10,000 grew to more than a million in year or two. He kept his holdings when the return of the miners began, preferring to retain them at their inflated values.

He continued to buy, confident of the town's future, and he invested with shrewd judgment. For a large piece of land at Post and Montgomery Streets he paid just $275 in gold.

Thoughts of the girl he loved and her father's challenge were with him constantly. He went to San Jose, purchased an enormous tract of land for $3,000 and built a flour mill which he believed was the largest in the country. Having now met the demands of the man he regarded as a prospective father-in-law, he returned to Fredericksburg to claim the girl. Thirty five years had passed and to Lick's disappointment he could find no trace of the family. However, he did locate a son born of the romance and adopted him.

Returning to San Francisco, he continued to accumulate money in more and more investments. Soon he was on his way to his second million.

In the late fifties he decided to build a hotel that would surpass in elegance any place of its kind of the Pacific Coast. On Montgomery Street near Sutter he erected what became known as the Lick House, a three-story brick building that many said was "a dizzy height." The hotel, completed in 1862, contained 60 complete suites, all luxuriously furnished. In the marbled corridors the elite of the city gathered for Sunday night dances or for brilliant socials but the man who owned the place lived in squalor in a poorly furnished room.

After a time Lick turned his attention to the Santa Clara Valley which he believed held a profitable future for fruit growing. He bought large pieces of land but for his own dwelling he erected a crude shack with the frame of an old grand piano as its principal furniture. Over the piano top he placed a badly worn mattress that served him for a bed.

Lick, with considerable knowledge of horticulture, believed that the valley would produce fruit if properly cultivated and fertilized. To prove his point he arranged with San Francisco cooks to save old bones for him. These he collected regularly during return trips to the city, making the rounds from one eating place to the other with sacks over his shoulders.

Back in his country shack he would grind the bones and dig the fragments into the ground. He planted fruit trees and proved that they would produce abundantly if properly fertilized.

He then turned his attention to Catalina Island in Southern California. He bought the Island for $80,000. Soon after his death it was sold for $250,000.

In 1873, now 77 years of age and in failing health, he told his friends that he wished to put his house in order. He decided to will the greater part of his millions to the people of the state in which he had acquired his fortune. Their comfort, pleasure and education were his chief considerations.

The observatory that would fulfill his longing for astronomical study, headed his list of benefactions with a bequest of $700,000. There were many others, in addition, bringing his total donations to more than $3,000,000.

Always concerned with the vocational training of young people, he bequeathed $540,000 for the erection and maintenance of the California School of Mechanical Arts, established in 1895 and better known for years as Lick School. In 1915 it merged with the Wilmerding School of Industrial Arts but retained its original name. A gift of $100,000 was made for the erection of public baths. The Mechanic's Institute and other institutions were well remembered.

He provided for a statue of Francis Scott Key in Golden Gate Park, a statute of his grandfather, William Luk in Fredericksburg, and others.

The son, born of the unfortunate boyhood liaison, was not forgotten. To him Lick left $500,000.

The bequests were made none too soon. In the early morning of October 1, 1876, little more than a year after the will had finally been executed, he died in the tiny, poorly furnished room of his luxurious hotel.

Before his death it had been suggested that his remains be interred in the Observatory. To this he had readily assented.

Pending completion of the project, the body was placed in a vault in the Masonic Cemetery, where it remained until January 9, 1887 when it was interred with fitting ceremony beneath the dome of the giant structure. Meanwhile his executors had proceeded with the building of the school, the baths and his many other philanthropies most of which, together with Lick Place, continue to perpetuate the memory of the man who had made his own fortune in his own way and chose to share it with his fellowmen.

Judah

Engineer with a
Dream

Theodore D. Judah

In 1858 SOME of the shrewdest men in California laughed at the young engineer Theodore D. Judah and said that he must be crazy. Who in his right mind, they asked scornfully, would propose so preposterous a venture as a railroad across the continent?

Judah, however, was confident that it could be done; he already had overcome difficult obstacles to build railroads in the East. He was correct, of course, but fate turned cruelly against him. He died before his dream was realized, never to know that those who ridiculed him most were to reap millions from his idea.

Born in Connecticut in 1826, he received his technical training at Rensselaer Polytechnic Institute in Troy, New York. In May of 1854 at the age of 28, he arrived in San Francisco, summoned on recommendation of New York's Governor Horatio Seymour to build a much-needed railroad from Sacramento to Folsom, a distance of about 110 miles. For the next decade, until his final departure for the East in 1863 he would be in and out of San Francisco on important business and to visit his many friends.

Judah well deserved the recommendation of the New York governor. While still in his teens he had not only planned railroad construction in his own state and in Massachusetts but had helped to build the Niagara Bridge Railroad.

Only months after establishing himself in Sacramento, work was under way on the short-line railway. Its completion in 1856 was celebrated with a round of festivities.

However, for Judah this accomplishment was of far less concern than the bigger plan that had been developing in his mind: the thought of a railroad that would traverse the country. He knew that some years earlier engineers sent west by Jefferson Davis, then Secretary of War, had made preliminary surveys and concluded that such a road was possible. In fact, they had mapped out four different possible routes. Little or no attention had been paid to their report.

Now Judah, fired with enthusiasm over his idea, undertook to carry on extensive surveys. As he progressed he became convinced that he had found a suitable pass through the Sierra Nevada Mountains. Further studies confirmed his belief that the project was not only feasible but practical. All that he needed was money and government approval.

For months he talked to influential men, seeking backers. No one was interested; especially those who had crossed the plains in wagon trains. But Judah was persistent. He continued drawing maps and diagrams, wrote articles for the newspapers, and spoke at every meeting that afforded an audience. Always he would emphasize California's isolation. A railroad from the East, he argued, would bring quick development to the state and the entire coast. No one was willing to invest.

On a forlorn hope he appeared before the State Legislature in 1860, to discuss his project and displayed his maps. Some of the lawmakers showed a degree of interest but they made it clear that they would not support a state appropriation. As a token gesture, they approved the calling of what they called a Pacific Railroad Convention, a gathering of important people such as had preceded railroad ventures in the East.

The meeting took place in San Francisco. Judah was authorized to take his plans to Washington, which he did at his own expense. He met with no success.

He returned disappointed but still determined. His first encouragement came when he met a druggist, Daniel W. Strong, in the little hydraulic mining town of Dutch Flat. Strong was impressed by what Judah had to say and they began exploring the mountain region together. Strong pointed out that Dutch Flat actually was situated on a natural ramp offering easy access to Donner Pass and beyond toward the East.

As an experienced engineer, Judah surveyed the area and found to his delight that it would be possible for a railroad to reach the 7,000-foot summit elevation over a distance of little more than 70 miles from the valley floor, with a maximum grade of only 105 feet to a mile.

He drew new maps, spread them over the counter of Strong's drug store, and studied them laboriously night after night. Convinced of their practical worth, Judah and Strong drew up tentative articles of association for what they chose to call the Central Pacific Railroad of California.

Again Judah went to San Francisco and called another meeting. Among those present were four men who had risen to wealth from humble beginnings. They were destined to be known as the "Big Four." Two of them, Collis P. Huntington and Mark Hopkins, ran a hardware store in Sacramento, selling picks and shovels to miners. The others, Charles Crocker and Leland Stanford, were successful drygoods merchants.

Funds were not forthcoming but the group was sufficiently impressed to graciously authorize Judah to go to Washington — again at his own expense — and plead with Congress for legislation permitting the building of a transcontinental railroad.

He found the congressmen far more concerned with other and more pressing issues — slavery for one. Then, as he continued to press his case, dissension developed over the feasibility of a southern route instead of the northern one. Once more Judah returned home reporting failure.

Still unwilling to drop his plans, Judah went once more into the mountains. He returned with a new proposal; if he could not construct a railroad across the continent, at least he could build one from Folsom to the Nevada boundary, some 150 miles, mostly over mountain grades.

Such a project, he believed, might interest the men in San Francisco — especially Huntington and his three associates, for money was their main concern and this latest plan promised big profits.

State law, however, required an initial capital investment of $115,000. Judah and Strong subscribed as much as they could afford. Townsfolk added more. But $70,000 still was needed.

Another San Francisco meeting took place and this time Judah presented an entirely new project, realizing that he must stress money-making opportunities. Businesmen, he knew, were profiting by supplying mining machinery and foodstuffs to the Comstock mines in Nevada, so he proposed a new and far shorter wagon road to the Comstock.

Huntington and his colleagues grasped at the idea and, since only $7,000 or less would be needed to finance initial surveys, they willingly opened their purses.

Judah, of course, recognized their short-sightedness, but he was content to be named chief engineer of the project while the others were quick to designate themselves as company officers.

The engineer went to work at once. Before long he told the officers that he had uncovered an even greater way for profit. He pictured the tons of low grade ore that lay piled at the head of the mining shafts. With a railroad, he told them, this abandoned ore could be salvaged and converted into money — into millions.

This time they were excited. Judah was instructed to return to Washington and plead for government funds. The time, however, was not propitious. The Civil War was on and high officials were deluged with problems.

Heeding the temper of the day, he boldly came forward with a new and timely argument. A railroad across the country, such as he originally had proposed, should be viewed as a vital wartime measure, especially since disturbing movements were afoot to drag California and Nevada into the Confederacy.

Judah's latest argument reached understanding ears. After long delays, Representative Aaron A. Sargent agreed to sponsor an appropriate bill in the House; Senator James A. McDougall of California would do the same in the Upper Chamber. As a mark of confidence, Judah was appointed clerk of the key railroad committees in both Houses, a position which enabled him to draft the necessary documents with supporting maps and blueprints.

When the law was finally enacted and signed by President Lincoln, Judah was astounded, for the government was offering far more than he ever had dared to expect. The railroad builders were granted free use of public land for the entire route, with ten alternate sections for every mile. And they received much more — millions in subsidies and many other valuable concessions.

The "Big Four" listened to his report with open mouths; it seemed unbelievable, so much so that those who had formerly ridiculed the plan were moved now to selfishly guard the fortune that they saw ahead — and to freeze Judah from their ranks. He quickly realized what was going on but all that he could do was protest.

Huntington and his three cohorts lost no time in organizing their own construction company since the railroad bill provided for a subsidy of $16,000 a mile in low country and fully three times as much over mountainous terrain. Despite his arguments, Judah failed to be included in the new concern.

Still more conniving was to come. The "Big Four" members were revising Judah's maps, altering his proposed route to cover more mountainous country to reap still greater funds from the government. Judah was outraged.

They pressed their efforts to force him out and finally succeeded. In the end he was compelled to accept $100,000 in exchange for his position as chief engineer.

Defeated and sick at heart, he packed up his belongings and prepared to leave by ship. With his wife, he embarked in October, 1863 for the East, intending never to return.

In Panama he was stricken with yellow fever and died in New York, a broken man.

The "Big Four" soon forgot him. But San Francisco, years later, remembered and gave his name to a street in the residential district known as the Sunset.

Broderick

The Duel at Lake Merced

Senator David D. Broderick

A SLAB OF granite with an inscribed bronze plate stands near the shores of Lake Merced in San Francisco, marking the site of the city's most sensational duel. It took place in the early morning on September 13, 1859. The victim was United States Senator David D. Broderick, felled by a single bullet from the pistol of Chief Justice David S. Terry of the California Supreme Court.

For Broderick, it was the tragic end of a brilliant and extraordinary career. His death climaxed a feud between the two men that had its basis in their bitter differences over slavery, Broderick having been an ardent abolitionist. Terry, a stormy Kentuckian, was always ready to pick a fight.

In San Francisco no man was more beloved than Broderick, an imposing figure, large and heavily built, gruff in manner and serious-faced, yet always concerned with the welfare of the common people. It was said that he was incorruptible.

In no way did his early life foreshadow his future. As a boy, he worked with his father as a stone cutter on the Capitol Building in Washington, D.C. In New York City he was employed as a city fireman, then became a saloonkeeper and a Tammany politician with high ambitions.

When he left the East for San Francisco, he was determined to return some day as a United States Senator — an outlook that seemed ridiculous. Yet — only six months after his arrival on June 13, 1849 — he was elected to the State Senate and rose to be its president. No one appeared to be surprised, for the newcomer had a way of making friends and knew how to acquire influence.

He had become the partner of an assayer, engaging in the business of buying placer gold and converting it into coins, a legitimate practice of the time. The venture profited and Broderick invested heavily in city lots which he was confident would increase in value.

Before two years had passed he became involved in his first duel. The challenge came from Judge Caleb Smith who had resented an innocent remark by Broderick concerning the jurist's father. Smith's bullet struck Broderick's heavy watch; the contest ended, and Broderick's apology was accepted.

In January, 1857 he launched a vigorous campaign for a seat in the United States Senate. He was successful and now his goal of only a few years before had been attained. He was regarded as one of the foremost Democrats in the State.

It was inevitable that he would clash with David Terry, also a self-made man, who firmly supported slavery and was a reactionary on every other issue as well. Fighting poverty, Terry had become a lawyer and was practicing in Texas when he closed his office to engage in the war with Mexico.

He came to California late in 1849 to practice law and to campaign unsuccessfully for the office of mayor in the city of Stockton. Six years later, running on the Know Nothing Party ticket, he became Chief Justice of the State's highest court.

He had been in office less than a year when he found himself in difficulties so serious that his career would probably have ended but for Broderick's powerful and timely help. Terry had stabbed a policeman without provocation. Jailed for more than a month, he was freed largely through Broderick's efforts. The subsequent challenge to a duel and its fatal ending cast Terry as an ingrate.

Their trouble had started at a political convention where Broderick, in complete control, had decided that he could not support Terry's campaign for reelection for political reasons. In a rage, Terry denounced the Senator in insulting terms in a public address shortly afterward, asserting that Broderick had turned against him in favor of a mulatto.

Broderick read the speech in his morning newspaper while breakfasting at San Francisco's International Hotel. Incensed, he called over to D. W. Parley, a former law associate of Terry, seated at a nearby table, referring to Terry as "a damned miserable ingrate."

The words were carried back to Terry who immediately challenged his one-time friend and defender to a duel. Broderick replied, stalling for time; he said that he was in the midst of a campaign for reelection. At its close, he stated, he would be ready to answer for any statement he made.

Terry obviously watched his calendar. The day after the election he sent his adversary a sharp letter referring to the remarks made two months before and demanding a retraction. It was not forthcoming. Instead Broderick replied that he had used the words in question and stated that it was for Terry to decide whether they were offensive.

Terry's answering letter brought the two to the dueling grounds. It stated that he saw no other way to settle the issue satisfactorily and that he had called on his friend, Calhoun Benham, a former District Attorney of San Francisco, to arrange the contest.

Under Benham's direction, seconds for the antagonists met. They decided that the duel should be fought at sunrise on the morning of September 11, 1859 on the shores of Lake Merced, on the outskirts of the city.

But the law was to have its say.

Word of the impending meeting reached Captain of Detectives Isaiah Lees, later to become one of the city's best known police chiefs. With Detective H. H. Ellis, Lees promptly obtained a warrant for the arrest of the combatants and hurried in a carriage to the scene. They waited until the distances had been measured off and weapons had been handed to the two men. Lees then stepped forward with his warrant and placed the pair under arrest. Dueling, however. was not uncommon at the time and when the two appeared before Judge Coon the following morning, their cases were promptly dismissed.

Broderick and Terry met again on the following morning at the same place and this time the law was not represented. Terry won the choice of weapons, an advantage he did not need, for his opponent was inexperienced in the use of firearms.

It had been agreed that they would fire at the count of three but as the word "one" was spoken, Broderick accidentally discharged his gun. The bullet struck the ground nine feet away but in Terry's direction. Then came the count of two. Terry fired, hitting the Senator squarely in the chest.

Broderick's large powerful frame quivered for an instant, then he fell sprawling to the ground. Paces away Terry stood motionless, his arms folded, gazing at the wounded man.

Within minutes Broderick was lifted into a carriage and driven to a hospital where it was diagnosed that he was probably mortally wounded. Terry started for his home near Stockton, accompanied by Benham and Thomas Hayes, for whom Hayes Valley was later named.

Three days later Broderick succumbed. His last words were: "They have killed me because I was opposed to the extension of slavery."

The city was in an uproar and quickly went into mourning. Stores and many homes were draped with black. Newspapers eulogized the Senator in glowing terms, castigating Terry for having provoked the duel. Many declared openly that it was a case of murder.

More than 30,000 people viewed the body lying in state in the Plaza and as many gathered for the funeral. The community took the Senator's death as an irreparable loss for all the people and calls for justice came from all quarters.

The law, meanwhile, was moving fast. A warrant charging murder was issued but, when Lees and Ellis undertook to serve it, they encountered unexpected and violent resistance. As they approached the house, a window opened and shotguns were drawn by the accused man, Benham, Hayes and Sheriff O'Neill.

The officers stood their ground, announcing their purpose. Terry replied that he would surrender in three days in Oakland, contending that he could not receive a fair trial in San Francisco.

He kept his word and received a change of venue to Marin County where his trial ended in a dismissal. An effort to try him again in San Francisco on a grand jury indictment failed because he could not be placed in double jeopardy.

Since no further action could be taken against Terry in a legal way, the community, saddened and outraged, showed its high esteem for Broderick sometime later by dedicating the street that still bears his name.

King
Preacher and
Patriot

Rev. Thomas Starr King

A DYNAMIC UNITARIAN minister, fired with a love of country, is credited by historians with having done more than any other single man to keep California in the Union in the trying days before and during the Civil War.

He was the Rev. Thomas Starr King, spiritual leader of San Francisco's First Unitarian Church, a man of extraordinary eloquence and force, with a deep devotion to humanity and fervent religious convictions.

With all of the power at his command, he campaigned relentlessly against the growing movement for California's secession. Demanding loyalty to country and denouncing supporters of the Confederacy as traitors, he stumped the State, using the pulpit and the rostrum to achieve his purpose.

Of his ultimate success in keeping California within the Union, one writer said:

"At this critical moment as if by the direct interposition of the Almighty, Mr. King stepped into the breach and became the champion of his country. Taking the Constitution and Washington for his text, he went forth appealing to the people. They had not before been taught their duty; they had been waiting to be told what course to pursue. He at once directed and controlled public sentiment and he lost no opportunity to strike a blow at the rebellion. Visiting different sections of the State he kindled the fires of patriotism wherever he went by his matchless eloquence and unanswerable arguments."

Starr King, as he was popularly known, was a native of New York born December 16, 1824. As a child he learned the basic tenets of religion from his father, a minister of the Universalist Church, who had spent his last years in the pulpit of a church in Charlestown, Massachusetts.

The boy, of his own accord, had decided to follow in his father's footsteps and his early education was in that direction. He was preparing for Harvard when his father's sudden death left him responsible for the family's support. From the age of 12 until his twentieth year he worked variously as a store clerk and a school teacher.

He continued his studies at night, usually absorbed in his books until early morning hours when he would be overcome by sleep. With only a few hours of rest he was ready for another day's work.

At 21 he was ordained in the ministry. He already had mastered several modern languages. In September, 1845 he preached his first sermon, surprising his listeners by his gift of oratory, his diction, and his depth of understanding. Some time later he was called to officiate in the church where his father had presided and at 24 he moved to the Hollis Street Unitarian Church in Boston.

In the Unitarian Universalist Church doctrines and forms of worship are determined by each congregation. He found members of his new congregation sorely divided, with many convinced that harmony could not be restored. The young clergyman faced the challenge and only months later, under his determined leadership, he was preaching to a happy united family.

Two years later he received an unexpected call from the Unitarian Society of San Francisco. For a time he remained undecided. In the end he accepted, despite the earnest pleas of his congregants to remain with them. He admitted that he was reluctant to leave but was doing so for two reasons — "my desire to do the will of my Master" and the need for a better climate for his health, which was poor. He sailed from Boston in April, 1850.

From the start his San Francisco congregation realized that it had selected a spiritual leader of rare strength and ability. His sermons, often philosophical, were forceful, penetrating and delivered with unusual eloquence. Often they were blended with a touch of humor.

Starr King, however, looked far beyond his pulpit. He soon identified himself not only with his new community but with all of California and its people. He rallied to vital public causes — sanitation, health and welfare. It was said that "he touched life at every point." He preached to crowded pews and with a gentle, understanding way he made friends with everyone.

His time was in great demand; people craved a chance to hear him on any subject. And when he gave a course of lectures at the Mercantile Library, standing room was at a premium.

Serious problems within the church demanded his attention. On assuming his new pulpit he found the congregation $20,000 in debt and lay advisors saw no way of meeting this obligation. The Reverend King told them that all indebtedness must be promptly cleared and that he would find a way of doing it. To set an example he contributed $7,000 of his own funds and called on others for assistance. Before a full year had passed every bill was paid and plans were started for the erection of a new church. This beautiful building, which still stands on Franklin Street, was completed three years later at a cost of $90,000 but the task had taken heavy toll of the clergyman's health and vitality.

In the meantime he had turned his attention to the preservation of the Nation. He was shocked by the serious threat of California's sucession and the support received by those who advocated joining the rebel forces. He threw his entire strength into the Union and campaigned vigorously with no thought of rest or his own health.

Friends suggested that he take a long leave of absence but he told them he had too much to do; that the country's preservation demanded his full attention.

Strangely, he had a premonition of impending death: it came to him in a dream only weeks before the end — a nightmare that he confided only to one of his closest friends.

Relating the details in his study, King said that in a vivid dream he had seen his razor slip while shaving, inflicting a gaping wound in his throat. He had heard physicians telling him that death was near; that nothing could be done.

In his sleep he had argued with the doctors, exclaiming that his windpipe was not severed and that they could save him if only the bleeding could be stopped. But the medics had merely shaken their heads, telling him that he must prepare to die.

Two weeks later he became seriously ill. His throat troubled him and he breathed with difficulty — a condition that must have brought the dream sharply to his mind, though he said nothing of it to his wife. Doctors were summoned and fearing for the outcome they ordered him to bed.

To his regret he was obliged to remain there a few nights afterward when guests whom he had invited to dinner gathered at his home. Alone in his bedroom he overheard a couple at the door announcing that they had come to be married.

Mrs. King advised them of her husband's condition and the young couple was about to leave when Starr King called down to them to wait. With characteristic self-sacrifice, he dressed himself and walked feebly to the parlor.

When the ceremony was over and the happy couple had departed, the minister was near collapse and friends were obliged to help him to his bed.

His condition grew steadily worse. On the following day he sent for his two-year-old son whom he adored, "Beautiful boy" he mumbled and threw the child a kiss. Then he lapsed into unconsciousness. A few hours later he died.

People of all religious faiths mourned his passing. The funeral drew crowds, a throng so large that a military escort was required to route the lines of mourners. He was eulogized as a man who never had a selfish thought; a man who never uttered a sentiment unfit for the most critical ear.

The esteem of the community was well expressed in this obituary published in *The Bulletin* on March 4, 1864:

"No other man on the Pacific Coast will be missed so much. San Francisco has lost one of her chief attractions, the State its noblest orator, the country one of her ablest defenders.

"Mr. King had been less than four years in California. In that short time he had done so much and so identified himself with her best interests that scarcely one public institution or enterprise or philanthropy exists here which will not feel that it has lost a champion."

Today a theological school in Berkeley and a street in San Francisco bear his name. At one corner of the church he helped to build on Franklin Street, Thomas Starr King is buried under a simple but impressive stone sarcophagus. Inside the church, in a room named for him, members of the congregation and other concerned San Franciscans often meet to discuss and actively deal with controversial social concerns of the day. Thomas Starr King would approve.

McAllister

"Learned and Eloquent"

The Hounds

BY COINCIDENCE OR by design, an imposing statue of Hall McAllister, one of San Francisco's most distinguished early lawyers, stands on the side of City Hall overlooking the street that was named in his honor.

The bronze figure, tall and erect, portrays McAllister with an open law book in his hands, looking out, as he did in life, as if eager to protect those about him with dedication and courage.

Below his name on the stone pedestal are engraved the nine words which epitomize his character and his career:

Learned Able Eloquent

A Fearless Advocate

A Courteous Foe

Hall McAllister was all of these and more.

Unlike many of the Forty-Niners who came West high in hopes but low in experience, McAllister had migrated from Georgia as a seasoned lawyer and important political figure, who abandoned a lucrative practice and a brilliant future to take part in a new and growing community. Two brothers soon followed him.

The son of a judge, he came from a prominent southern family whose members, for three generations, had won honors, mainly in law.

He was born in Savannah on November 26, 1800. After graduation from Princeton, he was admitted to the bar and practiced in his native city for 29 years before setting out with his wife for San Francisco.

In his earlier years he had shunned public life, considering himself too occupied with professional affairs but as time passed he gradually became involved in politics. At the age of 35, he was regarded as one of the most influential members of the Georgia Legislature and later became United States Attorney for the southern district of Georgia.

In 1845 he was nominated as the Democratic candidate for Governor of his state and though his party was in the minority, his popularity was such that he was defeated by only a small vote. He was a delegate to the Democratic Convention that nominated General Cass for President.

It was with such a background that Hall McAllister arrived in San Francisco to pursue his calling and to assume his place in community affairs. Word had been received in advance of his coming and he was warmly welcomed. It was not long before he was called on for public service.

Only months after his arrival the Hounds, a lawless gang of rowdies and troublemakers, climaxed a reign of terror by raiding the Chileno quarter, killing ruthlessly and putting the torch to many homes. Citizens rose in angry protest; the Vigilantes went into action, and McAllister took his place as commander of one of the four companies of 100 volunteers each.

After close to 20 of the ringleaders had been put in jail, McAllister volunteered to act as prosecutor. He soon found that his first duty was to calm the people and avert wholesale lynching. The accused Hounds were convicted and promptly shipped out of the country, some of them in the brig of a warship. Later McAllister was named attorney for the district.

By the early years of the 'sixties, Mrs. McAllister had become the leader of San Francisco's social set. They entertained extensively in their attractive Stockton Street home and the hostess, a talented vocalist, often sang for their guests. At such affairs her husband, usually serious and reserved, joined in the merriment. One Christmas Eve he surprised and even baffled his guests in a game of charades, appearing with a large wreath of flowers on his head to symbolize Spring.

He also enjoyed an occasional game of poker and his friends persisted with a story that he once had lost his home in a game with Captain Harry Lyon from New Orleans, who in turn presented it to his daughter as a wedding present. McAllister always semed to enjoy the tale and never took the trouble to deny it, although it was common knowledge that he had sold the house and bought a better one in South Park.

Despite their fondness for entertaining, religion was not neglected. McAllister served for years as a vestryman in the Church of the Advent, of which his brother, the Rev. F. Marion McAllister was rector.

Hall McAllister, a brilliant orator as well as a successful lawyer, held a deservedly high place in the community when he was suddenly stricken on December 19, 1865. He died a few hours later. Courts were adjourned in his memory and a saddened city paid him due honors.

Phelan

Father of an
Illustrious Son

James Phelan

JAMES PHELAN, A native of Ireland, arrived in San Francisco in 1849 to become a millionaire industrialist and banker. His greatest gift to his adopted city was his son, who bore the same name.

An avenue honors the father while the son, James D. Phelan, is remembered as one of the city's best mayors who finally served the Nation as a member of the United States Senate.

The senior Phelan, born in Queens County, Ireland in 1821, was barely six years old when he landed in New York with his parents. He received his education in the public schools and began a business career at an early age. Everything he touched seemed to turn to money. He invested wisely, choosing only ventures he believed were assured of profit. One biographer said that "his name is synonymous with financial strength on both sides of the continent."

As a young man he established valuable trade relations in the South and West. His travels took him far from home. He was in Cincinnati late in 1848 when he first read Larkin's dispatches briefly announcing the discovery of gold in California. The course of Phelan's career was suddenly changed.

Realizing new opportunities in California, he bought large stocks of goods whch he knew could be sold profitably in a land crowded with fortune hunters. He had them loaded aboard three ships destined for the West and booked passage for himself on the steamer *Eldorado,* intending to arrive ahead of his goods. At Panama, however, he was stricken with a fever. He probably would have succumbed but for his rugged constitution.

Considerably delayed, he arrived in San Francisco August 18, 1849 where he was met by his brother, Michael, who had preceded him by about three months.

They soon established a mercantile business under the firm name of J. & M. Phelan and advantageously disposed of the merchandise that James had shipped from the East.

Their business was booming when fires twice razed their store — once in 1850 and again a year later. But for their shrewdness, the brothers would have faced financial ruin in a day of slow transportation but, with unusual foresight, they had placed their orders so that vessels were constantly bringing new shipments.

Michael Phelan died in 1858 leaving his brother to manage all of the business affairs. He proved more than equal to the challenge, carefully weighing every move with chances for profit as his only guide.

When he heard of a need for wool in eastern markets in 1863 and 1864, he contracted with the many ranches in Northern California and soon was engaged in money-making trade with New York buyers. A year later he found opportunities with wheat and for the first time ships leaving San Francisco Bay for the Atlantic Coast were laden with California grain.

Profits rolled in; Phelan became one of the wealthiest and most respected members of the community.

By the end of the decade he had accumulated sufficient capital to launch himself into a new field — financing. In 1870 he established the First National Bank of San Francisco and became its first president. He invested heavily in real estate, always careful to select properties that could be turned to profit. It was said that he was interested only in ventures that were positively assured of gain.

In one of these, a dredging company that he organized, stock that was sold initially at $2 a share rose gradually to a value of $325 — and Phelan was one of the heaviest stockholders.

Another of his heaviest and best known investments was in a large piece of land at the gore of Market and O'Farrell Streets and Grant Avenue where in 1881 he erected a large structure that took the name of the Phelan Building. It was razed in the fire of 1906 and rebuilt, still bearing the name of the original builder.

The land, at the time of Phelan's acquisition, was occupied by a number of small ramshackle structures, all of them tenanted by stores. He bought the property piecemeal, giving one tenant after another a notice to vacate within sixty days. Having no alternative they complied — with one execption. Soon, all the old buildings but one had been demolished, only a small store occupied by Scholz Brothers remained.

Through a technical error in their notice the brothers did not understand that they must move and claimed the right to remain where they were. When excavations started for the Phelan Building, the Scholz store was hoisted high on stilts, remaining for a time like a pigeonhouse in a wasteland while digging went on beneath for the laying of foundations.

The city's wealthiest and most influential men were Phelan's close friends and business associates. In 1889 he joined James G. Fair and others in organizing the Mutual Savings Bank.

A lifetime Democrat, he associated himself with civic interests and became a director of the Society of California Pioneers and other organizations. His home near Mission Dolores was one of the show places of the city.

As he grew older, Phelan looked to his son, James D., to take over many of his extensive business affairs. Young Phelan, at an early age, was showing rare business sagacity, an ability for leadership and a desire for a worthwhile career. Though realizing that he was a rich man's son, he was determined to succeed through his own efforts and had high-reaching political ambitions.

Late in 1869 he was elected mayor, taking office January 4, 1897 as the twenty-third chief executive of San Francisco. In this capacity he gained an outstanding reputation as a leader in good, honest and constructive government. History records him as one of the best mayors the city ever had. He served until January 8, 1902 when he was succeeded by a labor candidate, Eugene E. Schmitz, who became one of the central figures in a city-wide graft prosecution.

Returning to private life, the younger Phelan continued his deep interest in civic and cultural endeavors. He was generous in many ways and it is said that he alone knew of his many helpful gifts to needy individuals and to causes for the city's betterment.

He established a large and imposing country estate with beautifully landscaped gardens near Los Altos. To this he gave the name of Montalvo, now preserved as a State park.

But the people of San Francisco were not content to allow a man of James D. Phelan's ability to remain in private life. His services, they insisted, were needed in Washington. He was persuaded to become a candidate for a seat in the United States Senate and was elected in 1914, serving a full term of six years.

He then returned to San Francisco. Soon afterward his health gradually declined and he died August 8, 1930.

Harte

The Storyteller of the Gold Rush

Bret Harte

ON AN AFTERNOON in the fall of 1865, the secretary of the United States Mint in San Francisco was pacing the floor of his office, his hands thrust into his pockets, deep in thought. Occasionally he stopped to stare blankly through the window, then he quickly resumed his nervous steps.

He was so completely absorbed that he even failed to observe a caller standing outside the open door, reluctant to intrude.

"Anything wrong?" the visitor finally inquired, breaking the silence. "Can I be of any help?"

Bret Harte merely shook his head and motioned to his friend to enter. "I'm simply waiting for the right word to come," he said. "It's simply got to be the right word to fit into a line I'm trying to put on paper."

A few pleasantries were exchanged and the writer explained briefly the thought he was trying to express. His friend, Charles Stoddard, ventured a few suggestions.

"No, no," Harte interrupted impatiently. "Can't you understand — it must be a word of two syllables. If it isn't, the rhythm of the whole sentence will be ruined."

It was typical of Harte, always the perfectionist, even in his early days as an author, when he was writing during every spare moment at the Mint. His meticulous ways never changed; they continued throughout a long career that brought him world-wide fame.

His works in prose and verse are still widely read. Less is known, however, of his life in San Francisco, in others parts of California, and abroad — of how he turned from tutor to stage coach messenger, to typesetter, newspaper reporter, novelist and poet; using his varied experiences and the unusual people he met to give life and color to the things he wrote. His characters were mostly drawn from life; his themes, sometimes with variations, from actual happenings.

His given name was Francis Brett Harte which he changed soon after he began writing in San Francisco. In his boyhood relatives and friends called him Frank.

He was born in Albany, New York on August 25, 1836. His father was Henry Hart, born in 1800, the son of Bernard Hart, a military man who had married a Jewish girl, Zipporah Seixas, with fifteen brothers and sisters.

Henry Hart died in 1845 leaving a rather impoverished widow and four children, two sons and two daughters. They remained in New York until 1853 when Bret and his sister Margaret left the family home for California.

As a small boy, Bret was precocious, a bright student with an unusual sense of humor. At six he was reading Shakespeare and at eleven he wrote his first poem, "Autumnal Musings" which was published in the New York *Sunday Atlas* much to his great delight and satisfaction.

At thirteen he left school and went to work in a lawyer's office; later he became a merchant's bookkeeper. Then he drifted into other work until his departure for the West, traveling by way of Nicaragua. He reached San Francisco in March, 1854.

Bret became a teacher and a tutor. Spare time was given to writing and occasionally he sent stories to eastern magazines. One of them was his popular "Bohemian Days in San Francisco."

He moved to Humboldt County in Northern California where he worked as express messenger, riding coaches that often were waylaid by stage robbers. These experiences would provide color and plots for writing later. However, he soon tired of this work and moved on to the town of Union, where he became a typesetter on the Humboldt *Times.* He apparently found the job boring, for he left it to tutor and afterward became a clerk in a pharmacy, a position that no doubt inspired the story of Liberty Jones.

Still restless, he moved back to San Francisco in 1857, and again turned to setting type, this time in the office of *The Golden Era.* It was a turning point in his career for *The Era's* editor, Joseph Lawrence, soon offered him a dollar for every column of prose. Harte accepted the challenge, was promoted to the editorial department, and wrote prolifically. In 1862, still a writer for the paper, he married Anna Griswold, a member of a New York family.

Now facing the need for more income, he accepted an offer of a better position. He had become friendly with R. B. Swain, then superintendent of the San Francisco Mint, and when Swain offered to make him secretary of the institution, the young writer eagerly accepted. He held that post for several years since its duties permitted him to utilize spare time in writing. With his wife he lived quietly, spending some time with such good friends as the Rev. Thomas Starr King and Mrs. Benton Fremont, wife of the widely-known military man. They encouraged him in his literary efforts, and that was what he needed, for Harte often took a dim view of his talents and his future.

He had given up his work at the Mint only a short time before a new publication, *The Californian* appeared and Harte was engaged to be one of its principal writers. In that capacity he met another journalist, a reporter on *The Morning Call* and a frequent contributor to *The Californian*. He used the nom de plume of Mark Twain. They became close friends.

Harte was not long in his new job before his work began to attract wide attention. A year later the first collection of his poems was published, followed by reprints of articles that had won special favor.

After a year there came another opportunity. He was engaged to edit a new San Francisco publication, *The Overland Monthly,* which came into almost instant popularity. Its new editor soon found himself in serious trouble, however, since the owner objected to his story, "Luck of Roaring Camp" insisting that it was indecent. Harte stood his ground and the article appeared in the second issue, only to be severely criticized by religious leaders and by the press. Harte was downcast but the piece proved to be a blessing in disguise.

A week later he received a letter from the editor of *Atlantic Monthly* with a generous offer for a story like the one that had created all of the controversy.

His next big success was his "Heathen Chinese" which attracted national attention at a time when "the Chinese question" was being hotly debated. By now Harte had truly "arrived." He was appointed professor of recent literature at the University of California. Other honors followed but he was not completely happy. People reading of his success were constantly at his heels begging money and he was too generous to ever refuse. More than that, the temper of the people was changing; San Francisco was growing into a more material, more commercial city. There was friction between people in high places.

Tempting offers were coming from the East and Harte, his talents now fully recognized, could not resist. He left San Francisco for New York in February, 1871 where he was received as a famous person whose presence was a tribute to the city.

He moved about with celebrated writers. He traveled to Boston and other cities where he was hailed as one of the most outstanding writers of the time. There were flattering offers from many publishers. He finally accepted one from *The Atlantic* which offered him $10,000 for the year, regardless of how much or how little he chose to write. He also lectured, traveling far, always appearing before large audiences.

With it all, he was constantly in debt, partly because of his charitable impulse and partly because of traveling expenses while maintaining a costly home in New York. Through the efforts of friends, President Hayes appointed him United States Commercial Agent in Crefeld, Prussia at a good salary. He left America in June, 1878, with no thought that he was destined never to return.

The post offered ample opportunity for continued writing and lecture tours. Harte made the most of it but at heavy cost to his health. In October, 1879 he wrote Washington requesting a leave to recuperate in a better climate; but business kept him in Crefeld until early in the following year.

He was finally transferred to Glasgow where he assumed the rank of Consul at a salary of $3,000 a year. He was contented there, though his wife had not joined him. The new berth continued until 1885 when the advent of a new administration in Washington resulted in the appointment of a successor.

He moved to London and was received by men and women important in literary life. He continued with his writing and found new interests in golf and photography.

Suddenly, toward the end of 1901, his health again began to fail. Doctors told him bluntly that he was suffering from cancer of the throat. His condition worsened and in March of the following year he underwent surgery which gave him little or no relief. Still he continued writing although he knew his life was coming to a close.

The end came on May 6th. That morning he had been busy at his desk when he was suddenly stricken with a hemorrhage of the throat. Doctors were summoned and were hopeful that he would rally.

He was resting peacefully in bed that afternoon when a second hemorrhage occurred. Harte lapsed into semi-consciousness. Friends were at his side, realizing that hope was gone.

Before night the career of the famous writer was at an end.

Stanford

Grocer to Governor

Leland Stanford

FROM A SIMPLE start as a grocer in Sacramento, Leland Stanford rose to become the Governor of California, a member of the United States Senate, a railroad builder, and finally the donor of one of the greatest universities in America.

He did it all in a life span of 69 years, much of it dedicated to public service and philanthropy. He was a man of great vision, always a hard worker, with a deep concern for the welfare of his fellowmen. Money was not his only goal; he saw more to life's purpose.

He was born in Watervliet, New York in 1824, the son of a poor and struggling innkeeper. After receiving a good secondary education, he decided to prepare for a legal career and went to work in a law office in Albany. On being admitted to practice he moved to Port Washington in Wisconsin where he opened his own office. His mind was on the West, however, thinking of his five brothers who already had gone to California to seek their fortunes, and before long he decided to follow them in the hope of better opportunities.

Unlike his brothers, he was not interested in working with pick and shovel. Instead he saw easier and more certain profits in selling supplies to those who did mine. He opened a store in Sacramento dealing largely in flour, tallow candles and other goods needed by the prospectors.

The business grew and he invested his profits shrewdly. He visited San Francisco frequently in behalf of his varied interests and soon became involved in politics.

Meanwhile in Sacramento he was developing a close friendship with three of the town's leading merchants — Collis P. Huntington, Charles Crocker, and Mark Hopkins — men of humble beginning who later were to become the "Big Four" that built the Central Pacific, western link to the country's first transcontinental railroad.

As early as 1858 they were listening with feigned indifference to a young engineer, Theodore Judah, who was seeking their support for what he considered a feasible project, a railroad through the western mountains and far into the East. That they were deeply interested appears certain, though publicly they called him a dreamer, shrewdly believing it would be to their advantage to turn deaf ears.

They were prepared to play a watchful, waiting game, in no haste to make any move that might betray their interest. They looked to Stanford to pave the way.

Stanford, with a gift for leadership, was steadily gaining strength in Republican ranks. Anxious for public office, he ran for State Treasurer in 1857 and for Governor two years later. He was unsuccessful in both campaigns, but he was not one to accept failure.

Early in 1861 he was mentioned again as a likely candidate for Governor. His mind was now on the railroad and, though his motives were not entirely selfish, he did realize that as the State's chief executive he could do much to gain support for the railroad project, benefiting himself, his three associates, and the country as well.

He won the nomination and this time he was elected, taking office in January of the following year.

As Governor he used the power of his office to win support for the railroad, not only in the State Legislature but in Washington as well.

The "Big Four" gradually rose to tremendous power, coming into possession of valuable lands and assuming a high place in the Nation's politics.

They organized the Central Pacific Railroad, elected Stanford president and on January 8, 1863 he broke ground for the historic venture near a levee at the foot of K Street in Sacramento. Six years later the last spike was laid; the transcontinental railroad had become a reality.

As a millionaire railroad president and former Governor, Stanford was recognized as one of the foremost men in his State and city. He moved in the best society and his time was always in demand.

His summer home in Palo Alto became a gathering place for the smart set of the time. The estate, once known as Mayfield Grange, had been built by a ne'er-do-well, George Gordon, the son of a wealthy Yorkshire family. Gordon liked his liquor all too well. One morning he awakened in his English home to find himself married to a barmaid he had met only the night before. Unwilling to disgrace his family, he took her to San Francisco and built the Palo Alto home, a mansion surrounded by large gardens. After Gordon's death in 1876 Stanford bought the property, remodeled it, and used it for a summer residence. It was badly damaged by the earthquake of 1906 but one wing later became part of the Stanford Home for Convalescent Children.

As befits a country gentleman, Stanford became deeply interested in horses. One day in a newspaper interview he insisted that a trotter, at a certain point, lifts all four feet from the ground at once. His statement was widely read by horsemen and soon vigorously challenged by Frederick MacCrellish, who then was publishing the *Daily Alta California*. The newsman declared that Stanford's view was ridiculous — and thereby a legend started, and an experiment which was to result in the advent of motion pictures.

Many still insist that the argument led to a $50,000 wager between the two. A photographer, Eadweard Muybridge, was hired to take pictures of Occident, one of Stanford's best trotters.

The photographs, however, were inconclusive, being badly blurred. Five years later Muybridge tried again, using improved equipment which could take faster exposures. The pictures, showing the complete sequence of the trotter's action, proved Stanford's disputed assertion correct. Whether the wager was ever paid is not recorded.

Through the years Stanford's political interests continued and in January, 1885 he was elected to a seat in the United States Senate. He was reelected in 1891 for a second term, which he was serving when he died two years later.

He had reached the height of his career when misfortune hit him a cruel and telling blow. The son whom he adored was stricken seriously ill at the age of eighteen and died. Stanford never fully recovered from his loss but his attention turned to finding a suitable way of honoring the memory of his only child.

After considering many plans, he finally decided to erect a university in Palo Alto that would provide educational opportunities for young people through the years. He gave much of his fortune to building the institution that he named the Leland Stanford Junior University, and San Francisco honored him by giving his name to a street.

Ralston

The Bon Vivant Banker

William Chapman Ralston

LATE IN THE afternoon of August 27, 1875 newsboys ran through the streets of San Francisco crying news so shocking that it seemed incredible.

"Ralston dead — Ralston drowned," they yelled.

Men and women, hurrying along, stopped as if they could not believe the words they heard. It appeared impossible that multi-millionaire William Chapman Ralston, one of the city's foremost bankers, industrialists and civic leaders, had met tragic death in the prime of life.

In little more than a month his fantastic Palace Hotel, the most luxurious in the country, was scheduled to open. He had planned elaborate ceremonies with the state's most distinguished citizens participating.

At 49 Ralston was often called "California's great empire builder." A bon vivant, he was a symbol of the flamboyant living of his time. He enjoyed the respect of everyone.

Born in 1826 in Plymouth, Ohio of Scottish and Irish ancestry, he had sailed to San Francisco by way of Panama as a young man, determined like many others to make his way in the young and growing West.

He was possessed of extraordinary energy, imagination and daring and was soon on his way to reach his goals. Everything he undertook always had to be on a bigger, better and more elaborate scale than that of anyone else. And he did just that, building the city's largest and most extravagant hotel, and founding one of the state's most powerful banks.

His grandiose ideas even extended to his building of the California Theater some time after the Civil War. "Find out the size of the biggest theater in the country," he told the architects. "Then make mine ten feet bigger."

Personal gain was not his only motive. He was filled with civic pride. It was said that anything for the good of California became a personal part of his life. He played a major role in developing the state's resources and furthering its industrial progress. Never did he turn down a friend or fail to support a worthy cause.

From the start he chose his associates wisely, and before long they came to be known as "the Ralston Ring." Together they first engaged in mining operations in Nevada's Comstock silver lode. Fortunes were quickly made and profits were invested. Ralston individually became the owner of a furniture factory, a carriage factory, woolen mills, and even a watchmaking enterprise. Nothing with a chance for profit was overlooked.

He moved in the city's most exclusive social set. His wedding on May 20, 1858 to Lizzie Fry, a popular belle, attracted wide attention. In strange contrast to his imposing ways, he chose to issue no invitations; the time and place of the wedding were simply announced by his pastor at Calvary Church the previous Sunday. Those who cared to attend were told to come.

The honeymoon was equally unusual for him — a camping party in Yosemite Valley — and when the bridal couple was followed there by a party of the groom's male friends, Ralston took it good-naturedly and became a gracious host.

For his bride he established a lavish estate in Belmont, some 25 miles down the Peninsula. There they lived like royalty, entertaining in a style befitting their wealth and social status. The horses stalls were made of polished inlaid wood and every harness was silver mounted. Ralston's entrances and exits through the gates of the palatial estate in a picturesque tallyho became a familiar sight.

In 1864 he founded the Bank of California with D. O. Mills. It soon became one of the richest and most influential institutions of its kind in the state. For a site they first moved the Tehama House from California and Montgomery Streets to Broadway and then erected a suitable building on the vacated lot.

William Sharon was selected as the bank's agent in Virginia City, Nevada and, with Ralston's approval, found it easy to tempt silver mine owners to borrow money at low interest. There were many foreclosures adding rich mining properties to the assets of the growing bank.

Ralston's love of country reached high levels during the Civil War, especially during its early stages when attempts were made to bring California into the Confederacy. It was then that he assembled the staunchest Unionists and organized the Union League, later to become the Union League Club. As its leader he drilled the members nightly in Union Square Pavilion and kept them ready for any emergency.

He was equally concerned with suppressing crime and violence in the community. When the Vigilantes took drastic action against the "Sydney Ducks," former convicts from Australia, Ralston assumed a major role, working closely with the Committee's leader, his friend William Coleman.

One of Ralston's business associates was Asbury Harpending, a reckless adventurer with a sharp business mind, who later gained worldwide notoriety as the victim of a fabulous diamond hoax perpetrated through a "salted" mine.

On a day in 1868 the two turned their backs on an offer of a large piece of land for which the owner, Selim Woodward, was asking $300,-000. Later in the same year there was a severe earthquake and Woodward, terrified, announced that he was leaving town for good. He happily accepted $150,000 from Ralston and Harpending for the property.

They decided to use the land for a large hotel, the Grand. At their own expense they cut through land for New Montgomery Street and began construction of the new hostelry. Ralston poured $2,000,000 of his profits from the Comstock mines into the venture.

Next came Ralston's dream of a hotel that would be even bigger and more luxurious: the Palace. The site he had selected was occupied by the Roman Catholic Orphan Asylum. He bought the property for $440,000 and razed the orphanage. Erection of the hotel was soon under way but not before Ralston built a reservoir, fed by four wells and with a capacity of 26,000 gallons, under the structure.

Money was no object in furnishing the new Palace. Ralston bought an entire furniture factory, ordered 30,000 specially made dishes from France, and imported Irish linens by the ton. For four months, 250 men worked on a 15-hour daily schedule on furnishing the hotel.

No example of the daring and resourcefulness which characterized Ralston's spectacular career is more dramatic than the story of a coup that saved the Bank of California from disaster. It happened after the Civil War when President Grant had forbidden banks to exchange gold bullion for coin at the mints. Rumors had spread that the bank was in serious trouble and a run was imminent. The vaults were filled with bullion but, if a run began, there would be a shortage of money to meet demands.

The directors, excepting Ralston, were in near panic. "Just leave it all to me," he told them. "I'll handle the situation. Don't worry."

Still skeptical, his colleagues assumed that he planned a new appeal to Washington, although previous calls for help had been refused.

An hour later Ralston summoned a few of his most trusted men to his office. Near midnight they left the bank carrying bulging bags of gold bullion and moved directly to the Mint on Commercial Street, only a few blocks away. The trips continued, the party returning each time with sacks of coin, an even exchange for the gold ingots. When dawn came the banks vaults were stacked with money, far more than would be needed to meet the most serious run. How this was accomplished no one but Ralston and his trusted group ever knew — and they never told.

As time passed, however, his personal extravagances and bold investments took their toll from his bank's stability. Personally he owed it $4,000,000. The directors, his close associates, were greatly worried.

The day of reckoning came on the morning of August 27, 1875. It was then that a directors' meeting was hastily called. They told Ralston that the bank was periled and demanded his resignation.

Crestfallen and humiliated, he acceded reluctantly to the request, stalked out of the bank and started walking toward the beach where he was in the habit of swimming almost daily.

A few members of the swimming clubs lining the shore watched him swim out to deep water as was his custom. Suddenly they saw him sink from view. There was no outcry. He never was seen alive again.

A few hours later the body was washed ashore. Whether the once-influential banker had decided to end his troubles or whether high nervous tension had induced a stroke never was determined. The question was on every tongue, with the community well-divided in its conclusions.

An insurance company readily accepted the accident theory and paid the widow $50,000, though the policy expressly provided that it would be void in the event of suicide.

At the opening of the Palace Hotel two months later, William Sharon, to whom Ralston owed more than $2,000,000 paid him a glowing tribute and the bank's directors voted the widow a liberal allowance for the balance of her life.

Ralston's greatest tribute, however, had taken place at his funeral, before one of the largest crowds San Francisco had ever seen assembled to pay its respects to a prominent citizen. There were bankers and laborers, men high in government, in business and in the professions.

The officiating clergyman, the Rev. Campbell Shorb, spoke the words that were in every heart when he said:

"Our loss is an indescribable calamity to the state. Had I the power to drape California in blackest crepe from Siskiyou to San Diego I would do it. . . . He has made California a synonym for princely hospitality and generosity to the utmost bounds of the universe."

Haight

Tribute to Four

Henry Huntly Haight

GUARDED TALK OF a dark horse filtered through the Democratic State Convention when it assembled in San Francisco early in June of 1867.

The party was determined to elect the next Governor of California but it needed a winner. For weeks its leaders had met in caucus considering one name after another, only to eliminate them as good men but without sufficient political strength to carry the election. Not until the night before the Convention opened officially was a decision reached — and then it was too late to ask the approval of the candidate.

"Give him the nomination and he'll have to accept it," someone said near the close of the last-minute session. Others nodded their agreement.

The convention was called to order. By previous agreement, J. B. Crockett, a stalwart of the Party, jumped to his feet and asked for the floor.

Silence fell over the crowded room; at last the secret choice would be disclosed.

"I rise to perform an agreeable duty," Crockett began. "I rise to present as a candidate for Governor of the State of California a gentleman whom I have known from boyhood. I have known him for 20 years and I can say truthfully that I have never known a truer, better, more honest man than he whose name I now present to this convention. I do now nominate for the office of Governor of California Henry Huntly Haight."

The delegates burst into wild applause and all eyes turned toward the nominee, whose face showed his complete amazement. He had never taken an active part in politics and on several occasions when his name was mentioned for judicial appointments he had flatly refused.

Haight now rose to his feet amid more rounds of handclapping.

When order was finally restored he began to speak and expressions suddenly changed. "Gentlemen," he said, "you do me great honor but I must decline. I'm a lawyer and I wasn't born for politics."

Cries of "No" came from every delegate. A short adjournment was ordered and Haight found himself surrounded by a group of insistant friends. They adjourned to an anteroom and there the surprised candidate finally acceded to the wishes of his supporters.

When the convention reconvened and heard Haight's decision the place again rang with cheers. He was escorted to the rostrum and formally announced his final decision.

A heated campaign ensued, with Haight winning easily over his opponent, George Graham; in fact, the entire Democratic ticket was victorious. He was inaugurated December 5, 1867 and served with credit to himself and his Party until the expiration of his four-year term in 1871.

Thus ended the political career of another pioneer who arrived in San Francisco a stranger and rose to the highest office in the State.

Henry Huntly Haight, the eldest son of a large family, was a native of Rochester, New York, born May 20, 1825. His paternal ancestors had come from England; his mother, of Scottish descent, took pride in her relationship to the Clan Cameron.

At the age of fifteen, Henry had entered Yale, graduated in 1844. He continued his law studies in the office of his father, Fletcher M. Haight, and moved with him to St. Louis where he was admitted to practice.

Late in 1849 he joined the many travelers to the West, arriving in San Francisco on January 20, 1850. He practiced first with J. A. McDougall, a well-known attorney of the time, later establishing an office with his father, who had followed his son to San Francisco in 1854. Their office in the Old Custom House soon became one of the busiest in the town. It continued so until both Haights were in elective office: the younger Haight as Governor, his father as a Judge of the United States District Court.

Most chroniclers of the early days assume that Henry Huntly Haight's name was given to a street in recognition of his brilliant career. A few historians are inclined to differ, however, for in that period there were four Haights — all related and all active in San Francisco affairs.

Aside from the Governor and his father, there was another Henry Haight (with no middle initial) who headed the important banking firm of Page, Bacon & Company; and Samuel, another son of Fletcher, who had come to California as a member of Stevenson's regiment.

Haight, the banker, was a founder of the Protestant Orphan Asylum and gave the land on which the building was erected.

Certainly, all four Haights made their individual contributions to the community and the street perpetuates the memory of them all.

Nevertheless, in the light of recent developments that have turned the nation's spotlight on the Haight-Ashbury neighborhood, many now point to the irony of social change that still associates the name of a distinguished lawyer with an area marked by lawlessness, police problems and judicial burdens.

Huntington

From Peddler to Plutocrat

Collis P. Huntington

WHEN YOUNG COLLIS P. HUNTINGTON, son of a poverty-stricken Connecticut tinker, proudly counted his savings on his four-teenth birthday and found that he had put aside $100 of his earnings, he little dreamed that he was destined to become a multimillionaire.

He had known privation and hard work from early childhood, com-pelled not only to support himself but to contribute to household needs. He did chores for neighbors, receiving only meager pay, and during hot summer vacations he worked on a nearby farm.

Before his eighteenth year he was traveling about, ambitiously grasp-ing every opportunity to earn a few dollars and to advance himself. He peddled jewelry through Ohio and Indiana. For a time he was a bill collector in the deep South and in New York City he profited by selling butter in the poorer neighborhoods. Once he and his brother operated a small shop, but it was a disappointing venture.

With little education, he had no fixed goal but he did have a sharp mind, a pleasant manner, resourcefulness and a determination to succeed. He was far-sighted, too, always seeking new ways to improve himself.

Soon after the first news of the gold discovery reached the East, Huntington decided to move to California to seek his fortune along with many others. By then he had saved a considerable amount of money. After paying for his passage by way of Panama, he had some funds left which he planned to invest when he arrived in San Francisco.

Landing in Panama he found that quick ship passage to the West was not available and that he would be obliged to remain there for weeks. Quickly realizing that there was an opportunity for profitable trading during his enforced stay, he rented a little schooner, invested in foods and merchandise, and sailed about selling his wares. In a month he had netted $1,000, a tidy sum with which to launch his career in California.

Once in San Francisco, he remained only a few days before leaving for the gold country. He started out with pick and shovel but his career as a prospector lasted less than a day; in fact, it took him only six hours to decide that this type of work was not for him. He chose to become a merchant trading with miners.

Returning to Sacramento, he rented a small store, bought a stock of pickaxes, spades, nails and other hardware, and went into business. A steady line of customers proved the wisdom of his quick decision.

He was making money rapidly and the store had been enlarged when he met three other ambitious pioneers, merchants like himself. They were soon fast friends. Of his three new-found associates, two of them — Mark Hopkins and Leland Stanford — had come West as he had by way of Panama. The third, Charles Crocker, had crossed the plains, intending to make his fortune at mining but like Huntington he also had opened a store.

They asked high prices and made large profits. Their funds grew fast and with success they gradually became influential in politics. The four were reaching out into new fields, buying land and investing in mining properties when they were approached with plans for building a transcontinental railroad. It was in an upstairs room over Huntington's hardware store that the engineer, Theodore Judah, often unfolded his maps and drawings to explain his plans for the railroad.

When the "Big Four" finally undertook the gigantic task of building the Central Pacific, each played a different but vital role. Huntington, a large man with broad, heavy shoulders, was a figure personifying power. Beyond doubt, he was the leader of the partners. To him fell the tremendous task of influencing Congress, state legislatures and city governments to grant them land, rights of way, subsidies and other moneys. Far greater financing than the four builders could provide was needed. Huntington became responsible for obtaining this help.

Mark Hopkins was the bookkeeper. Leland Stanford undertook much of the political maneuvering, backing Huntington in his demands for official privileges. Charles Crocker assumed charge of actual construction, with responsibility for providing the vast quantities of materials of all sorts for the project.

Once they had as many as 39 ships sailing to Northern California at the same time, carrying construction materials for the railroad. "Get me everything I need and I'll build a mile of railroad each day," Crocker was quoted as having told Huntington, and the request was fulfilled.

Huntington's power over Senators, Representatives and State legislators was barely short of phenomenal. He has often been pictured as sitting at his desk long into the night, a black skull cap pulled down over his bald head, planning political maneuvers. One biographer has written that politically he controlled all of California and Nevada.

He came to San Francisco frequently. He was often seen on the California Street cable cars. He greeted gripmen as old friends and to show their esteem they would stop in front of the door of his large pretentious home on Nob Hill.

Despite his wealth and influence neither he nor his family was ever conspicuous socially. His adopted daughter, Clara, was educated abroad and was married there to a German prince.

For years San Francisco had a picturesque memento of Huntington — an artificial waterfall on Stow Lake in Golden Gate Park which was named for him. He made the gift, at a cost of thousands of dollars, in response to a request from John McLaren, the park's superintendent.

McLaren had been driving the famous railroad builder through the Park when he stopped suddenly at a spot on the lake and pointed upwards. "There, Mr. Huntington," he said, "would be a perfect place for a waterfall if we only had the money to build it."

Huntington asked for details and finally wrote a check to cover the cost.

In 1900, thirty-one years after driving the last spike for the railroad in Utah, Huntington died. In his memory, his nephew, Henry E. Huntington who had inherited millions from his uncle, erected the famous Huntington Library and Art Gallery in Pasadena.

Flood

The Nabob of
Nob Hill

James Clair Flood

JAMES CLAIR FLOOD, one of the multi-millionaire members of California's famous Big Four silver kings, adored the bronze fence surrounding his palatial home on Nob Hill — and with good reason. The fence alone cost him $30,000. It would cost far more today.

It is said that the sight of a single tarnished post would spoil his day and, since money was no object, Flood engaged a man whose sole duty was to keep the costly fence clean, bright and glistening at all times.

People passing the Flood mansion — now the exclusive Pacific Union Club — on California and Mason Streets would pause to watch the servant at his work. They said that he was always polishing.

Were Flood to return today, he would be chagrined to observe the fence now dull and black. But the house that the wealthy mining man built years ago at fabulous cost of Connecticut brownstone remains a landmark and a reminder of times gone by.

James Clair Flood's early life permitted no such indulgences. In San Francisco he began as a bartender. But he kept his ears open as his wealthy patrons exchanged valuable information on investments in the mines. What he heard Flood put to good and profitable use.

To follow him in his meteoric rise to wealth and influence, one should know of his partners in the Big Four combine — James G. Fair, John W. Mackay, and William S. O'Brien — though only Flood and Fair have had streets named for them.

The monarchs of the silver mines had come from Dublin, Ireland with the exception of Flood, who was born in New York City only a short time after the arrival of his parents there.

Three of them — Flood, Fair and O'Brien — arrived in California in 1849; Mackay two years later. In appearance, personality and background the four were widely different. Flood, probably the most ambitious, had received some schooling before being apprenticed to an eastern carriage maker.

Flood was a heavy man, short and with broad shoulders. Soon after setting foot on San Francisco he hastened to the Mother Lode and found work as a carpenter for $16 a day. He did not keep the job long. He was eager for money and stories of quick fortunes made by miners lured him away. He turned to the Feather River from which he took fully $3,000 in relatively no time.

One night he started comparing experiences with a stranger, O'Brien, who had been working with pick and shovel with similar success. Striking up a friendship, they decided to move together to San Francisco, where they were told they could invest their earnings profitably. Flood, relying on his old trade, opened a carriage shop; O'Brien a store selling general merchandise. All went well until a depression in 1855 took nearly all their money.

Probably because misery seeks company, the two talked of a partnership. As they walked about, dejected and confused, wondering how they might recoup their losses, they noticed numbers of half-empty stores and crowded bars; evidently everyone had money for liquor.

With no experience and borrowed funds they opened a saloon. It became successful almost from the start. They sold two drinks for 25 cents and made friends with their patrons. Flood, working behind the bar, wore neatly pressed business clothes while his partner, in a high silk hat and a cutaway, stood outside to greet their customers who soon numbered some of the wealthiest brokers and financiers in the town. Neither partner, however, liked the business. Both were convinced that they were fitted for something better.

A few years later, with fat bank accounts, they sold the bar and profiting by tips from friendly customers, they became stock brokers with an office on Montgomery Street.

Meanwhile in Nevada events were shaping in a way that would radically change their course of operations. Two successful mining men, Fair and Mackay were in bitter competition with William Sharon who then was facing heavy losses due to a sudden slump in Hale and Norcross mining stock. Output had dropped to an alarming rate.

With covetous eyes on these properties, Fair and Mackay decided to consult the new brokers whom they had met before and trusted. The result was a four-way partnership, with its members investing almost all of their funds in the stock then selling at ridiculously low prices. In fact, the partners secured a controlling interest and Sharon lost his place on the board.

The four were convinced that fortunes still could be taken from the Hale and Norcross mines. The slump, they reasoned, was due to inefficient operations.

A few years later, their judgment vindicated, stockholders received dividends of half a million dollars.

Now the Big Four bought new mines, erected a mill of their own, and took over a decadent water company that Sharon believed was worthless. In two of their new mines they lost heavily but their confidence was not shaken; nor was their daring.

Their attention turned to the Consolidated Virginia, whose mines they were certain had not been fully worked though many others believed otherwise. Again they theorized that operating from the right direction and to proper depths would make the mines yield rich rewards.

Sharon and his associates were still in control of the Consolidated Virginia. So the four partners decided to acquire stock cautiously and in small amounts, each man for himself. They did not want to arouse the suspicions of their competitor.

They were investing in six mines at the 1300-foot level when the shrewd Sharon became aware of what was going on and succeeded in manipulating the remaining stock so that the Big Four members were forced to pay fully $100,000 to gain control.

Sharon was positive that he had engineered a clever coup; the properties, he told his colleagues, were not worth a cent more than $40,000. But he was unaware of the cleverness of the others, their thorough knowledge of mining, and their confidence.

Flood and his associates, realizing that their plans called for more money than they had, levied a heavy assessment which produced adequate funds. Then they went to work, knowing precisely what to do.

Boring in new directions started early in May, 1872. Each day the Big Four gamblers looked hopefully for some indication of the results they had predicted. Disappointing weeks slipped by; they had reached the 1200-foot level with no sign of what they wanted.

"Go down deeper," they told their engineers and waited.

Success did not come until four months of impatient watching had passed. Early one morning Flood, standing at the mouth of the shaft and closely watching the rock coming to the surface, hailed those about him. "Look," he cried, "Here's what we've been looking for."

It was a sample of one of the richest veins of silver ever tapped in Nevada. He and his three partners knew that great fortunes lay ahead.

The Big Four soon purchased all outstanding shares of stock and became sole owners.

Despite efforts to keep their luck secret, the news soon spread and brought experts to the scene, anxious to confirm what they had been hearing. One of them estimated the value of the vein at $230,000,000. Others set even higher figures.

Now new levels were explored with results as exciting. Four men of humble beginnings were to become multi-millionaires while the mining world marveled at what they had done.

Flood, with more money than he could spend, moved to San Francisco, erected his palatial Nob Hill home, and purchased real estate as freely as most people were buying groceries. At one time his monthly rents were estimated to exceed half a million dollars.

O'Brien remained in San Francisco, living modestly, and took pleasure in sharing his wealth with his brothers, sisters and a host of other relatives. Of the mining colleagues, he was the first to die and his fortune was divided among his kin.

Mackay chose to settle in the East and use his fortune for purposes other than real estate. He became the head of Postal Telegraph, an active competitor of Western Union.

Fair, with political ambitions, took a different course, and became a United States Senator.

For both Fair and Mackay, however, millions failed to buy domestic happiness. Fair gained the unhappy distinction of being the first Senator to be sued on adultery charges and when the case was settled he found himself $5,000,000 poorer.

Mackay's wife, once a dressmaker, had dreams of high society which she could not satisfy in America. She went to Europe, gained the position to which she aspired, and rarely saw her husband.

Flood may not have lived to see his name on a street post in a section of the Mission where he had heavy land holdings but since no records can be found, his descendants, still living in San Francisco, are convinced that he was intended for that honor.

William Sharon

Sharon

The Scandalous
Senator

A LOVE AFFAIR that was in no way secret struck multi-millionaire William Sharon a humiliating blow in 1883. He became the laughing stock of San Francisco and the central figure in a scandalous courtroom drama that proved costly to his pride and pocketbook.

By his own standards Sharon had a right to haughtiness — and a right to guard his fortune. Overcoming business failure, he had worked his way to a position of wealth and power as one of the state's foremost bankers and mining men. He had been a member of the United States Senate and by his own cleverness had saved the Bank of California from disaster. These were the unusual achievements of a man who had abandoned a small law practice in Mississippi to come West in 1849, whose little store in Sacramento had been forced to the wall, and who had found himself compelled to go hat in hand to the influential William Ralston begging for a job.

People looked at Sharon in the streets or in the clubs — a small man with a black mustache, habitually dressed in a long frock coat and a dark, broad-brimmed hat — and marveled at his success. They even condoned his tobacco-chewing habit.

Everyone seemed to know how he had overcome adversity. It was common knowledge that after the failure of his Sacramento store he had come to San Francisco to gamble in real estate and had emerged with a profit of $150,000. But this man of Quaker birth was always looking for bigger things. His eyes had turned toward the Comstock mines in Nevada in which he had great confidence despite a serious slump that was taking place.

Sharon decided to invest all of his real estate gains in one of the largest Comstock companies but he was soon defrauded of his money by crooked, manipulating brokers. For a second time he had tasted failure.

And once more he had decided to use his wits.

This time he called on Ralston, head of the Bank of California, who was seriously worried over the sharp decline in Comstock operations. Many of the pits were flooded; miners were losing their lives. There were many other problems. Stocks had dropped to alarming levels and with millions of his bank's funds invested in the mines, Ralston had good reason to be concerned.

No doubt Sharon understood the situation and believed this to be a propitious time to come forward with a bold proposal. He asked to be hired as the bank's agent in Virginia City where its business had been ruinously mismanaged by a representative who had recently decamped.

Ralston was not too much impressed with Sharon but with affairs as they were he, too, decided to gamble. Sharon looked like a man of courage, understanding and imagination. He got the job and hurried to Nevada.

By masterful strokes he soon turned the tide in Ralston's favor. He grasped opportunities that had been overlooked and converted them into profit. Small mining companies that were borrowing from rival banks were persuaded by offers of low interest to do their business with Ralston's institution. Some of them went into bankruptcy and the Bank of California acquired new and valuable assets.

Then Sharon turned his attention to a newcomer, Adolph Sutro, who daringly had begun to bore a tunnel that he believed would increase the Comstock yield at greatly reduced operating cost. Sutro, who had failed to obtain Ralston's support, was working independently and in competition.

Sharon fought this project with vigor, delayed it by litigation, and won the confidence of disgruntled miners.

By this time Sharon was making money fast for the bank and for himself. He had attained a place of influence, moving in high social circles and with men of affairs in the two states.

Such was his status when San Franciscans picked up their newspapers on a morning early in September, 1883 and read the astounding report of a suit just filed against Sharon by an attractive, 30-year-old woman, Miss Sarah Althea Hill.

Sharon, a widower twice her age, was alleged to have entered into a marriage contract with her three years before and then ruthlessly thrown her out after fourteen months of supposedly-married bliss. The lurid facts of the ill-fated love affair continued to unfold in a courtroom.

Throughout the days of sensational testimony that followed, every seat was taken and spectators cupped their ears fearing they might lose a word.

Miss Hill naturally became the star witness — a striking, well-dressed figure, who already had been dubbed "the rose of Sharon."

Sparing no details, she unfolded the entire sensational story of her romance. She had met Sharon by chance and after a brief courtship had accepted his marriage proposal, agreeing to keep it secret, she said, because of an earlier affair of Sharon's that might cause complications.

He signed a marriage contract, she testified, and established her in fitting style in a suite at the Grand Hotel. They went about together, attending social functions given by his friends and relatives, and in no way did her wealthy husband seek to keep their association secret.

The denouncement came when Sharon fell seriously ill and demanded possession of the marriage contract. Sarah admitted telling him, falsely, that it was lost. A quarrel followed, she testified, and she was pummeled, later to be evicted from the suit and abandoned.

Sharon, however, told a far different story when he took the stand. He emphatically denied having signed the contract and branded it a forgery. He was equally positive that love letters produced in court by his accuser were likewise spurious. And he repudiated her claim that he once had offered her a fabulous sum to forsake their marriage and go her way.

The trial went on for days with each session providing new sensations. It soon became obvious that Sharon's hired detectives had been digging deeply into the plaintiff's background. One witness who tried to besmirch her character was jailed as a perjurer.

Suddenly there came another surprise. David Terry, who had finally returned to California after leaving in disgrace following his fatal duel with Senator Broderick, walked into the packed courtroom and told the judge that he had been retained to join Sarah's battery of six attorneys.

The trial dragged on for months, a bitter contest in which the accuser tried her utmost to prove her claims, while Sharon countered with repeated charges of fraud and forgery.

When she finally produced the much-disputed marriage contract, he looked at the signature and insisted that it was spurious.

Both sides had their supporters. Some branded the former Senator as a gadfly who had been lured into marriage by the woman's charm and beauty; others took his side, criticizing Sarah for agreeing to such a relationship and insisting that her only purpose was to share his fortune. Her tempestuous outbreaks in court did much to sway many against her.

At last the long protracted hearing ended and Judge Sullivan's decision was anxiously awaited. He had chosen not to rule at once.

His judgment, rendered on December 24, 1884, was a victory for Sarah Althea Hill. It upheld the validity of the disputed marriage contract, granted her a divorce and a half share of all of the community property. Sharon listened white with rage and announced that the fight had just begun.

His lawyers appealed to the United States Circuit Court which was in no haste to render an opinion. The case was still under consideration when Sharon died November 13, 1885. To the end he had hoped to emerge the victor. Fate was to deny him the privilege of knowing that in the end he would win.

The city still was buzzing over his sudden death when two developments came in rapid-fire succession. The first was a decision by the federal court. It declared the marriage contract to be a forgery.

Two weeks later Sarah Hill, chagrined and disappointed, married her lawyer, Terry, who promptly announced that he and his bride were unwilling to accept defeat.

They appealed to the State Supreme Court which after much delay upheld the trial judge and the legality of the marriage. The federal court decision, however, remained against them and they appealed for reconsideration. What they no doubt did not know was that Justice Stephen J. Field of the United States Supreme Court would be given an interim assignment to decide the appeal along with two other jurists. Field had been a close friend of Senator Broderick, the victim of the duel with Terry.

When Justice Field, some time later, announced judgment against the Terrys they became enraged, created a scene in the crowded courtroom, and were sent to jail for contempt.

The last chapter in the prolonged struggle was written by the State Supreme Court which reversed itself and invalidated the marriage. The Sharon estate had won the final victory.

Today in San Francisco a short street bears the name of Sharon. In the absence of official records, his surviving relatives are quite certain that it was named for the former Senator and banker.

Hearst

Father of an
Empire Builder

George Hearst

WHEN GEORGE HEARST, a strapping awkward Missouri boy with little more than two years of schooling went to work in a lead mine near his father's plantation, he little dreamed that this experience would help him to accumulate millions in Nevada mining. Or that eventually he would win a seat in the United States Senate.

Despite his wealth and political power, Hearst is perhaps best remembered as the husband of an affable friendly philanthropist, Phoebe Apperson Hearst, and as the father of William Randolph Hearst who built the vast empire of newspapers, movie studios and radio stations.

Biographers are critical of the Senator himself, sparing no words in referring to his lack of education, his sloppy appearance and his total lack of manners. He chewed tobacco in the best of company and often paid no attention to the nearby cuspidor.

W. A. Swanberg, in his popular biography of William Randolph, makes the most generous comment on the father as a Senator. "No one would have called Uncle George a statesman," he writes, "but his unassuming kindness had won him warm friends."

Born in 1820, George Hearst as a boy divided his time between working with slaves on his father's properties in Franklin County, Missouri and in digging in the lead mine, a kind of labor that he fully enjoyed. He liked to mingle with seasoned miners. He asked them many questions and gained more knowledge of the earth's secrets in this way than he did from the few books that he was able to read.

He was 26 when his father died, leaving the plantation heavily encumbered. George, who was the eldest son, accepted his responsibilities and by hard work succeeded in supporting his mother, sister and a brother, while he gradually cleared all of the debts he had inherited.

Barely had the last debt been liquidated than news from California gave the young man's life new purpose. Gold had been discovered and with his rudimentary knowledge of mining he looked westward for his fortune.

A later year, in May, 1850, he joined a small party on the Overland Trail. On the way he was stricken with cholera in Wyoming and probably would have died but for unusual strength and vitality. Months later he arrived in California and went directly to the Mother Lode, where he began to hunt for nuggets and gold dust. Success eluded him though he moved from place to place, always hopeful that he would strike a rich vein.

Late in 1859 he was looking for still another location when news spread about a lucky find in Washoe County, Nevada. Hearst packed his pick and shovel, rolled up his blankets, and started off on his mule. On the way he met two friends. Together they had $450, just enough to buy a half interest in a new mine in Virginia City. They began to dig and soon struck a vein of silver, so rich that it started a march of prospectors to the area. Their mine, it developed, was the fabulous Comstock Lode. Hearst was on his way to millions.

Unlike many of those about him, he remained away from gambling halls, choosing to invest his profits in other properties that would increase his dividends. He bought a large interest in the Ophir Mine, which soon proved to be an even richer producer than his first. Flushed with money and success, he moved to San Francisco and continued to buy heavily into gold and silver mines.

Into his busy and prospering life there came a sudden interruption that was to end his bachelor days. A letter came telling of his mother's critical illness. Hearst hastened to her side, traveling on a steamer by way of Panama, and remained with her for a considerable time before her death.

During this time, he fell in love with an eighteen-year-old schoolteacher, Phoebe Apperson, whom he had known as a child. Despite the disparity in their ages — he had just reached his fortieth year — he proposed marriage and immediately faced the bitter opposition of her parents, well-to-do farmers on the Peramec River.

Never were two people more opposite to each other than Hearst and the girl he wooed. Phoebe was well-educated and spoke perfect English. She had gentle manners which went well with her daintiness. Hearst was a large heavy man, gruff and uncouth; yet he had handsome features.

He pursued his courtship for more than a year, painting glowing pictures of romantic life in the West. Finally Phoebe gave him the answer that he wanted. They eloped and were married in her native State.

They came West by steamer, settled in San Francisco, and took up temporary residence at the Lick House, later moving to the Stevenson House at California and Montgomery Streets. Less than a year later a son was born. They named him William Randolph. The three lived in a new brick home that Hearst had built on Rincon Hill, then the fashionable section of the town that housed less than 100,000 people.

While the young mother bestowed unusual care and protection on the child, putting his comforts far above her own, Hearst busied himself with his mining operations, frequently leaving home for trips into Nevada. Phoebe Hearst was a perfectionist and she was determined that her son should become the same. From early childhood his upbringing was directed to that end. No nurse or governess was too costly if she could aid in the child's advancement.

By now Hearst's properties were valued in the millions. He was constantly investing, selling at profit, and buying again. There was frequent litigation but even those opposing him admitted his extreme honesty. They said that he always kept his word. Some called him "one of God's noblemen."

When young William Randolph was ten years old, his father sustained serious reverses. Close to half a million had been lost in a single deal and George Hearst was being pressed by some of those from whom he had borrowed heavily. However, he kept his confidence and courage; his way of life did not change, not one of his many domestic servants was dismissed.

Seeking to recoup his losses, Hearst formed a business alliance with two wealthy men from Kentucky, Lloyd Tevis and James Haggin, who were eager to increase their fortunes. They knew nothing about mining, but guided by Hearst's knowledge and experience, they invested heavily. Again success came Hearst's way.

By this time, his wife had decided that their son's education demanded a trip abroad; it was an indulgence of all wealthy people of the day. She engaged a tutor and together they left early in 1873.

Their home-coming after little more than a year's absence, was a sad one. For the second time Hearst had suffered serious losses. The lavish home was sold, along with its horses and carriages. Mother and son went to board with friends. The father returned to the mines, confident that he could overcome adversity again.

His luck turned in 1875 when the Ontario Mine in Nevada, which Hearst had purchased with high expectations, suddenly began to yield new fortunes.

Nevada no longer demanded all of his attention. Boldly he looked to other areas — to South Dakota and New Mexico. In Pinos Altos, New Mexico three prospectors whom he had grubstaked uncovered one of the richest gold mines in the country's history.

Mother and son returned to Europe, for Phoebe believed that her young Willie would not receive the thorough education she believed he required in America.

In their absence, George Hearst — an ardent Democrat — began to dabble in politics. To further his ambitions for public life, he had contributed generously to *The Examiner* which had been losing money steadily. The idea came to him that if he owned the paper he might make it pay, and certainly its columns could be used to further his political hopes, which were now focused on a seat in the United States Senate.

He bought the paper and finally decided that the Governorship of the State would be a logical steppingstone to higher office. Aided by his own newspaper, he campaigned vigorously for the nomination in 1882, striking out against railroad monopoly as a popular cause. He was defeated by General George Stoneman, who was to become his good friend.

He then decided to focus his attention directly on the Senate. Again *The Examiner* took up his cause, devoting columns to his attacks on the Southern Pacific.

Meanwhile young William, now approaching manhood, was an unhappy student at Harvard. *The Examiner* intrigued him and he spent his time thinking of ways to improve it. At last he wrote his father, begging for a gift of the newspaper.

At first George Hearst laughed at the request, thinking that his son regarded the paper as a new toy. He did not relent until William was expelled from Harvard for a prank; then he wrote the young man to come West and try his hand. *The Examiner,* he believed, could not lose much more money that it had.

What young William Randolph Hearst did with *The Examiner* is newspaper history.

The year 1886 was the high point in George Hearst's varied career. In March an incumbent Senator had died and Governor Stoneman appointed Hearst to fill the vacancy. Elated, he hastened to Washington with his wife.

The unexpired term was brief but the new Senator ran for reelection and was successful. Some of his adversaries insisted that he had paid a good price for the plum — a price estimated at fully a million dollars. The victor was not embarrassed.

Late in 1890, now 69 years of age, he became ill and hurried to New York to consult his doctor who told him that while he was suffering from "a complication of diseases resulting from a serious derangement of the bowels," he had a good chance to recover.

He went back to Washington but his condition soon worsened. His wife and son were summoned. Near the end the dying man called William to his bedside to urge him, in whispers, to devote his life to useful constructive endeavors.

The Senator breathed his last on February 28, 1891. Both Houses of Congress eulogized him and among those at the funeral were President and Mrs. Harrison.

McLaren

Conqueror
of the
Sand Dunes

John McLaren

IN THE WOODSHED of a small farm in Stirling, Scotland, a boy sat on a box, day-dreaming. He was bored on this warm Spring morning, for he had nothing to do. His thoughts, wandering far, were suddenly interrupted by the sound of footsteps. He knew his father was approaching and that he would be reprimanded for idleness.

Moments later, Donald McLaren, a thrifty hard-working Scot, was eyeing his son reproachfully. "As fine a day as we've had this Spring," he said "an' here ye are, doin' exactly nothing."

"But Father, I really have nothing to do," the lad answered, groping hard for an excuse.

"Son," the other retorted, "if ye've nothing to do, go plant a tree and it'll grow while ye sleep."

Years later in California, half the world away from home, immigrant John McLaren took his father's advice literally — and on a scale that Donald McLaren could not have foreseen. For nearly 56 years, as Superintendent of San Francisco's world-famous Golden Gate Park, John McLaren planted 2,000,000 trees not only in the city but in many other parts of Northern California. He continued planting until his death in 1943 at the age of 96.

John McLaren is often called "The Edison of Golden Gate Park." He was responsible for the transformation of 1,017 acres of barren, desolate windswept sand dunes into what is recognized as the largest, most beautiful man-made park in the world, providing pleasure and recreation for millions of men, women and children the year round.

McLaren, though a young man, was already a master horticulturist when he left Scotland seeking better opportunities in California. He had been in charge of large estates in his native country but departed for the Far West with no thought that he would assume charge of San Francisco's now famous park.

However, on undertaking the job, he fully realized the tremendous obstacles to be overcome. He understood that most parks in large cities had the benefit of natural resources in ideal settings. In San Francisco, he knew he faced the problems of shifting sands, ocean winds and lack of water. City Hall politicians laughed at him and said he would simply be wasting public money. "How are you going to nail down those sand dunes?" they asked sarcastically.

"Just wait and see," he told them. "It can be done and I'll prove it."

To keep the vast expanse of sandy wastelands from shifting, McLaren began a series of experiments with native plants. Unsuccessful, he sent abroad for seeds and vegetation. At last he obtained from France the seeds of what is known as bent grass, used in many coast countries of Europe. He set the seeds out in nurseries and watched the young plants with almost fatherly care. Two years later they were taken out and planted closely together over the loose dunes where their unusual root growth held the sands together. McLaren had proved his critics wrong. He was now ready to haul in tons of soil and loam to cover the wide expanses of ground for cultivation and prove that flowers could be made to bloom in San Francisco in every season.

He sent to many countries for seeds: New Zealand, China, Japan, the Alps, Algeria, and Madagascar among others. All of these he made to grow. He planted Rhododendrons by the thousands and introduced many exotic plants. His gardeners often said that he knew almost to the minute when a plant would bloom. In a year he planted more than 700 trees that were new to California. It was his boast that in Golden Gate Park were trees from every country except Bolivia.

He accomplished all this in the face of bitter political opposition that would have thwarted a less determined man. In City Hall there were those who constantly accused him of extravagance; some even called his project "McLaren's great white elephant." But he worked on, ignoring criticism and brooking no interference that would mar the beauty of the park. "You tend to your politics; I'll mind my trees and flowers," he often told his opponents.

His severest test once came when a group of city officials insisted on plans to run a streetcar line across the Park to link two fast-growing residential sections. "You can't do that," the boss gardener protested. "You can't ruin the park with a trolley line."

The politicians laughed. "There is no cultivation where these cars will run," they countered.

"There certainly is," McLaren shot back. "Why don't you come out and see?"

A formal inspection was arranged. When the officials arrived two days later, they found the disputed area covered with blooming flower beds, shrubs and trees. The proposed car line was abandoned. What the inspection team did not know was that on the night before their visit, McLaren had assembled a crew of 200 gardeners and kept them working from darkness to early morning, hauling the plants and trees and setting them out to give the appearance that they had been there for months.

McLaren loved the Park and protected it as though it were his own. Until the time of his last short illness he arose habitually at five o'clock and was at work an hour later. A little man, sometimes described as "an over-sized elf," he was a strict disciplinarian and a perfectionist. He was blunt with his men, sometimes even gruff when his orders were disobeyed. Yet he was always fair and ready to explain his reasons for his directions. Sometimes a gardener, choosing to follow his own ideas, defiantly planted a tree or shrub at a spot other than that McLaren had designated. Usually the change was quickly detected. "Dig it up and plant it where I said," he would command.

Through his long career he never relaxed in his firm resolve to make Golden Gate Park a place of constantly increasing beauty. The proof of his achievement lies today in a wooded paradise extending nearly four miles, from the heart of a densely populated residential section to the shores of the Pacific. Within its borders are vast expanses of forests and glens, hillocks and glades, lakes and waterfalls, and great stretches of sprawling green lawns on which McLaren permitted no "Keep off the grass" signs. One writer has described the Park as "A recreational department store with something for everyone."

McLaren planned every foot of it, yet much has the appearance of being completely natural and untouched by man. He abhorred formal planting. It was not Nature's way, he said. He was meticulous in following natural patterns and always cautious not to outdo natural beauty. "Nature is beautiful enough," he often said.

Another of his many achievements, a work of years, was the building of an esplanade along the Pacific shoreline, the western boundary of the park. Many said it could not be done because a beach driveway, laid out years before, had proved to be a constant source of trouble. Heavy tides and winds were sweeping tons of sand along the road and moving it inland into the Park.

"You can't fight the sea," McLaren was told but he merely shook his head. "I can make the sea work for me," he answered.

First he laid thousands of lathes and tree boughs for miles along the water's edge, piling them higher and higher. When the job was finished nearly 20 years later, he had built an espalande 20 feet high, 300 yards wide, paralleling the Pacific shore for miles and covering 150 acres. The ocean and its shifting sands were conquered at last.

Time and age meant nothing to McLaren. When he had reached the age of 70 a friendly Mayor sent for "Uncle John," as he was affectionately called and pointed out regretfully that the City Charter would require his retirement. But McLaren protested that he still had much more to do and was capable of doing it. The result was an amendment to the Charter permitting him to retain his job. In addition, the Park Commissioners increased his salary.

On his 92nd birthday, 2,000 admiring citizens gathered at a testimonial dinner to honor him as the city's Number One citizen. Before the affair they asked him what he wanted as a gift. "Give me 10,000 yards of manure for my trees — that's all I need," he told them. He received the gift he had requested.

His death in 1943 threw his beloved city into mourning and tributes came from all parts of the nation. His epitaph was spoken by Mayor Angelo Rossi as he stood by the bier in City Hall, paying the community's final tribute to "Uncle John."

"He is gone," the Mayor said, "but the living plants and flowers will ever remind us of a life offered in the interests of giving our people the cultural delights which these beauties of Nature bring. Let us hope that, as he derived much of the spiritual from what he created, so will we, as the days roll on, approach to some degree at least the joys which men who live in the spirit and with beauty experience. As appropriate for him as for Sir Christopher Wren could be the inscription on the tablet to that great architect in St. Paul's Cathedral in London. It simply says: 'If you would see his monument — look about you.' "

And a grateful city paid him a final tribute — an avenue near Golden Gate Park was given his name.

Cameron
The Angel of Chinatown

Miss Donaldina Cameron

FOR MANY YEARS Miss Donaldina Cameron was known by two widely different names in San Francisco's Chinatown, depending on who spoke of her.

Owners of little slave girls, and others who trafficked in vice, called her Fahn Quai, "The White Devil."

To all law-abiding people in the Oriental quarter she was Lo Mo, "The Mother," for they knew of her dedication and fearlessness in rescuing young Chinese girls who had been smuggled into the United States, kept in hiding, and forced to become prostitutes.

No one knows how many were saved through Donaldina's relentless work as Superintendent of the Chinese Presbyterian Mission. She never counted. She was too busy following slender clues that led to a hidden child in a brothel, or in providing happy home life and Christian education for those she sheltered.

The lone woman crusader labored from year to year, often risking her life in a daring raid of an opium den or a brothel disguised as a modest private home.

She knew the ways of those who profited from unfortunate slave girls; how children were sold by parents or entrusted to deceitful strangers with promises of bright opportunities in a strange land across the ocean.

Once carefully secreted in dingy crowded tenements of Chinatown, these luckless children had but one hope of escape — to smuggle word to Donaldina Cameron, risking torture if they were caught, and to pray that she would come to save them.

Such escapes, she well knew, often led to bloody tong wars when the owner of a rescued girl suspected a rival tong of invoking Miss Cameron's intervention. Without warning, hired hatchetmen or highbinders went slinking through dark alleys or narrow streets heavily armed, hunting those on whose heads prices had been set. And rarely did they fail.

At such times Chinatown would be blockaded by the police. Some merchants would close their stores and Chinese leaders would exert their influence to keep other tongs from joining in, for such warfare was always costly in business as well as in human life.

Donaldina Cameron had learned the risks involved, yet when a child's freedom and future were at stake she never hesitated to respond to a smuggled message.

Such a note, typical of countless others, reached her at her mission home late one night. It came on a tiny scrap of paper that bore only an address. With it was half of a blue handkerchief, the only clue to the identity of a captive girl.

The slender blonde-haired woman read the note and knew she must act quickly, for the girl's owner might sense trouble and spirit her away. She called the police and they responded, equipped with sledge hammers and crowbars, necessary tools for such an errand.

With Miss Cameron in the lead, they hurried to a shabby two-story building in a filthy alley where they demanded admittance. There was no response and, when further demands went unheeded, the officers tried the front door and found it barred.

They shouted a final warning; then went to work with their sledges. Slowly the heavy door yielded and went crashing to the floor. The party entered, only to be confronted by a tiny child playing with a doll.

Donaldina Cameron knew this ruse; she had faced it many times before. As expected, a fat pale-faced Chinese came hurrying toward them, bowing with false graciousness, while he insisted that they had invaded a peaceful private home.

Brushing him aside, the woman started up a narrow rickety stairway, calling to the police to follow. Moments later they were in a dark, unfurnished room.

Now Miss Cameron's experienced fingers groped about the walls, hunting unsuccessfully for a loosened panel. "Guess we've got the wrong address," one of the officers suggested, ready to leave.

The woman shook her head. "Not so soon," she answered. "I've only begun to look."

On her knees she began to examine the worn linoleum. With the help of the men she raised one corner of the floor covering, then a little more. Before them was a trap door, barely discernible in the dimly lighted room.

The policemen tried to lift it but it was securely fastened. Crowbars came into play, the door was raised, and there, huddled in a narrow tight compartment between the floor and the ceiling below, were two forms — a girl of 12 and an old woman, acting as her guard. The child, with a dazed look, held up her half of the torn handkerchief, her only means of identification.

Half an hour later the rescued child was being bathed and fed in the warm atmosphere of the mission while the woman and the Chinese who had guarded his "home" so cautiously were in jail. Donaldina Cameron had saved another life from degradation.

Through the years she encountered many obstacles in addition to barred doors and protesting brothel keepers. There were lawyers to defend those who had bought slave girls and seemingly endless immigration red tape to untangle. Damage suits were filed but Miss Cameron had dedicated her life to humane service and was never dismayed. She knew that with the strong support of the devoted board of the mission and the cooperation of the authorities she would win, in spite of all the barriers that could be thrown in her way.

She had entered upon this unique career as an unsophisticated, pampered young woman in her twenties. Within her was strong sympathy for the oppressed and a firm belief that all people were God's children regardless of their race.

She was born in New Zealand on July 28, 1869, the youngest of six children in a family originally from Scotland, where her industrious father had suffered financial reverses.

She was only two when the family arrived in San Francisco. There, from a hotel window overlooking the crowded Oriental quarter, she watched Chinese men, women and children hurrying about. It was her first sight of Orientals. A short time later the family settled in the warm San Joaquin Valley. Dolly, as she was affectionately called, first learned of human bondage as a young woman, scarcely older than some of the slave girls she would later help. A friendly visitor, Mrs. L. P. Browne, spoke of a courageous woman named Margaret Culbertson, who headed a mission in San Francisco and devoted herself to rescuing Chinese slave girls and rehabilitating them. Young Dolly, deeply concerned, asked many questions every time her friend returned. She learned that of more than 60,000 Chinese then in California, fully half were crowded into nine blocks of San Francisco's Chinatown.

In cellars and attics of the congested area, Mrs. Browne explained, lived the imprisoned little slaves. They were bought in China for little more than $100 and sent to America in steerage where they were met by unscrupulous procurers who posed as doting fathers waiting for their children.

Shocked by such lurid details, Dolly asked anxiously how such an inhuman practice had started. She was told that the first Chinese entering California in numbers had come as contract laborers, their fares paid by the railroads which had no interest in transporting the wives of imported workers. Then, in 1862, Congress enacted the rigid Chinese Exclusion

Act barring practically all men and women. Under such circumstances, Mrs. Browne said, it was understandable that an illegal traffic in women should result.

"How do these unfortunate girls find out about the Mission?" Dolly inquired curiously, "and how do they make themselves known?"

Mrs. Browne answered that there were many good people in Chinatown who secretly helped in the work of the Mission; people who had devised ways of getting word to and from the hidden girls.

Dolly was fascinated by what she heard and one day Mrs. Browne dared to ask a question: "Would you care to help Miss Culbertson? She needs assistance badly."

The suggestion brought enthusiastic response but when the young woman sought the approval of her father and her sisters, the idea shocked them, Dolly pleaded, begging for a chance to spend her time in a useful way.

"For just one year, then," they finally agreed, and Dolly who had known only comfort and protection, started for San Francisco.

Soon after this first year had passed, Miss Culbertson became ill and left for what was intended to be a vacation. She died during this absence and there was only one person ready to succeed her.

Donaldina Cameron assumed full charge of the Mission which had been established for some years in a tall red-brick building at 920 Sacramento Street in the heart of Chinatown. It had become far more than a haven for rescued girls. Often, young mothers and other needy young women were comfortably housed there and taught the principles of practical housekeeping.

As the years slipped by Miss Cameron became a powerful force not only in the city but throughout the State. And she wielded influence wherever she went.

Once she was obliged to fight a stubborn Legislature for a new law that would give her temporary custody of rescued girls until the courts could determine their legal status. A similar measure had been vetoed by the Governor a year before; strong influences were at work to balk her.

But she had learned as much about politics as she knew about the ways of Chinese slavers. She pressed hard for the necessary statute and it was passed. There were many other victories of similar nature.

In 1937 Donaldina Cameron, now white haired and worn, retired. Her one-year tenure had lengthened into 42 years.

She moved to Palo Alto where she lived until her death on January 4, 1968.

Yorke

The
Crusader-Priest

Father Peter C. Yorke

THE PHENOMENON OF the labor priest may seem new. But over a half-century ago a fiery and dedicated priest, Father Peter C. Yorke, was the moving force behind one of San Francisco's bitterest and most bloody labor conflicts: the teamster-waterfront strike of 1901.

Then 37 years of age, Father Yorke battled the powerful employers organization, attacked the police and other city authorities for protecting strikebreakers, and turned adverse public opinion in favor of the workers. He finally brought about a settlement through persistent negotiations that ended with full recognition of the unionists' right to organize and to bargain.

Long before the strike, tensions had been mounting between the city's unions and the influential Employers' Association, whose desire to break the back of organized labor was common knowledge. No doubt management realized even then that San Francisco was potentially one of the strongest "Union towns" in the nation.

Antagonisms reached a sudden climax early in 1901 as leaders of the Epworth League convened in San Francisco. The contract for handling their baggage was given to a non-union firm, which soon found itself unable to fulfill its obligations. Though new arrangements were made with a drayage firm that recognized organized labor, the union leaders were furious when they learned that the initial negotiations had been made for non-union workers. With tensions as they were, even such an issue was enough to bring matters to a boiling point.

Union members now refused to touch the luggage; they were locked out and strike-breakers were hired as quickly as they could be recruited. Labor leaders first considered calling a general strike. But, instead, the City-Front Federation decided that all of its members should refuse to work the busy docks. 20,000 workers left their jobs and the waterfront soon faced complete paralysis. Before long fourteen unions were on strike.

Almost at once it became obvious that the police were supporting Big Business and the City Establishment. Uniformed officers rode on the trucks beside strike-breaking teamsters and when clashes occurred the union men were the losers. Bitter and bloody street fights were a daily occurrence.

In the face of this fast-worsening situation, two of the teamster leaders, Michael Casey and Andrew Furuseth, looked about for a fearless champion to uphold their cause and negotiate in their behalf. They soon thought of Father Yorke, who had achieved a position of high respect and influence not only in San Francisco but throughout the state.

A native of Ireland, ordained by Cardinal Gibbons in 1887, he already had distinguished himself in a number of ways. He had been instrumental in organizing the League of the Cross, a temperance organization then enjoying great popularity in San Francisco. Even more significantly, he had succeeded against powerful odds in breaking the back of the viciously anti-Catholic American Protective Association, better known as the APA, in 1894. At this time he was functioning as the Chancellor of the San Francisco Archdiocese and as head of *The Monitor,* the official archdioecesan publication.

Furuseth and Casey called on the crusading priest and asked him to be their spokesman. It was not an easy decision for Father Yorke to make.

As he sat alone at his desk, he reviewed the situation from every viewpoint. Neither wages nor hours were a factor in the controversy. But it did not take him long to realize that a principle of far greater importance was at stake: the right of workers to organize for their own benefit and to bargain collectively.

Soon, the words of a papal encyclical of Pope Leo XIII — Rerum Novarum — upholding the right of all working men to organize for their own betterment ran through his mind. Here, he understood, was a directive from the Supreme Pontiff. It gave him the answer he was seeking but still he desired the counsel of his friends. They assured him that if he followed the dictates of his conscience he was certain to receive the support of the Vatican.

With the relentless energy that had marked his earlier campaigns, Father Yorke threw himself into the bitter struggle. By this time much of the city's business was at a standstill.

His chief weapons were his gift of oratory and his pen. Only a week after the strike began, he appeared with civic leaders and clergymen of other faiths at a mass meeting called by the strikers. Before long he was recognized as the dominant figure of the gathering. "A strike is war," he asserted, speaking with characteristic vigor, "While you desire peace you cannot afford to accept any peace but peace with honor!"

Tumultuous applause interrupted him. "It is a crying shame," he went on, "that while you have been orderly and shooting has been done only by those taking your places, the police force, paid with your taxes, has been turned into the guardian angels of the draymen. If the government of this city, when the strike began, had stood for even justice between employer and employee, you would be back to work by now."

In similar tone and sometimes even harsher, he appeared at other meetings of the strikers, assuring them that their cause was right and admonishing them to stand firmly united.

Encouraging the working men, however, was not the most difficult of his problems. More vexatious was his attempt to swing public opinion from the employers. The city's newspapers were divided. Hearst's *Examiner* supported the strikers and Father Yorke enjoyed the publisher's friendship and confidence.

In daily columns and in letters to the editor, the determined priest refuted what he regarded as false and misleading claims put forth by the opposition, as well as personal attacks.

Fearlessly, he excoriated the police chief, repeatedly charging that the city's uniformed officers had official backing for brutality against the strikers. And he vigorously denied police accusations that his campaign was responsible for the rioting.

His accusations fell on deaf ears. As bloody clashes continued Father Yorke in an open letter to the public called on Mayor James D. Phelan to remove George Newhall, a prominent figure in the Chamber of Commerce, from the presidency of the Police Commission. His plea was ignored and in many quarters the strikers continued to be blamed for disorders.

To counter such accusations, the priest called on the workers for scrupulous obedience of the law and, as a further step, he organized a waterfront patrol to see that order was kept.

As Father Yorke pressed for negotiations between the warring factions, the California Board of Trade called on Governor Henry T. Gage to order the state militia into San Francisco. The Governor, who once had publicly recognized the help of Father Yorke in bringing about his election, flatly refused. The strikers were jubilant.

Still the strike dragged on. Finally a sudden and wholly unexpected complication developed — dissension in the union ranks. Some strikers, discourged by what Father Yorke called the employers' "divide and conquer startegy," were suggesting that they give up and return to work.

The news reached the priest as he lay ill in bed, exhausted by his efforts to restore peace. Ignoring his health, he jumped out of bed and dictated a plea to the men. "Don't give up now," he urged. "You are standing on a gold mine and you don't know it." He went on to charge that the employers were spreading lies and that a bribery charge against a leading unionist had been framed deliberately.

Gradually Father Yorke's public messages were making their impact and public opinion was swinging away from management. Meanwhile he waited for a propitious time for a make-or-break move he had been contemplating.

Close to two months after the strike had started, he appealed to his good friend Governor Gage to intervene and use the influence of his office to bring about a settlement. Hopeful that Gage would consent, the cleric already had encouraged the unions to formulate peace terms.

Governor Gage, however, was skeptical as to the wisdom of intervention. First he came to San Francisco and discussed the problem with Father Yorke, questioning whether martial law was really necessary. "The men already are behind you," the priest told the Governor. "You won them over when you first declined to call out the militia. I'm sure you can bring both sides together."

Now ready to accede, Governor Gage hastened to the Palace Hotel and summoned leaders of the three opposing factions to his suite — the Brotherhood of Teamsters, the City-Front Federation and the Employers' Association.

Facing them a short time later, the Governor minced no words. "Arbitrate or you'll have martial law," he said firmly. "That's my ultimatum."

An hour later an aide sent out a hurried call to the newspapers. "The strike is over," Governor Gage announced.

Working men had won the right to organize and to bargain through their unions. Father Yorke's practical application of the Papal encyclical had achieved a victory.

This, of course, was only one chapter in the colorful and dedicated life of Father Yorke during which he fought relentlessly for social justice.

In 1903 he moved to Oakland to become the pastor of St. Anthony's Parish, a position he held until 1911 when he returned to San Francisco as pastor of St. Peter's Parish. He was still in this post when he died in 1925.

Some time later it was decided to name a street in his honor.

Appropriately it lies close to the site of old St. Mary's Cathedral which was destroyed by fire and to the magnificent new edifice that now takes its place.

General Frederick Funston

Funston

The Hero of
The Earthquake

SAN FRANCISCANS WHO experienced the earthquake and fire of April 18, 1906 never forgot the invaluable services rendered to the stricken city by Brigadier General Frederick Funston, for whom a busy avenue in the Richmond District is named.

As acting commander of the Army's Pacific Division, the popular Funston assumed full responsibility for maintaining order through one of the most difficult situations ever faced by an American community.

Only hours after the temblor, while devastating flames were spreading fast in many districts, Funston had received a hurried call from the city's Mayor, Eugene E. Schmitz, asking for an immediate meeting.

"We need the Army's help to maintain order," the Mayor said. "Can we depend on you?"

General Funston went into immediate action. First he called Colonel Charles Morris, the Presidio Commander, directing him to report at once with his entire artillery command at Portsmouth Square. Companies of Army Engineers were summoned from Fort Mason, and later the Twenty-second Infantry from Fort McDowell.

Soldiers, with rifles and fixed bayonets, were dispatched through various districts with strict instructions to keep order in the burning city that appeared completely doomed. Funston, cooperating with civil authorities, kept a close eye on the disaster, as calls for help came from one quarter and then another.

For days his men guarded against looting and other lawlessness. Engineers directed the dynamiting of buildings in a desperate attempt to halt the spread of flames, while others joined with Red Cross and other workers to render relief to the homeless and the sick.

During this critical situation the General issued many proclamations to the people and orders to his forces. He demanded strict obedience but his directives at all times were tempered with cool judgment and understanding. Once, less than a week after the earthquake when much of the city was in ruins, there came complaints from a few intolerant people protesting that soldiers had ordered them to clear away rubble to make a way for ambulances and police patrols.

Despite his annoyance, Funston took the messages with amazing coolness. He simply issued a directive to all men in uniform to carry out their orders but not to abuse their authority. There were no further complaints.

When the work was over and people began to think of rebuilding the devastated areas, newspapers and public officials were loud in their praise of General Funston. "The smallest man did the biggest and most important job in saving the city from total annihilation," said one writer, and others expressed their sentiments in similar vein. Years later this was written in an editorial on an anniversary of the disaster:

"The amount of life and property that Funston's regulars preserved is impossible to ascertain but had it not been for General Funston's quick and decisive action on the day of the quake and those following our memories today would be more unpleasant than they are."

Funston's brilliant services to San Francisco, however, were but a chapter in an outstanding military career that took him to the Philippines, the Hawaiian Islands and into Mexico.

Before joining the Army he had followed a number of widely different callings. Born in New Carlisle, Ohio on November 9, 1865, he moved westward with his parents at an early age. They settled in Kansas where he studied at the State University, earning his way by working during vacations, sometimes as a railroad conductor and at others as a newspaper reporter.

In 1891 he obtained employment with the Department of Agriculture as a botanist. He had taken courses in this subject at the University, with the thought of perhaps making this his life's work. In that capacity he was assigned first to an expedition into Death Valley. Two years later he was sent to Alaska to report on flora. The commissions, at times, led to dangers, as on one occasion when he was obliged to travel down the Yukon alone in an open boat.

His career changed suddenly in 1896 when the government sent out a call for volunteers to serve in Cuba during tense times that preceded the Spanish-American War. Funston was commissioned a Lieutenant-Colonel, then promoted to full Colonel when the war began and he was dispatched to the Philippines with the Twentieth Kansas Regiment.

Before his return home, some years later, he had distinguished himself in a number of ways. He was awarded the Congressional Medal of Honor for his "exemplary conduct" in the Battle of Calumpit in 1899 during the Philippine Insurrection and advanced to the rank of Brigadier-

General of volunteers.

Sometime later he won widespread recognition by the capture of the insurgent leader, Emilio Aguinaldo, whom he had cleverly trailed to a closely guarded camp. As a reward he was promoted to the same rank in the Regular Army.

In this capacity he came to San Francisco as Commander of the Department of California, a post he held together with his responsibilities as acting Pacific Division Commander at the time of the disaster.

In 1914 he was dispatched to lead a force to Vera Cruz. Funston became the city's Military Governor, performing his duties in so humane and efficient a way that he was commissioned a Major General.

In 1916 he was put in command of forces on the troublesome Mexican border and in the same year he organized a punitive expedition sent into Mexico in pursuit of Pancho Villa.

General Funston died in San Antonio, Texas on February 13, 1917. Two years before he had published his "Memoirs of Two Wars," a book relating many of his varied military experiences.

Rolph

"The People's
Mayor"

James Rolph, Jr.

THEY CALLED HIM "Sunny Jim."

It was a sobriquet that fitted perfectly the personality, character and temperament of James Rolph Jr., who served as Mayor of San Francisco for nineteen consecutive years before becoming Governor of California.

The name also reflected the spirit of the city at the time. The flamboyance of the early days had passed but there remained a friendly way of life in what was known as "the Paris of America."

Rolph was a handsome man, bald and of splendid physique. A native San Franciscan, he was raised and educated in the city with which his life was closely interwoven. He probably knew more people and their personal affairs than any other person in San Francisco.

It was an everyday occurrence for the Mayor to stop his car beside a streetsweeper to inquire "how's your uncle's rheumatism" or to hail a newsboy to ask about his mother's health. He had a pleasant smile and a ready handshake for everyone. He was referred to as "a gregarious optimist."

Born August 23, 1869, he attended city schools and received his diploma from Trinity Academy in 1888. Weeks later he found his first job. He became a messenger boy for the shipping and commission firm of DeWitt, Kittle & Company and advanced rapidly.

The turn of the century marked a significant change in his career. Then 31, he married Annie Marshall Reid. Shortly afterward, he accepted an invitation to join his old friend, George U. Hind, in a shipping concern that took the name of Hind, Rolph & Co. The new venture launched Rolph into an important place in the city's shipping and financial life.

Three years later he became a founder of the Mission Bank and its president.

He was heavily involved in his new ventures when much of San Francisco was destroyed in the great earthquake and fire of April 18, 1906. Thousands were left homeless. People camped in city parks, and many found refuge in public squares in Rolph's home district, the Mission. It was then that he grasped the opportunity to help those in want. He organized the Mission Relief Committee which later grew into the influential Mission Promotion Association, with Rolph as president.

When business began to return to normal months after the disaster, Rolph found chances to further expand his interests. Three new firms — Rolph Navigation and Coal Company, the Rolph Shipbuilding Company, and the James Rolph Company were established.

Then, with World War I came a crying need for ships. Again Rolph saw an opportunity, not only for himself but to meet a national emergency. Sensing the value of wooden ships that could be built quickly and economically, he established a shipyard on Humboldt Bay. Soon wooden vessels were coming off the ways with amazing speed. However, the venture floundered at the end of the war when the market collapsed and Rolph was left with a personal loss of more than $3,000,000. It took him until 1927 to recoup his fortune. Meanwhile, however, he continued to advance rapidly in the city's business and civic life. He became president of the Merchants Exchange, the Chamber of Commerce, and the Shipowners Association of the Pacific.

Rolph's political career started in 1911 when the people were looking for a new mayor who would represent all interests; they were tired of the labor administration of the incumbent, P. H. McCarthy, a strong unionist. Rolph was the man they nominated. He accepted with some reluctance and easily defeated McCarthy.

He ran for reelection not once but four times, on each occasion emerging victorious by a heavy majority. He ran the city with efficiency and there were no hints of graft or corruption.

When he finally neared the completion of his nineteenth consecutive year in the Mayor's chair, he looked about and saw the realization of many dreams. A new City Hall and a civic auditorium had been completed, an expansive Civic Center had been planned; he had established the first municipally-owned streetcar system in the country and a city-operated water department to take the place of a private corporation. More than that, two tunnels had been completed to expedite public transportation and much needed street paving had been done.

Before that time, in 1918, Rolph's eyes had turned to higher horizons. He aspired to become Governor. Under a peculiar cross-filing system then in vogue, Rolph declared himself a candidate for both the Republican and Democratic nominations. Ironically, he won on the Democratic ticket but lost the nomination of his own party which disqualified him from the final election, since state law then required that a cross-filing candidate win the nomination of his own party. Thus defeated, Rolph turned again to vigorous work in City Hall but his political ambition was not stilled.

He waited twelve years before trying for the governorship again. This time he threw himself into a state-wide campaign on a scale never undertaken before. In characteristic style, he chartered an airplane, an innovation in California politics, and covered more than 28,000 miles before election day.

This time Rolph's warm personality and splendid record raised him to the highest office in the State. He took the oath of office on January 6, 1931 and delivered a ringing Inaugural Address in which he pleaded for harmony to meet the needs of California. From the start he declared himself firmly against increased taxes and pledged greater government aid to the farmers.

This was in what many have since referred to as his "honeymoon year" for thereafter he found himself in many bitter clashes with the Legislature — and in many he emerged the loser. Gradually political observers noted a decline in Rolph's popularity but the Governor was not perturbed. He continued to go about with his usual smile and appeared to be as carefree as ever. Rolph was a good actor but inwardly he felt the sting of public criticism and he was not accustomed to it.

In December, 1933 an unexpected and unfortunate blot marked his spotless political career. The trouble started in San Jose where the popular young son of one of the city's prominent merchants had been kidnapped and ruthlessly murdered.

Brooke Hart's disappearance was a mystery until his body, bound and heavily weighted, was taken from the Bay. Soon after two young men, Thurmond and Holmes, were arrested for the crime. The evidence against them was overwhelming.

Indignation was running high and threats of lynching were heard in many places. For a time the city authorities were confident they could protect the prisoners but the temper of the people — or at least of some of them — became alarming.

Fearing that they might be unable to hold their prisoners, San Jose officials appealed to Governor Rolph to call out the state militia. His reply was a flat refusal. The situation worsened rapidly.

A day later, on a Sunday, an angry mob gathered, marched to the jail and demanded Holmes and Thurmond. The sheriff and his men, forewarned, stood their ground courageously, pleading with the crowd to let the law takes its course. Their pleas were jeered.

Soon angry men appeared with a battering ram. The jail doors gave way and the two cringing prisoners were dragged from their cells and taken to St. James Square in the center of the "Garden City."

Ropes were quickly tightened about their necks, tossed over the limbs of trees, and moments later the two bodies dangled in midair. Mob violence had taken the place of justice.

Repercussion came at once. Many in San Jose and throughout the state decried the act and blamed the Governor for his refusal to heed the call for troops.

Rolph, however, not only justified his stand but praised the mob. The issue quickly assumed nationwide proportions. Newspapers throughout the country took the Governor seriously to task and one of them dubbed him Governor Lynch. "The Nation" quoted him:

"Why should I provide troops to protect those two fellows? The people make the laws, don't they? When they have confidence that troops will not mow them down, they will protect themselves against kidnappers and there is liable to be swifter justice and fewer kidnappings. Hangings provide a good lesson for the country."

Rolph continued to support his position, even promising to pardon anyone arrested for the lynching. He suffered badly from the publicity and some supporters turned against him. It was a hard blow to a man who had been a favorite and whose judgment had once been unquestioned. Those who knew him best realized the extent of his emotional hurt.

On February 28, 1934 he collapsed in Marysville in Northern California while conducting government business. He was rushed to San Francisco and a few days later his physicians allowed him to be moved to his Santa Clara ranch to recuperate.

He recovered quickly and weeks later returned to his office in the San Francisco City Hall. But he was not the same jovial man.

On May third he collapsed again and on his recovery announced that he would retire at the end of his term.

A month later, on June second, he suffered a heart attack and died at the age of 65.

His funeral was the largest ever held in California for a public official. Men and women from every section of the State gathered to pay him homage. Forgotten for the moment were the schisms in political factions and the ill-spoken words about the kidnapping. "Sunny Jim" was gone and his career was to remain a legend in the city of his birth, the city that he loved so dearly and served so long.

O'Shaughnessy
The Master Builder

Michael Maurice O'Shaughnessy

ONE APRIL MORNING in 1885, a 21-year-old engineer, tall and powerfully built, landed in San Francisco from his native Ireland. He dropped his only suitcase in a cheap lodging house and with the confidence of youth started out to find a job.

An hour later he stood before the manager of a large construction company. "My name's O'Shaughnessy," he said. "I have a degree in engineering from the Royal University of Dublin and I want to go to work."

The other shook his head. "Son, you'd better look for some other kind of a job," he said bluntly. "There are too many engineers in California already."

Surprised but not dismayed, the newcomer tried several other firms, only to receive the same response.

On that disappointing day in April, Michael Maurice O'Shaughnessy determined that while there might be too many engineers in California, there must be opportunities for a good one with imagination, skill and an eagerness to work. And he set out to prove it.

In the years that followed he built dams and aqueducts, bridges and railroads from one end of the Pacific Coast to the other, in Hawaii and in distant Eastern cities. His works have added to the comforts of millions of people; they have supplied water and electric power for industrial developments and for urban use. His whole career is an epic of achievements, many of them in the face of bitter political opposition and stubborn physical obstacles.

For 22 years he served as San Francisco's chief engineer, building tunnels and boulevards and a municipal street car system. Finally came his greatest triumph, the world-famous Hetch Hetchy water and power system costing more than $86,000,000; a project supplying San Francisco and its environs with fully 400-million gallons of water a day.

Jack London, one of O'Shaughnessy's closest friends, called him a "daring engineer who conquered gorges and jungles, and built enduringly in concrete and masonry."

He was born in Limerick on the banks of the Shannon in May 23, 1864. As a young man, his mind set on engineering, he studied first at Cork, then moved on to Galway and finally to Dublin's Royal University, now the National University of Ireland.

As soon as he earned his degree of bachelor of engineering, he headed directly for San Francisco. Unable to find work, he moved northward and soon landed his first job, as an assistant engineer for a small railroad. The pay was low but it met his modest needs and he was convinced that some day an opportunity would come in San Francisco.

Soon he was being hired for work that was more lucrative and important. For a time he was employed by the Southern Pacific; then he was chosen to lay out the picturesque town of Mill Valley, north of San Francisco, and to provide it with adequate water.

Other towns called for his services; they, too, needed planning, water and power facilities. Years slipped by and O'Shaughnessy's reputation as a skilled and imaginative engineering expert spread fast,

One day he received a call from owners of Hawaiian plantations who were facing a desperate need for adequate water. He sailed to the Islands to face a challenge that had baffled other engineers. For seven years he labored on one island after another, often hacking his way through jungles. He built 30 miles of tunnels, connected them with aqueducts and ditches, and revolutionized the sugar and pineapple industries. He constructed the famous Olokele aqueduct at Kaui, the Kojola on the island of Hawaii and the Koolau on Maui, where his friendship with London began.

The work was barely completed when he received shocking news from San Francisco — the earthquake and fire had devastated much of the city where he had so longed to work. Engineers were badly needed. He returned at once and was engaged to direct the restoration of public works. He designed a high-pressure water system with giant reservoirs in key positions against future conflagrations. And he assumed charge of various other projects designed to make the new city a better and safer place in which to live.

When this work was completed near the end of 1907, he responded to a call from the Southern California Mountain Water Company in San Diego to become its chief engineer, a position that he held for five years. He built the Dulzura Conduit, more than 13 miles in length, and 262-foot high Monero Rock Fill Dam, then the largest of its kind in the world. In recognition of his skill the American Society of Engineers awarded him the coveted James Lowry Prize. Some time later San Diego was swept by a destructive flood that inundated a large area with a heavy loss of life. Only the Monero Dam withstood the rush of torrential waters and saved the city from a water famine.

Appreciating what O'Shaughnessy had done, San Diego appointed him its consulting engineer to direct restoration and to construct two new dams to augment the Monero.

Important assignments followed. He used his skills in rectification work on the channel of the Salmas River, in constructing a dam on the Merced River, and in erecting a waterworks at Fort Costa, across the Bay from San Francisco.

By this time O'Shaughnessy, who was receiving preference over noted Eastern engineers, became anxious to settle down. He had married and his constant moves made home life impossible.

Fortunately he was sent for by the Mayor of San Francisco in August, 1912 and asked to accept appointment as city engineer. The offer meant the fulfillment of his dreams, though its annual salary, then $12,000, was only half of what he had earned the year before in private practice.

He established his growing family in a permanent home, rolled up his sleeves and undertook a long list of civic improvements that have left his name indelibly inscribed in the city's hall of fame. The Municipal Railway, then a fledgling project, was transformed into a model street car system with 68 miles of track. Over intensive opposition, he built the 12,000 foot Twin Peaks Tunnel that others said could not be done. Completed 11 months ahead of schedule, it opened up 4,000 acres of new home sites.

He constructed the Stockton Street tunnel, linking two important city areas. There are many other lasting examples of his skill in San Francisco — a main sewer system running under Golden Gate Park into the Pacific; the Ocean Beach esplanade, the Twin Peaks and Telegraph Hill boulevards, among others. The projects constructed during his tenure as city engineer cost more than $180-million altogether.

While all these public works were in progress, he found time to help other communities — including Detroit, Seattle, Tacoma and Portland, Oregon— with public utility problems.

All these accomplishments, vitally important as they are, were dwarfed by his fabulous achievement in constructing the Hetch Hetchy water and power system in Hetch Hetchy Valley in Yosemite National Park. It proved conclusively that the engineer from Ireland could do what other experts considered impossible.

For years San Francisco and her neighbors had faced the problem of an inadequate water supply. Various plans were studied and abandoned. One called for harnessing the Hetch Hetchy waters and it was this which O'Shaughnessy undertook.

He went into the High Sierra, explored the region, and returned convinced of the feasibility of the project. He reported that it would require a tremendous dam and the building of a railroad 68 miles long to carry men and supplies to the focal point of operations.

Opposition developed at once. Politicians insisted the cost would be prohibitive; conservationists said that it would ruin the natural beauty of the entire region. But O'Shaughnessy was obdurate, as he always was when he knew that he was in the right, and this time he had the support of the administration and of public-spirited citizens.

He went to Washington to lay his plans before the government and to seek official permission to use and drastically alter land belonging to one of the Nation's first national parks. Political skirmishing developed; almost an entire year was lost.

He later renewed his pleas in the Nation's capital and finally succeeded in bringing about the passage of the Raker Act which gave the city sanction to tap public lands.

That, however, was only the beginning. Highlighting his enormous engineering triumph were construction of a dam in Hetch Hetchy Valley at a height of 344 feet, making it one of the highest — if not the highest — in the world; another dam, somewhat similar at Lake Eleanor; a railroad; a power plant at Moccasin Creek with a transmission line 98 miles in length; a main aqueduct 137 miles long; and many miles of mountain tunneling.

It was a Herculean task, beset with countless obstacles, but he insisted that the engineering problems were relatively simple compared with the many complex political issues that pursued him throughout the undertaking.

A grateful city gave his name to the gigantic dam and long afterwards to a boulevard. At public ceremonies marking the dam's completion, conservationists who had opposed his plans viewed the graceful mass of steel and concrete as a thing of beauty in an awe-inspiring setting.

Completion of the entire enormous project was to be marked by a great civic celebration that would do just honor to the genius of Michael O'Shaughnessy. The date was set for October 28, 1934 but fate had other plans for O'Shaughnessy.

In the midst of preparations, he was stricken with a heart attack and died suddenly at his San Francisco home, just 16 days before the contemplated festivities.

The occasion, instead, was a day of mourning. The grieving city awarded Michael O'Shaughnessy a gold medal posthumously in recognition of all he had done for his adopted city.

Rossi
Posies and
Politics

Mayor Angelo J. Rossi

AT THE AGE of seven Angelo Rossi was mowing lawns to help support his family.

Forty-six years later he was Mayor of San Francisco, an office he was to hold for 14 years.

On his way up the ladder this kindly self-educated man held other public offices, winning advancement by his deep concern for public welfare. His door was always open and as Mayor he refused an unlisted telephone in his home, preferring to be called at any hour of the day or night by citizens with suggestions or complaints.

In private life he was one of the city's leading florists. Many years in the business gave him a deep, personal love for flowers. He regarded them as living things and could not bear to see them mishandled. It even annoyed him to see women wearing corsages with the stems turned upwards. "They didn't grow that way," he would say. "Why don't you wear them as nature made them?"

He was never without a white flower in his lapel and there was always a large bowl of blossoms on his desk at City Hall from which he would select a flower for every woman who called on him.

Whether in his home or at public meetings, he habitually touched the earth in potted plants to make certain that they had been properly watered.

Like his predecessor, James Rolph Jr., Angelo Rossi was a people's Mayor. He was an ardent supporter of municipal ownership of public utilities. With the interests of property owners foremost in his mind, he fought for low tax rates and usually got them.

Throughout his long life in politics, he refused to carry grudges. "Always look for the good in people," he often said. "Look hard and you'll find it." Frequently political opponents became his close friends.

Rossi was proud of his Italian ancestry. He traced his family back to 1180 in Italy, where many of his relatives had been mayors or prominent physicians. One of them had been a friend of a Pope and a great-grandfather had marched with the famous Garibaldi.

His father, also named Angelo, came to California in about 1845, leaving his native Genoa to escape from English raiders. He left behind his young sweetheart, a pretty girl named Madeline, promising to send for her as soon as he could support a wife.

Soon after his arrival in San Francisco, he opened a store on Market Street but when the Gold Rush offered better opportunity in the Mother Lode, he closed the place and moved to the little town of Volcano in Amador County. There Rossi's general merchandise store served the whole community.

As soon as business prospered he sent for Madeline and they were married in Stockton. They became the parents of six children. Angelo Joseph was the youngest, born January 22, 1878.

He had just turned seven when his father died, leaving his widow in a difficult situation. She had never become fluent in English, so she decided to move with her brood to San Francisco, hoping that life would be easier among the city's Italian community.

They all went to work and young Angelo, still in school, contributed his share by cutting lawns and doing other chores in his spare time. He was still in knee pants when circumstances forced him to leave the classroom but he did so with a firm determination to continue his education. He was always studying, fitting himself to meet problems that arose in private or public life. Economics, finance and business administration all received his serious attention.

When he was twelve, he found his first fulltime job as delivery boy for the Pelicano Floral Company, the largest in the city. He advanced rapidly, saved his money, and eventually became a partner. The firm took the name of Pelicano, Rossi & Co. and opened a new and larger store on Kearny Street. Years later he bought out his partner and the store, one of the two largest florists in the city, changed its name to the Angelo Rossi Floral Company.

In spite of increasing business responsibilities, he became actively interested in civic and fraternal affairs. He was proud of his California birth and took a leading part in the activities of the Native Sons of the Golden West. He rose to high office in the organization and frequently served as marshal of the colorful parades with which members celebrated the State's Admission Day.

He also played an important role in business organizations, especially the powerful Downtown Association, of which he was president for years.

While all of these activities would be enough for any man, Rossi also faced unusual responsibilities at home. His eldest daughter, Eleanor, stricken with polio as a child, was a helpless invalid. The two high points of her day were in the morning when her father tenderly carried her to a front window chair and at night when he lifted her back to bed. For the devoted father it became a habit with which neither business nor civic duties were allowed to interfere. On Sundays he drove her through Golden Gate Park in his carriage and later in the family automobile. And once when Eleanor sadly complained that she would be unable to view the Admission Day procession her father was to lead, he changed the line of march to pass their home on Union Street so she could watch from an upstairs window.

Today his daughter, long since fully recovered, follows in her father's footsteps. Now Mrs. Eleanor Rossi Crabtree, she is an energetic leader in a diversity of communal affairs, a member of more boards than she can count.

Rossi's first taste of public life came in 1914 when his close friend, then Mayor Rolph, appointed him to the city's Playground Commission. Seven years later he was selected as a candidate for the Board of Supervisors on a ticket sponsored by prominent downtown business men and was successful.

Elated over victory, he confided his policies to his daughter and voiced a secret ambition that he shared only with his family. "Do you think I could ever become Mayor?" he asked her anxiously.

"You can be anything you want to be," she answered, pressing his hand.

But four years later, Rossi suffered bitter disappointment. A candidate for reelection, he was defeated largely because of an unpopular stand on a controversial issue — a stand which time later proved correct.

He ran again in 1929 and received the highest vote, which made him President of the Board. "Now I've been vindicated," he said to Eleanor, never dreaming that his highest goal now was within his reach.

Some time later Mayor Rolph left City Hall to become Governor of California. On Rolph's recommendation, Rossi was chosen to be Mayor by the Supervisors. He was elected for his first full term in 1931, again four years later, and reelected for a third term in 1939.

These were busy times as he devoted all of his energies to the improvement of the city. The spacious Civic Center, planned and begun during the Rolph regime, was completed. There were many other constructive programs and Rossi prided himself in reducing the tax rate to its lowest in 25 years.

He tried for a fourth term in 1943 but opposing political forces had aligned against him and he was defeated. It was a loss that he took seriously to heart and from which he never fully recovered.

He became seriously ill the day after the election and was confined to his bed at Franklin Hospital for months. He was finally allowed to return home but his health declined steadily and he was never able to resume his old way of life. The business was sold and he lived quietly until he passed away on April 5, 1948. His widow died five years later.

The city that he loved so well honored him in death. Public officials and citizens in every walk of life gathered at his funeral to pay their final tribute. As a further honor a statue of the former Mayor was unveiled in the rotunda of City Hall.

Cleary

The City's Trouble Shooter

Alfred John Cleary

AT NOON ON February 18, 1941 Mayor Angelo J. Rossi stood in the rotunda of San Francisco's City Hall beside the bier of his close friend and long-time associate, Alfred John Cleary, the city's chief administrative officer, whose sudden death at 56 had shocked the community.

Surrounded by sad-faced men and women from all walks of life, the Mayor, speaking with obvious emotion, praised the departed for his many achievements in public life, his devotion to duty, and his unfaltering assistance to everyone who came to him for help.

"His works among men will be eternal monuments to his memory," Rossi said: "He was honesty personified; he was loyalty itself. We shall remember him as one who placed before any personal advancement the well-being of this city he so deeply loved."

The service ended the brilliant career of a native San Franciscan who loved his city and in many ways typified its spirit. By profession an engineer, he found a thrill and a challenge in every project he undertook. His friends were legion; they revered and respected him for his sincerity and integrity.

Born in the Mission District, he spent most of his life in San Francisco. From grade schools he went to St. Ignatius College which granted him a Bachelor of Arts degree, and then to the College of Engineering of the University of California, graduating as a Bachelor of Science.

One of his first professional assignments took him into the sandswept wastes of Death Valley. Then he built oil pipe lines for a private company, finally being engaged by the city's Department of Engineering, first as an assistant city engineer and later as chief assistant to City Engineer M. M. O'Shaughnessy. In this capacity he played an important role in the construction of the Hetch Hetchy water project. He concerned himself, also, in the study of plans for construction of the San Francisco Bay Bridge. Engineers had diverse ideas for the mammoth project.

Cleary's proposed route was finally adopted.

Ten years later, with his responsibilities fulfilled, he resigned to become chief engineer for the Construction Company of North America, supervising the boring of an eighteen mile tunnel through which Hetch Hetchy water was brought to San Francisco. From this work, continuing over three years, he gained many practical ideas on water and achieved a reputation as an expert in the field. He was called on to develop the widely-known $75,000,000 Mokelumne project carrying water to East Bay communities.

During this period Cleary won a long and difficult battle with the sea, evolving a way to prevent the incursion of salt water into the delta of the Sacramento and San Joaquin Rivers. His success was hailed as an unusual engineering feat effecting tremendous financial savings.

Then the State of California summoned him. From 1921 to 1929 he was its consulting engineer in development of water resources, his work involving the American River dam and hydro-electric project.

South America sent for him to direct a number of complicated mining undertakings. On their completion, he returned to San Francisco to become Mayor Rossi's executive secretary, a post that kept him at his desk from early morning until late hours long after City Hall had become deserted for the night. His work day usually lasted a full twelve hours. An eloquent speaker, he was often called on to represent the Mayor at important public functions. It was said that his remarks, usually short, went directly to the point without flourish or unnecessary flights of oratory, yet always appropriate to the situation. He was known as the Mayor's most effective trouble-shooter.

In January, 1932 a new City Chapter became effective, creating a new office — chief administrative officer with authority "to exercise supervision and control over all administrative departments . . . including health, public works, electricity, finance and records, real estate, welfare, tax collection, the coroner and the recorder."

Appointing the first man to fill an office with such involved and widespread duties was Mayor Rossi's responsibility. His first thought was of Cleary. Rossi hated to lose the services of his personal secretary but decided on a sacrifice for the city's good.

The appointment met with general approval and Cleary, facing new responsibilities, proved his capabilities from the start. It is said that his interpretation of the new office and its demands did much to shape the change in the form of government.

His success and popularity, however, did not come only from professional and administrative accomplishments. It was Cleary, the man, who won the public's heart. He loved people and enjoyed serving them in personal ways — and they gave him many opportunities to do so. Those who knew him say that he had more friends than any single City

Hall official before or after.

In his busy life there was little time for recreation but he did enjoy golf whenever time would permit and for years it kept him physically fit. He often met friends at Harding Park precisely at six o'clock in the morning. They would play nine holes after which Cleary would hurry away to his desk at City Hall.

Death came sudenly from a heart attack at his home on the night of February 16, 1941.

Next day his body was taken to City Hall to lie in state until the formal ceremonies and his funeral.

The city honored him posthumously some years later when a new residential area was developed in the Western Addition under the redevelopment program and a court there now perpetuates his name.

Ahern

The Man in Blue

Francis J. Ahern

SAN FRANCISCO'S POPULAR Chief of Police Francis J. Ahern won the unique distinction of being the only member of the department whose name was given to a street. Appropriately, Ahern Way, one block long, runs at a right angle to the Hall of Justice.

He was unusual in many ways, a man of driving force, dedicated to his work, tireless and scrupulously honest.

In pursuit of criminals or in search of a clue, hours and personal needs or comfort were entirely ignored. He would forget about meals when duty called and sleep was of no concern. But there was one exception — no matter where he was, at home or far away, he never missed early morning mass and communion, regardless of difficulties or personal inconvenience.

He gained national prominence in 1950 when he was loaned to the United States Senate Crime Investigating Committee at the request of its chairman, Senator Estes Kefauver. For six months he covered the country with his partner, Thomas Cahill, who succeeded him as chief, in an intensive investigation of crime syndicates, gangsters and the Mafia. Their sensational findings became the basis for the widely-known Kefauver Report.

From then on he was honored by appointments to other important posts in the city, state and country, recognition that he accepted with innate modesty.

In his 29 years in the Department, he denied himself many pleasures and recreation. Baseball was his only hobby but on rare occasions, when time and circumstances permitted, he would spend a free day or sometimes a week-end at his summer cabin at Felton in the Santa Cruz Mountains. There he would enjoy himself with carpenter's tools building fences or just tinkering. Idleness was something he could not endure.

He was never known to swear or curse despite the most aggravating circumstances. "He's a no good bum" was the worst he was ever heard to say of anyone.

Throughout his life he was known as Frank, though as the head of the Department he liked to be addressed as "Chief." He was of average build, muscular, with a kindly face that could express sternness when the occasion justified. His men respected him and though he set a hard example, they did their best to follow. He demanded hard work and honesty. For the most part he got them both from the force.

"He was honest from the day he was born," say those who knew him best. They recall his anger at the slightest suggestion of a bribe as on one occasion when he went with warrants to arrest a notorious abortionist, Inez Burns, and to search her home. Hidden under a rug he found $300,000 in crisp greenbacks, the obvious profits of her illegal operations.

"Take what you want of it; take it all," said Inez Burns. With an angry look, Ahern wrapped up the currency and saw that every dollar was accounted for when he left the bundle in the property clerk's office. He related the incident at her trial which ended in a long penitentiary sentence.

Ahern was born in San Francisco March 25, 1900 and he loved the city to the last. He was a studious boy. His spare time spent at baseball, the only sport that interested him. During all of his life he would follow the careers of professionals on the diamond, study their ratings and their performances.

After graduation from Polytechnic High School, he found his first job with the Southern Pacific Railroad as an investigator in the claims department and finally became the bureau's head. But Frank Ahern's ambitions were far from satisfied. He wanted to suppress crime and to see the lawless punished. What he really craved was more action.

He resigned to join the police force July 15, 1929 and after the usual period of beat patrolling, he was assigned to undercover work of various kinds, including vice. Soon his tirelessness and dynamic energy came to the chief's attention. A vice squad was created and Ahern became its head.

Later came appointment to the detective bureau where he advanced rapidly. Every case was a new challenge; he would spend hours at the scene of crime hunting for the smallest clues and he often unearthed them when others had failed. Through days and nights he would pursue those he wanted; time made no difference once he was on the trail. And for him no case was ever closed until it had been solved.

He frequently recognized criminals by sight. He became a one-man bureau of identification.

In 1948 he was appointed head of the Homicide Squad with the full rank of inspector. New units were added — the gangster, the narcotics and the racket squads. He assumed command of all of them as one assignment.

His work gave him a broad knowledge of criminology and related sciences but he craved more knowledge in his chosen calling. With the permission of his superiors he attended the National Academy of the Federal Bureau of Investigation and was not only graduated with honors but personally commended by J. Edgar Hoover.

He had been back on duty only a few months when the Police Commission received a call from Senator Kefauver who, with his colleagues, had become alarmed over the powerful crime syndicates that were operating with little interference.

"Lend us your two best men," the Senator asked. "The Crime Investigating Committee of the Senate wants to find out everything it can about the mobs, the gangsters and the Mafia."

Without hesitation, the authorities selected Ahern and his working partner, Cahill, for the job. The pair spent six months traveling about the country, probing deeply into the underworld, gathering every shred of available information. It was a gruelling, back-breaking assignment for these two men, both eager to justify the confidence that had been placed in them.

"I never saw a man work so hard," says Cahill of his partner. "Time and meals and sleep meant nothing to him. And I recall one stormy night in an eastern city. We were on the Kefauver assignment and it was later than two a.m. when we piled into bed after working since early dawn. But Frank was up and dressing at five; he wanted to go to early mass before we set out for the day."

They returned to San Francisco in April, 1951 and Ahern resumed his command of the Homicide Squad with its affiliated units. That year he was appointed by the Governor to serve the State as a member of the Alcoholic Rehabilitation Commission, to which he made valuable contributions while still continuing his police duties.

In January, 1956 George Christopher was the Mayor and with the Police Commission he felt the need for complete reorganization of the Department to increase its efficiency. He sent for Ahern.

"We've selected you to be the new Chief of Police," Christopher said. "What we want is a program that will elevate the San Francisco Police Department to a position of respect and efficiency that will make it the number one Department in the country. We think you're the man to do it. Go ahead."

Ahern accepted the challenge and took the oath of office on January 15, 1956. He knew his men, their capabilities and their weaknesses. He also knew the problems that confronted him. No time was lost in bringing about constructive changes. Men were shifted; the able ones assuming important posts; others were moved to duty in the "fog belt."

It was not long before Ahern and his innovations were attracting wide attention throughout the State and Nation.

Only months after his appointment he realized the need for closer cooperation between police in all large American cities, especially in the exchange of vital information necessary in crime detection. He discussed the matter with his friend, Captain James Hamilton of the Los Angeles Department, and through their efforts the Law Enforcement Intelligence Unit came into being, an organization with members now extending from coast to coast. Ahern was chosen to serve as chairman.

A year later when the Governor took notice of an increasing crime rate and the westward drift of eastern mobsters, Ahern was asked to serve on a newly-created body, the Governor's Law Enforcement Advisory Committee, to which the twelve largest metropolitan police departments in the United States and Canada were invited to send representatives.

There was still further recognition. In November, 1957 he was elected to the Board of Governors of the Federal Bureau of Investigation's National Academy Association in Washington, and to the chairmanship of the California Peace Officers Assocation and several important committees of the International Association of Chiefs of Police.

Law enforcement officers were coming to him from all parts of the country for advice while numbers of his innovative services were being emulated by departments in other large cities.

His career was at its height on the afternoon of September 1, 1958, a day when he was tired and worn from an unusually difficult case that had occupied his close attention for weeks. Associates, noting his drawn face, urged him to spend a few hours at the ball game, his only means of relaxation.

He was sitting in the bleachers in the old ball park at Sixteenth and Bryant Streets enjoying the game as he had so many times before, when he suddenly collapsed from a heart attack and died.

He was survived by his widow and two children, Bernardette and Francis.

He was borne to his final resting place with all of the honors a grieving community could bestow. The highest officials of the city were present.

Some time later it was noted that the short, narrow thoroughfare off Sixth Street leading to the Hall of Justice was unnamed and the suggestion that it be called Ahern was readily accepted. Each day it is traveled by many of the men who once were proud to serve Ahern and who have profited by his example.

Appendix

The 1909 Name Commission

Many San Francisco pioneers and other distinguished citizens who were overlooked in the early-day naming of streets received belated recognition through the work of an unusual commission of prominent men appointed in 1909 to recommend necessary changes in street nomenclature.

The task was considered essential for a number of reasons aside from the fact that so many worthy people had been excluded in the earlier selection of names. There were duplications that created serious confusion in the Post Office; designations by a single letter of the alphabet were considered undesirable; and many names were regarded as unsuitable.

The need for a study of these problems in depth with necessary recommendations had been discussed for some time before Mayor Edward Robeson Taylor appointed the official study group in 1909. Its report is of absorbing interest, not so much because of the extensive changes it recommended but rather for its fascinating use of language in defining what the commissioners considered the essential requirements for San Francisco street names.

Of the more than 400 changes recommended by the Commission, less than half were approved by the Board of Supervisors.

Chairing the Commission was Supervisor Charles A. Murdock. His associates were Supervisors Henry Payot and W. W. Sanderson; J. D. McGilvary Jr. of the Board of Public Works, R. W. Madden, the Post Office's superintendent of delivery; Zoeth S. Eldredge, noted historian; and Charles Sedgwick Aiken, editor of *Sunset* Magazine.

The Commission's report opens with this explanation:

"Assured by the postal authorities that not less than 500 letters daily go astray or are delayed in delivery through the chaotic conditions existing, the necessity of action in relief is forcibly impressed upon us; but bearing in mind disturbance and annoyance incident thereto, the presumption has been against change, and for all recommendations made there seems to be either absolute necessity or clear desirability. . . .

"The main cause of irregularity in mail delivery is the duplication in the use of names. For instance, we have a Virginia Street, a Virginia Avenue, a Virginia Place and a Virginia Court. The use of the same name for a street and an avenue is common. To remedy this inexcusable state of affairs, hundreds of changes are required. In determining which name to change in case of duplicates, we have taken the least important or the shortest — that the fewest residents may be affected.

"The word avenue has been greatly misused. It should be reserved for important streets or used for thoroughfares at right angles to streets. Some of our avenues are little more than alleys. . . ."

More than six printed pages of recommended name changes follow, after which the Commission set forth in the following paragraphs its concept of how street names should be selected:

"The first consideration in selecting a street name should be use. It should not be difficult to pronounce or spell, nor should it be very long. So far as possible, a name should be pleasant to the ear — musical in sound. Beyond that it should have significance. It should mean something or commemorate some character or event. The names of persons are the best street names, especially those of historic or patriotic significance. It is wholly fitting that men who have served their country well, or who have been local pioneers, or who have made their names conspicuously respected in a community, should have them perpetuated in the names of streets and made familiar to those who are to follow them. San Francisco began well, but as the city has extended good example lost its force, and the result is a great confusion and serious loss. Among the conspicuous mistakes are the use of the alphabet and the numeral.

"The use of the letters of the alphabet as names for streets is a cheap and indefensible expedient resorted to only when imagination is lacking. It is, in a way, conventional and easy but without meaning or beauty, and its only advantage can be secured by means that have none of its disadvantages. We have two sets of lettered streets in San Francisco — one in the western part of the city and one of the southern border, to which we add South. For both of these we recommend names, having the present street designation as an initial, preserving all the utility and giving names of significance and character. For the South, which will be a business district, we propose the names of men who have rendered public service or borne an honorable part in the business life of the city. They are short, and certainly no objection can be made to substituting them for the letters with which they begin."

Lengthy consideration then is given to the use of numerals for both streets and avenues, the commissioners explaining their views in these words:

"In San Francisco we are unfortunate in having both numbered streets and numbered avenues, and are absolutely without excuse in having two sets of numbered avenues, one of them distinguished with the suffix 'South.'

"The confusion is aggravated in the Potrero district where letters addressed, for instance, to Fifth Avenue South, San Francisco, are often sent to South San Francisco, a distinct post office. It is obvious that the numbered streets must remain, although it is confusing that since First Street was named six other streets have been laid out on the filled land, so that First Street is the seventh from the Bay. . . .

"California is blessed with a historic background of peculiar interest, romantic and picturesque. It is a distinct asset that we cannot afford to ignore. It should in every way be fostered and stimulated. The beauty of the Spanish nomenclature of California is admitted, and the railroad companies entering the State have proved its direct commercial value.

"San Francisco has neglected its opportunity. Other California cities of Spanish origin have availed themselves of the musical names associated with its discoverers and founders, and made the most of our common heritage. We have made very little of it."

In conclusion came this explanation of how East Street finally became The Embarcadero:

"We have discouraged the use of points of the compass as parts of street names as it leads to confusion in the delivery of mail and is otherwise objectionable. The most conspicuous instance of this faulty naming of streets confronts the stranger who arrives at the waterfront and passes to East Street North or East Street South, as the case may be. We have a beautiful building at our ferry gate, and in time the esplanade fronting will be very attractive. It should have a distinctive and fitting name. We propose to ask the state authorities, under whose control it is, to call it The Embarcadero, which has a meaning, is beautiful, and fits in with other city names like the Potrero and the Presidio. The Board of Harbor Commissioners have concurred with our recommendation. The change will give our waterfront a name that will be of world-wide renown, associated with the Spanish antecedents of the city."

Alvarado Street	*named for* Juan Bautista Alvarado, Mexican Governor of California from 1836 to 1842. Joined Castro and Pico in Mexican opposition to occupation by the United States.
Armstrong Avenue	*named for* General Samuel Strong Armstrong, founder of Hampton Institute.
Arthur Avenue	*named for* Chester A. Arthur, twenty-first President of the United States.
Balboa Street	*named for* Vasco Nunez de Balboa, discoverer of the Pacific Ocean.
Bancroft Avenue	*named for* George Bancroft, noted American historian, who served as Secretary of the Navy and U.S. Minister to Great Britain.
Bartol Street	*named for* Abraham Bartol, president of the Board of Assistant Aldermen, 1850.
Battery Street	*so named* because it orignally led to the battery erected by Lt. Misroon at Clark's Point.
Beale Street	*named for* Edward F. Beale who, in the summer of

1848, was sent to Washington to officially report the California gold discovery. He served as a naval officer in the Mexican war and was an Army Lieutenant in California after the Bear Flag revolt; later became surveyor general of California. When Jefferson Davis was Secretary of War, Beale led an unsuccessful expedition to California deserts, bringing camels intended to be used for transportation purposes. He is perhaps best known for his daring rescue of Col. Stephen Kearny after the battle of San Pascual where Kearny was seriously wounded.

Bernal Heights Boulevard
named for Juan Francisco Bernal, a soldier in Anza's expedition of 1776. Forebear of family whose 4,400 acre ranch included land now known as Hunter's Point and part of San Mateo County.

Bluxome Street
named for Isaac Bluxome, Jr., pioneer merchant. Commanded action against The Hounds in 1849, served as Secretary of the Vigilante Committees of 1851 and 1856.

Boalt Street
named for John Henry Boalt, an Ohioan, who devoted himself to mechanical engineering and mining as a young man; came West at the close of the Civil War and practised first in Nevada, then moved to San Francisco. He was appointed to the California State Supreme Court, later becoming Chief Justice. Following his death some years later his widow presented a gift of $100,000 to the University of California School of Law that now honors his name — Boalt Hall.

Buchanan Street
named for John C. Buchanan, who came overland in 1846 and joined Fremont's Company; later joined firm of McDonald & Buchanan, autioneers; served as clerk to Alcaldes Bryant and Hyde.

Burke Avenue
named for General John Burke of the Revolutionary Army.

Bush Street
presumed to have been named for J. P. Bush who reached Yerba Buena in 1845 as cabin boy on whaler *Margaret*. Assisted Jasper O'Farrell in making first city map.

Cabrillo Street
named for Juan Rodriguez Cabrillo, famous navigator. Commanded an expedition to cross the Gulf of California and explore uncharted sea. In 1542 he sighted California from the sea.

Carroll Avenue
named for Charles Carroll, a signer of the Declara-

	tion of Independence.
Castro Street	*named for* Jose Castro, descendant of a soldier in Anza's Company. He was active in resisting United States rule after Monterey and Yerba Buena were taken by American forces. Failed in effort to regain Monterey.
Clay Street	*named for* Henry Clay.
Cleveland Street	*named for* Charles Cleveland, a '49er who became a banker.
Cole Street	*named for* Cornelius Cole, an Auburn, New York lawyer, who arrived in San Francisco late in 1849, mined for a time, practiced law in San Francisco, became one of principal organizers of Republican Party; later became publisher of the Sacramento *Daily Times.* Elected to House of Representatives in 1863; to U.S. Senate in 1866.
Columbus Avenue	*named for* Christopher Columbus.
Corbett Avenue	*named for* a pioneer family. In early '50s John, a son was a deputy county clerk under Thomas Hayes.
Custer Avenue	*named for* General George A. Custer who was killed in a battle with Sioux Indians under Sitting Bull on Little Big Horn River, Montana, June 25, 1876.
Colin P. Kelly Jr. Street	*named for* Colin P. Kelly Jr., a member of the famous Kelly-Cohn team that dropped first bomb to sink a Japanese warship in World War II.
De Boom Street	*named for* Cornelius de Boom, Belgian consul. He was associated in the real estate business with Dr. John Townsend.
Divisadero Street	*named for* its position — the summit of a "great hill," a place from which to view distant land. Spanish name for Lone Mountain was El Divisadero.
Dolores Street	*named for* Mission Dolores.
Donner Avenue	*named for* leader of the ill-fated party of immigrants perishing in the high Sierra.
Dow Place	*named for* William H. Dow, a merchant in the '50s.
Drumm Street	*named for* Lieutenant Richard Coulton Drumm USA, who served in the Mexican War. During the Civil War he was adjutant general of the Department of the Pacific, stationed in San Francisco.
Dupont Street	*named for* Captain Samuel F. DuPont, USN, commander of flagship *Congress* that brought Commodore Robert F. Stockton to California in July, 1846. He took active part in conquest of California. The

street later was renamed Grant Avenue.

Ecker Street   *named for* George C. Ecker, a pioneer watchmaker.

Eddy Street   *named for* William M. Eddy, city surveyeor, who in 1847 completed a new enlarged map of the city extending streets laid out by Jasper O'Farrell. He later became surveyor general of California.

Egbert Avenue   *named for* Colonel Egbert, USA, killed in the Philippines.

Ellis Street   *named for* Alfred J. Ellis, who reached Yerba Buena in 1847. He operated a popular saloon and boarding house on Montgomery Street. He was a member of the Auyntamiento of 1849 and of the State Constitutional Convention. He commanded a company of Vigilantes.

Evans Avenue   *named for* Rear Admiral Robley D. Evans, known as "Fighting Bob Evans," credited with an important part in modernizing U.S. Navy and building steel ships. In command of the Atlantic fleet, he led a world tour of his vessels in 1907, putting into San Francisco Bay for a visit.

Fair Avenue   *named for* James G. Fair, associate of Mackay, Ralston and Sharon, Comstock kings. Born in Dublin in 1831, he first worked in California as a pick and shovel miner. He occupied a modest Pine Street home near Nob Hill.

Fairfax Avenue   *named for* Thomas Fairfax, sixth Baron Fairfax, who became an American colonist; a friend of Washington. Died near Winchester, Virginia, March 12, 1782.

Fallon Place   *named for* Thomas Fallon, who arrived from Canada in 1844 and took an active part in Bear Flag Revolt. He raised American flag in San Jose; became prominent in San Francisco business.

Fanning Way   *named for* Charles Fanning, a well-known engineer.

Farragut Avenue   *named for* Admiral David Glasgow Farragut, who in 1840's was sent West from Washington to establish Mare Island Navy Yard, which he commanded for a time. Fought in War of 1812 at age of eleven.

Fell Street   *named for* William Fell, native of Denmark, who arrived in San Francisco in 1849. He became a popular merchant.

Fitch Street   *named for* George K. Fitch, a well-known pioneer.

Fitzgerald Avenue   *named for* Edward Fitzgerald, an English poet and translator.

Franklin Street	*believed named for* Silim Franklin, a pioneer businessman.
Galindo Avenue	*named for* Jose Galindo, grandson of Nicholas Galindo, who came in 1776 with the Anza Party as a settler. Jose owned 2,200 acres extending through present San Francisco County and into San Mateo.
Galvez Avenue	*named for* Don Jose de Galvez, Visitador-General of Spain and member of the Council of the Indies. He organized exploring expedition led by Don Gaspar de Portola in 1768.
Gilbert Street	*named for* Lieutenant Edward Gilbert USA, a printer arriving with Stevenson's Regiment in 1847. He became part owner and editor of *Alta California;* later elected to Congress. Killed in a duel over an editorial in his paper.
Gilman Avenue	*named for* Daniel Coit Gilman, president of the University of California 1872-75. A native of Connecticut, he did graduate work at Yale; served as an attache of American Embassy at St. Petersburg; returned to Yale as a faculty member; finally accepted a call to U.C. where he distinguished himself by developing the campus. Advocated changes in educational policies with less attention to classical subjects.
Golden Gate Ave.	*named after* the opening of Golden Gate Park when it became a driveway to the Park. Avenue originally was Tyler Street, named for John Tyler, tenth president of the United States.
Gordon Street	*named for* George Gordon, an Englishman, who in early '60s developed South Park as select residential area for wealthy people.
Gough Street	*named for* Charles H. Gough, popular milkman in early '50s, delivering milk on horseback. In 1855, when he was named on a committee to lay out streets west of Larkin, he gave his own name to one of them.
Griffith Street	*named for* Millen Griffith, a well-known pioneer.
Guerrero Street	*named for* Francisco Guerrero, a popular Mexican landowner who held several local offices before and after American occupation.
Harlan Place	*named for* George Harlan, who arrived in California in 1846 leading an overland party.
Harrison Street	*named for* Edward H. Harrison, who arrived in 1847 as quartermaster's clerk of Stevenson's Regi-

ment of First New York Volunteers. He became the collector of the port.

Hawes Street   *named for* Horace Hawes, who came as a poor man from New York in 1849 and attained prominence as an attorney and member of the California Legislature. He was a prosecutor of The Hounds; later appointed chief executive officer of the city under Mayor Geary.

Hayes Street   *named for* Colonel Thomas Hayes, San Francisco county clerk from 1853-1856; he owned a large piece of land in Hayes Valley.

Heron Street   *named for* Ensign James H. Heron, USN, who arrived in California in 1846.

Hollister Avenue   *named for* Sergeant Stanley Hollister of California, killed in Cuba.

Hudson Avenue   *named for* Henry Hudson, English navigator, discoverer of Hudson River and Hudson Bay.

Hunt Street   *named for* Henry Brown Hunt, a pioneer merchant.

Ingalls Street   *named for* General Rufus Ingalls.

Ingerson Avenue   *named for* Dr. H. H. Ingerson of San Francisco.

Inness Avenue   *named for* George Inness, a noted American painter.

Irving Street   *named for* Washington Irving.

Jennings Street   *named for* Thomas Jennings, Sr. a San Francisco pioneer active in civic affairs. His son, Thomas, Jr., was a member of the Board of Supervisors 1900-1; again in 1908-9. Once served as acting mayor.

Jerrold Avenue   *named for* Douglas William Jerrold, English dramatist and humorist.

Jones Street   *named for* Elbert P. Jones, a Kentucky lawyer who came to Yerba Buena in 1846. He was second proprietor of town's first hotel, Portsmouth House, on Clay St. near Kearny. Also edited Sam Brannan's newspaper, *The Star,* for a time.

Keith Street   *named for* Sir William Keith, born in England in 1680. Came to America and became governor of Pennsylvania and Delaware colonies. Later returned to London, lost his money, and was imprisoned for debt. Died in Old Bailey in 1749.

Key Avenue   *named for* Francis Scott Key, composer of "The Star Spangled Banner."

Kirkham Street   *named for* General Ralph W. Kirkham.

Kirkwood Avenue   *named for* Samuel J. Kirkwood, a governor of Idaho.

Laguna Street   *named for* Washerwoman's Lagoon, a pond.

Lane Street   *named for* Dr. L. C. Lane, a prominent physician.

La Salle Avenue	*named for* Robert Cavalier de la Salle, the French explorer; discoverer of the Ohio River.
Lawton Street	*named for* Brig. General Henry W. Lawton, who became military governor of Santiago after its surrender in Spanish-American War. In 1886 he led troops into Mexico and captured Indian chief Geronimo. Killed in action in 1909 in campaign against insurgent leader Emilio Aguinaldo.
Leavenworth Street	*named for* Rev. Thaddeus M. Leavenworth, an Episcopalian minister and physician. He arrived in San Francisco in 1847 as chaplain of Stevenson's First New York Volunteer Regiment. He served as alcalde in 1848-49.
Le Conte Avenue	*named for* Dr. John LeConte, a physician, who became the third president of the University of California after extensive teaching in eastern colleges. Earlier he had served the Confederate forces during the Civil War. Before heading the Berkeley institution, he served there as a professor of physics and is credited with the establishment of scientific courses, preparing curricula and setting new entrance requirements. Died at his Berkeley home April 29, 1891.
Lee Avenue	*believed named for* Lieutenant Curtis Lee, a son of General Robert E. Lee. Curtis was an aide to General Clark, commanding Department of California.
Lyon Street	*named for* Captain Nathaniel Lyon, West Point graduate who fought in war with Mexico. He came to California as captain of Troop C of the First Dragoons. In 1849 he successfully attacked Indians at Clear Lake to avenge the murder of Captain William H. Warner.
Macondray Lane	*named for* Frederick William Macondray, son of a Scottish sea captain. Arriving in San Francisco in 1849 after an early career at sea, he established the large mercantile firm of Macondray & Co., dealing largely in tea.
Market Street	*named for* Philadelphia's Market Street.
McCoppin Street	*named for* Frank H. McCoppin, ninth mayor of San Francisco, 1867 to 1869. In 1860 he was general manager of the Old Market Street Railroad Co., which ran steam trains on Market Street as the city's first mechanical public transportation.
McKinnon Avenue	*named for* Father McKinnon, chaplain of First Cali-

fornia Volunteers in Spanish-American War. He died in the Philippines.

Meade Avenue	*named for* General George G. Meade, a commander in the Battle of Gettysburg.
Mendell Street	*named for* Colonel George H. Mendell, a West Point graduate; active in Army Engineers Corps until retirement in 1852. Many Pacific Coast defenses were established under his direction. In San Francisco he served from 1900-03 as president of the Board of Public Works.
Mint Street	*named for* proximity to old U.S. Mint.
Mission Street	*named as* first street opened in the southern portion of the town. It followed the old road from the waterfront to the Mission.
Moraga Street	*named for* Lieutenant Jose Joaquin Moraga, second in command of Anza Expedition that founded Yerba Buena. Later he took command of the Expedition when Anza returned to Mexico; he founded the San Francisco Presidio and Missions in Yerba Buena and Santa Clara. Died July, 1785.
Muir Loop	*named for* John Muir, famous naturalist and conservationist; a native of Scotland, he spent his boyhood in a Wisconsin farm before coming West. He explored parts of Yosemite Valley and upper Sierra. He led a successful campaign to have the Valley taken over by United States as a national park. Founded Sierra Club in 1905. Died in 1914.
Natoma Street	*named for* an Indian tribe on American River. This originally was named Mellus Street honoring Henry Mellus, business partner of William D. M. Howard.
Newcomb Avenue	*named for* Samuel Newcomb, a distinguished astronomer.
Newhall Street	*named for* Henry M. Newhall, a native of Massachusetts who came to California in 1849 after a business career in Tennessee. In San Francisco he became a leading auctioneer; later a large buyer of real estate. Founded town of Newhall, Southern California.
Noe Street	*named for* Jose de Jesus Noe, a large ranch owner and last Alcalde under Mexican rule. His rancho was in the center of what is now San Francisco.
Otis Street	*named for* James Otis, twelfth mayor of San Francisco. A native of Boston, he arrived in San Francisco in 1848, became a member of the importing

and exporting firm of Macondray & Co. Active in civic affairs and was known for his high ethical principles. Died November 4, 1875 while serving as mayor.

Pacheco Street
named for Juan Salvio Pacheco, a soldier under Anza. He is often referred to as one of the founders of San Francisco.

Pacific Avenue
known earlier as Pacific Street. It was originally named for Alcalde Washington A. Bartlett. Records do not disclose reason for change.

Page Street
named for Robert C. Page, who served as clerk to the Board of Assistant Aldermen from 1851-56.

Palou Avenue
named for Fray Francisco Palou, a companion of Father Junipero Serra and his historian. Formerly with the Anza party, he took an active part in establishing Mission Dolores and the San Francisco Presidio.

Peralta Avenue
named for Gabriel Peralta, who arrived in San Francisco in 1776 as a corporal in Anza's forces. When California became American territory in 1846, his family owned much of what now are Oakland, Alameda and Berkeley.

Perry Street
named for Dr. Alexander Perry, major and surgeon in Colonel Stevenson's First New York Volunteer Regiment which arrived in 1847.

Phelps Street
named for Timothy Guy Phelps, a New Yorker arriving in San Francisco in 1849. Engaged in real estate operations; elected to California Legislature in 1856 on state's first Republican ticket; in 1869 appointed collector of customs for San Francisco.

Pico Avenue
named for Pio Pico, last Mexican governor of California 1845-46. Joined Alvarado and Castro in opposing American occupation.

Pierce Street
named for President Franklin Pierce.

Pioche Street
named for Francis Pioche, a financier regarded as one of city's great builders; a partner in mercantile firm of Pioche & Bayerehque of Clay Street near Portsmouth Square.

Pixley Street
named for Frank Pixley, an early day editor of *The Argonaut*.

Polk Street
named for President James A. Polk.

Post Street
named for Gabriel B. Post, a member of the Ayuntamiento in 1849; known for his efforts in behalf of economy in government.

Powell Street	*named for* Dr. William J. Powell, surgeon of the U.S. sloop-of-war *Warren,* often in San Francisco Bay. He was active in the conquest of California. Established an early sanitarium for sailors.
Quesada Avenue	*named for* Gonzales Ximinez de Quesada, a Spanish explorer and conqueror of New Granada.
Quint Street	*named for* Leander Quint, a native of New Hampshire, who came to California in 1849 with a law degree. After working the mines, he opened a law office in Sonora; later elected a judge in Tuolumne County. Came to San Francisco in 1865, practicing law until his death in 1890.
Quintara Street	*named for* an old Spanish family.
Rankin Street	*named for* Ira P. Rankin, well-known pioneer.
Riley Avenue	*named for* Brigadier General Bennet Riley, a native of Maryland, who became Military Governor of California in February, 1849. Lacking Congressional direction for governing the newly-acquired territory, he issued a proclamation calling for election of delegates to a state convention that drafted a constitution for what later became a state.
Ringold Street	*named for* Lieutenant Cadwalader Ringold, U.S. naval officer and surveyor. Later as commander of *U.S. Porpoise* he directed a survey mapping Sacramento River and parts of San Francisco Bay.
Rivera Street	*named for* Capain Fernando Rivera y Moncado Rivera, early commandante of California.
Sacramento Street	*originally named* Howard Street honoring William D. Howard. Reasons for name change not recorded.
Sanchez Street	*named for* Jose Antonio Sanchez, one-time commandante of San Francisco Presidio. An Indian fighter; his family once owned 15,000 acre ranch running from today's South San Francisco to Burlingame.
Sansome Street	*originally named* Sloat Street honoring the Commodore. Name changed in 1847 on request of Philadelphians desiring to use Sansome, the name of a street in their city.
Scott Street	*named for* General Winfield Scott, commander of Union Army in Civil War.
Selby Street	*named for* Thomas H. Selby, a New York merchant, who came to San Francisco in 1849 hoping to earn enough to pay his creditors after the eastern business had failed. Establishing the firm of Thomas H. Selby & Co., metal importers, he became suc-

cessful and met all of his former obligations. In 1851 he was elected a member of the Board of Aldermen, led an effort to reorganize the Police Department, and rendered various other civic services.

Serra Boulevard
named for Fray Junipero Serra, San Francisco padre who established first Alta California Mission at San Diego; served for years as Father-president in the region. Died in 1784.

Shafter Avenue
named for General William R. Shafter, commander of U.S. forces in Cuba.

Shotwell Street
named for J. M. Shotwell, cashier in Alsop & Co.'s bank; secretary of Merchants Exchange.

Sloat Boulevard
named for Commodore John S. Sloat, commanding U.S. Navy Squadron in Pacific waters. After the war with Mexico was declared, he took Monterey July 7, 1848; then ordered Montgomery to take Yerba Buena two days later.

Stanley Street
named for Lee Stanley, a '49er.

Steiner Street
presumably named for L. Steiner, who delivered water from house to house in pioneer days.

Steuart Street
named for William M. Steuart, secretary to Commodore Thomas Catesby Pones on *U.S.S. Ohio*. Arrived in San Francisco in 1848; member of Ayuntamiento 1849-50.

Sutro Heights Avenue
named for Adolph Sutro, twenty-first mayor of San Francisco 1895-97. Starting as a cigar dealer, he educated himself, becaming a noted mining engineer, winning fame and fortune by driving a five-mile tunnel into the Comstock Lode in Nevada.

Taraval Street
named for an Indian guide in Anza expedition.

Taylor Street
named for Zachary Taylor, twelfth president of the United States.

Thomas Avenue
named for General George H. Thomas, "The Rock of Chickamauga."

Tiffany Avenue
named for Robert J. Tiffany, head of the People's Homestead, a property development.

Toland Street
named for Dr. Hugh Toland, noted surgeon who pioneered correction of club feet. He reached San Francisco in 1853; called "The Great Surgeon of the Pacific Coast." Founded Toland Medical College in San Francisco; died 1880.

Treat Avenue
named for George Treat, an early settler, who owned noted race horses.

Turk Street	*named for* Frank Turk, attorney. He came to San Francisco in 1849, first working for John W. Geary in the post office. He once served as second alcalde.
Ulloa Street	*named for* Antonio de Ulloa, first Spanish governor of Louisiana; served previously in Spanish Navy and in administrative posts. In 1835 he accompanied a scientific expedition to South America; author of "A Voyage to South America."
Underwood Ave.	*named for* General Franklin Underwood, US Army.
Valencia Street	*named for* Candelario Valencia, son of Jose Manuel Valencia, one of Anza's soldiers. Candelario owned Acalanes Rancho near Lafayette, Contra Costa County; lived on property near Mission Dolores.
Van Dyke Avenue	*named for* Walter Van Dyke, a native of New York State and a lawyer, came overland to California soon after the gold discovery; served in both houses of the state legislature; elected as first district attorney of Trinity County. In 1873 he was appointed United States District attorney with headquarters in San Francisco; elected to the superior court in Los Angeles in 1888; six years later elected to the State Supreme Court. Died in Oakland December 25, 1905.
Van Ness Avenue	*named for* James Van Ness, sixth mayor of San Francisco 1855-56; author of Van Ness Ordinance which confirmed title of possessors of property west of Larkin on January 1, 1855.
Wallace Avenue	*named for* William Thompson Wallace, a Kentuckian, who came West in 1852, first practiced law in San Jose and became district attorney of Santa Clara County; in 1869 he was elected a justice of the State Supreme Court and later became Chief Justice. Also served as a regent of the University of California.
Waller Street	*named for* R. H. Waller, city recorder in 1851 and 1854.
Webster Street	*named for* Daniel Webster.
Whipple Avenue	*named for* Major-General Emile W. Whipple; died of wounds in battle of Chancellorville May 4, 1863.
Yorba Street	*named for* Antonio Yorba, sergeant in the Catalan Volunteers with the Portola expedition in 1769; also served as sergeant of a San Francisco company in 1777.

Index

Howard Presbyterian Church, 112
Howard, William D. M., 107, 110-112, 235, 237
Hubert, Numa, 39
Hudson Bay Co., 17, 110
Hudson, Henry, 233
Humphrey, Isaac, 85
Hunt, George T., 39
Hunt, Henry B., 233
Huntington, Collis P., 146-148, 166-167, 176-178
Huntington, Falls, 178
Huntington Library & Art Gallery, 178
Hyde, George, 52-54, 64, 78, 111

Indians, 2, 44, 59, 66, 84, 235; Walla Walla tribe, 49-50; Yuma tribe, 5-7
Ingalls, Gen. Rufus, 233
Ingerson, Dr. H. H., 233
Inness, George, 233
Irving, Washington, 233

Jansen, J. C., 76
Jenkins, John, 75, 114
Jennings, Thomas, 233
Jerrold, Douglas W., 233
Jessie Street, *ix*
Johnston, Capt. Abraham, 67
Johnston, George P., 40
Jones, Elbert P., 233
Jones, John R., 32
Judah, Theodore K., 145-148, 167, 177

Kearney, Dennis, 65, 116
Kearny, Gen. Stephen W., 47, 56, 65-68, 70, 81, 229
Keith, Sir William, 233
Kefauver, Crime Commission, 221, 223
Kelly, Colin P., Jr., 230
Key, Francis Scott, 233
King, James (of William), 40, 115
Kirkham, Gen. Ralph W., 233
Kirkwood, Samuel J., 233

Lake Merced, 149, 151
Land grants, 16, 36, 53, 67-68, 70, 81, 84
Lane, Dr. L. C., 233
Larkin, Thomas O., 31-34, 81, 106, 107, 108, 109
LaSalle, Robert Cavalier de, 234

Lawrence, Joseph, 163
Lawton, Brig. Gen. Henry W., 234
League of the Cross, 200
Leavenworth, Dr. T. M., 76, 106, 234
LeConte, Dr. John, 234
Lee, Lt. Curtis, 234
Lees, Isaiah, 151, 152
Leese, Jacob, 10, 15-17, 24, 35-36, 47
Leese, Rosalie, Vallejo, 17, 24
Leidesdorff, William A., 26-30, 50, 61
Leidesdorfer, Wolf, 29, 30
Lick House, 143, 188
Lick, James, 97, 98, 141-144
Lick Observatory, 141, 143, 144
Lincoln, Pres. Abraham, 121, 127, 148
London, Jack, 211
Los Angeles Star, 22
Lugo, Maria Antonia, 19
Lyon, Capt. Nathaniel, 234

MacCrellish, Frederick, 168
Mackay, John W., 179-182
Macondray, Frederick W., 234
Maiden Lane, *x*
Mare Island Navy Yard, 231
Marshall, James W., 80, 83, 85
Marston, J. D., 105
Martinez, Ignacio, 9
Martinez, Maria Antonio, 9
Martinez, Susana, 36
Mason, Col. Richard B., 68, 80-82, 111, 126
Masonic Order, 57, 58
Mayfield Grange, 167
McAllister, Hall, *x-xi,* 157-158
McAteer, Eugene, 105
McCarthy, P. H., 207
McCoppin, Frank H., 234
McDougall, James A., 148, 174
McGloin, Father John B., 129
McGlynn, John, 108-109
McKinnon, Father, 234
McLaren, John, 178, 191-194
Meade, Gen. George G., 235
Mechanic's Institute, 139, 144
Mellus, Henry, 110, 235
Mendell, Col. George H., 235
Mexican War, 56, 60, 66, 91, 238
Mills, D. O., 170
Mission Dolores, 4, 6, 236
Missions, 2, 67-68, 235, 238
Monero Dam, 211, 212
Monitor, The, 131, 200
Montalvo, 161
Montgomery, Mrs. Allan, 107
Montgomery, Comm. John B., 38-40 53, 62, 238